D1527124

KINSHIP AND MARRIAGE IN THE SOVIET UNION

KINSHIP AND MARRIAGE IN THE SOVIET UNION

Field studies

edited by

Tamara Dragadze

Routledge & Kegan Paul
London, Boston, Melbourne and Henley

First published in 1984
by Routledge & Kegan Paul plc

14 Leicester Square, London WC2H 7PH, England

9 Park Street, Boston, Mass 02108, USA

464 St Kilda Road, Melbourne,
Victoria 3004, Australia

Broadway House, Newtown Road,
Henley-on-Thames, Oxon RG9 1EN, England

Printed in Great Britain by
T.J. Press (Padstow) Ltd, Padstow, Cornwall

Library of Congress Cataloging in Publication Data

Family and Kinship in the Soviet Union.
Bibliography: p.
1. Kinship -- Soviet Union -- Addresses, essays, lectures.
2. Family -- Soviet Union -- Addresses, essays, lectures.
3. Ethnology -- Soviet Union -- Addresses, essays, lectures.
4. Soviet Union -- Social life and customs -- 1917 -
Addresses, essays, lectures. I. Dragadze, Tamara.
GN585.S65F36 1984   306.8'3'0947   83-24607

British Library CIP data available

ISBN 0-7100-0995-X

Contents

860879

Acknowledgments

This work has taken an extremely long time to come to publication, the major cause being difficulties over Soviet copyright procedures. The intervention of Academician Julian Bromley, Director of the USSR Academy of Sciences Institute of Ethnography, eventually resolved the problems and I am extremely grateful to him. I am also indebted to my teachers and their colleagues who first interested me in Kinship and Marriage: Professor P. Stirling, the late Professor E. Evans-Pritchard, the late Professor Vera Bardavelidze and also the late Professor Maurice Freedman who suggested the title of this book. Besides Academician Julian Bromley my thanks also go to all the members of the Miklukho-Maclay Institute of Ethnography of the USSR Academy of Sciences who helped me with the preparation of this volume, in particular Dr V. Basilov, Dr E. Ekimova and Dr L. Kusmina. Dr Anthony Alcott did a first rendering in English of two papers which were useful indeed. Katherine Vivien did her Georgian language translation without any delay. Academician G. Chitaya and Dr I. Chqonia of the Institute of Ethnography in Tbilisi helped with the Georgian text. My thanks also go to Dr G. Lienhardt, the late Professor M. Fortes and to Professor E. Gellner and to each of the living authors of the articles themselves whose comments have been invaluable. I also thank Mrs M. Gothelf, Mrs C. Smith and Mrs L. Kelly of Leeds University who typed the manuscript. My family gave me unending support. Joanna Seddon, however, has been the most invaluable colleague, persevering with the translations while working in Leningrad, Moscow, Oxford and London and she was patient at all times. The opinions expressed in the introductions are entirely my own responsibility.

T. Dragadze

Notes on contributors

Shikhberdy ANNAKLYCHEV   Born 1931, Doctor of Historical
Sciences, Ashkhabad (Dotsent), Lecturer of the Polytechnical
Institute at Ashkhabad.   Chief publications:
'The life of the oil-men of Nebit-dag and Kum-dag (a histori-
cal-ethnographical sketch)' ('Byt rabochikh-neftyanikov Nebit-
daga i Kum-daga (Istoriko-etnografichesky ocherk)'),
Ashkhabad, 1961.
'The life and culture of the workers of Turkmenistan' ('Byt i
kul'tura rabochikh Turkmenistana'), Ashkhabad, 1969.
'The formation of national cadres of workers in the cattle-
rearing districts of the republics of the Soviet East (based on
the example of Turkestan SSR)' ('Formirovanie natsional'nykh
rabochikh kadrov v skotovodcheskikh raionakh respublika
Sovetskogo Vostoka (na primere TSSR)'), Moscow, 1971 (11th
International Congress of Anthropological and Ethnographic
Science).

Khadel A. ARGYNBAEV   Doctor of Historical Sciences, Head of
the Department of Ethnography of the Institute of History,
Archaeology and Ethnography of the Academy of Sciences of
Kazakhstan SSR (Alma-Ata).   Chief publications:
'Family and marriage among the Kazakhs' ('Sem'ya i brak u
kazakhov'), Alma-Ata, 1973 (in Kazakh).
'Family and marriage among the Kazakhs', Alma-Ata, 1975
(summary of his doctoral thesis in Russian).
Marriage and wedding rituals of the Kazakhs in the past and
present (Svad'ba i svadebnye obryady u kazakhov v proshlom
i nastoyashchem), 'Sovetskaya Etnografiya' , 1974, no. 6.

Vera BARDAVELIDZE   Born 1899, died 1970, Tbilisi.   Candidate of Historical Sciences 1933;   Doctor of Historical Sciences,
1956.   Professor from 1957.   Head of Department of Ethnography at the Georgian SSR Academy of Sciences' Institute of
History, Archaeology and Ethnography.   Entered Tbilisi University in 1918 and in 1931 became the first woman postgrad-
uate from Georgia to study with the orientalist and controversial linguist, Nico Marr, in Leningrad.   With her husband,
Academician Giorgi Chitaya, she founded the school of Ethnography in Georgia.   She had more than 140 publications but
her principle work which is easily accessible and in Russian is:
'Drevneyshie religiozriye verovaniya i obradovoe graficheskoe
iskustvo gruzinskikh plemen' ('Ancient religious beliefs and
ritual graphic art of the Georgian tribes'), Tbilisi, 1957.
ix

Vladimir Nikolaevich BASILOV   Born 1937, Candidate of Historical Sciences, Senior Researcher, USSR Academy of Sciences Institute, Moscow, Institute of Ethnography.   Publications: 'The cult of Holy men in Islam' ('Kul't svyatykh v islame'), Moscow, 1970.
Articles:
The origin of the Turkmen-ata (simple popular forms of Central Asian sufism) (O proiskhozhdenii turkmen-ata (prostonarodnye formy sredneaziatskogo sufizma)), in the book 'Premusselman beliefs and rituals in Central Asia' ('Domusul'-manskie verovaniya i obryady v Srednei Azii'), Moscow, 1975.
Tashmat-bola, 'Sovetskaya Etnografiya', 1975, no. 5.
Traditions of female shamans among the Kazakhs (Traditsii zhenskogo shamanstva u Kazakhov), 'Field work of the Institute of Ethnography' ('Polevye Trudy Instituta Etnografii'), t. 98, Leningrad, 1973.

Nella Gregor'evna BOROZNA   Born 1926 in Bobruisk, died 1973 in Moscow, Candidate of Historical Sciences.   Educated Moscow University, Researcher at the USSR Academy of Sciences, Institute of Ethnography in Moscow.   Publications:
On the question of the forms of the family among the seminomadic Uzbeks (based on materials from the Uzbek-durmen) (K voprosu o formakh sem'i u polukochevykh uzbekov (na materialakh uzbekov-durmenov)), in 'The family and family rituals of the people of Central Asia and Kazakhstan' ('Sem'ya i semenye obryadov narodov srednei Azii i Kazakhstana'), Moscow, 1978.
The economy of the Uzbeks of Babatag and Kafirnitani (Material'naya Kul'tura uzbekov Babataga i Kafirnitana), in 'The economy of the peoples of Central Asia and Kazakhstan' ('Material'naya kul'tura narodov Srednei Azii i Kazakhstana'), Moscow, 1966.
Contributed to: 'Premusselman beliefs and rituals in Central Asia' ('Domusul'manskie verovaniya i obryady v Srednei Azii'), Moscow, 1975.

Lev Abramovich FAINBERG   Born Moscow 1929, Doctor of Historical Sciences, Senior Researcher Institute of Ethnography, USSR Academy of Sciences.   Chief publications:
'The social system of the Eskimos and Aleuts' ('Obshchestvenny stroi eskimosov i aleutov'), Moscow, 1964.
From the ethnographical history of the Amazons, in 'Nations in Latin America' ('Natsii v Latinskoi Amerike'), 1964.
The Indians of Brazil, in 'Modern Brazil' ('Sovremennaya Braziliya'), 1963.
The primitive communal relationships of the polar Eskimos of Greenland and their disintegration (Pervobytnoobshchive otnosheniya i ikh razlozhenie u polyarnyk eskimosov Greenlandii), in 'The disintegration of the tribal kinship system and the formation of class society', Moscow, 1968.

'Sketches of the ethnical history of the Non-Soviet North'
('Ocherki etnicheskoi istorii zarubezhnoi Severa'), Moscow,
1971.
From the history of the Indians of British Guyana (Iz istorii
indeitsev Britanskoi Gviany), in 'Guyana', Moscow, 1969.
The aboriginal population of Canada (Aborigennoe naselenie
Kanady), in 'Natsional'nye protsessy v Kanade', Moscow, 1972.
The rise and disintegration of the kinship system, (Voznik-
novenie i pazlozhenie rodovogo stroia), in 'Primitive society.
Fundamental problems of development' ('Pervobytnoe
obshchestvo. Osnovnye problemy razvitiya'), Moscow, 1975.

Nikolai Mikhailovich GIRENKO   Born 1940, Leningrad, Candidate of Historical Sciences, USSR Academy of Sciences Institute of Ethnography, Leningrad branch.   Chief publication:
'The traditional social organisation of the Nambezi (the main
tendencies of development in the pre-colonial period)'
('Traditsionnaya sotsial'naya organizatsiya n'yambezi (osnovnye
tendentsii razvitiya v dokolonal'ny period)'), Leningrad, 1975.

David Moiseevich KOGAN   Born 1913, in Belaya Tserkov',
Junior Researcher USSR Academy of Sciences Institute of
Ethnography, Moscow.   Publications:
A study of contemporary kolkhoz life. (The Kolkhozes of Kirov,
Vladimir and Gorky Regions) (Izuchenie sovremennogo
kolkhoznogo byta.(Kolkhozy Kirovskoi, Vladimirskoi i Gor'-
kovskoi oblasti), 'Sovetskaya Etnografiya', 1964, no. 5.
Materials from questionnaires carried out in the town of Kaluga
(Materialy anketnogo obsledovaniya v g. Kaluge), 'Sovetskaya
Etnografiya', 1970, no. 6.
Special features of the life of the village population working in
the town (using materials from the towns of the central area
of the RSFSR) (Osobennosti byta sel'skogo naselniya rabot-
ayushchego v gorode (po materialam gorodov srednei polyusy
RSFSR)), 'Sovetskaya Etnografiya', 1975, no. 6.

A.V. KOZENKO is the son of L.F. Monogarova.

Mikhail Vasilevich KRYUKOV   Born 1932 Moscow, Doctor of
Historical Sciences, Senior Researcher USSR Academy of Sciences Institute of Ethnography, Moscow.   Main publications:
The most ancient settlements,. in the book 'The peoples of
Eastern Asia' ('Narody Vostochnoi Azii'), Moscow, 1965.   'The
forms of social organisation of the ancient Chinese' ('Formy
sotsial'noi organizatsii drevnykh kitaitsev'), Moscow, 1967.
Social differentiation in ancient China (Sotsial'naya different-
siatsiya v drevnoi Kitae), in the book 'The disintegration of
the kinship system and the formation of classical society'
('Razlozhenie rodogo stroia i formatsiya klassicheskogo
obshchestva'), Moscow, 1968.
Types of kinship system and their historical relationships
(Tipy sistem rodstva i ikh istoricheskoe sootnoshenie), in the

book 'Problems of precapitalist society' ('Problemy dokapitalist-
icheskogo obshshestva'), Moscow, 1968.

Lidiya Fedorovna MONOGAROVA   Born 1921, Moscow, Candidate of Historical Sciences, Senior Researcher, USSR Academy
of Sciences Institute of Ethnography, Moscow.   Chief publications:
Family and family life, in 'Ethnographical sketches of the rural
Uzbek population' ('Etnograficheskie ocherki uzbekskogo
sel'skogo naseleniya'), Moscow, 1969.
'The transformation of the life and culture of the Pamir
peoples in the years of socialist construction' ('Preobrazovanie
v bytu i kul'ture pripampirskikh narodnostei za gody
sotsialisticheskogo stroitel'stva'), Moscow, 1973.
'Changes in the family structure of the Pamir peoples in the
years of socialist construction' ('Izmenenie semeinogo uklada
pripampirskikh narodnostei za gody sotsialisticheskogo
stoitelst'va'), Moscow, 1973.

Alexander Alexandrovich POPOV   Born 1902, Ugulyatski
Village in Yakutsk.   Died 1960.   Graduated from Leningrad
University in 1929 and worked in the Siberian section of the
USSR Academy of Sciences' Museum of Anthropology and
Ethnography and at the Leningrad Institute of Ethnography
from 1931.   Dotsent of Leningrad University from 1940.   At
time of death 37 publications and several large ms in the
archives of the Institute of Ethnography in Leningrad.

Margarita Sergeevna SHIKHAREVA (now publishes under the
name Kashuba)   Born 1931, Moscow, Candidate of Historical
Sciences, Senior Researcher, USSR Academy of Sciences,
Institute of Ethnography, Moscow.   Publications:
Peoples of Yugoslavia, in 'Peoples of Non-Soviet Europe'
('Narody zarubezhnoi Evropy'), 1964.
Peoples of Yugoslavia, in 'General ethnographical sketches'
('Ocherki obshei etnografii'), 1966.
The social and cultural life of the population of the Kuban,
family customs (Obshchestvennaya i kul'turnaya zhizn'
naseleniya Kubani, semenye obryady), in 'Kuban settlements'
('Kubanskie stantsii'), 1967.
The winter calendar festivals of the peoples of Yugoslavia
(Zimnie kalendarnye prazdniki narodov Yugoslavii), in the
book 'Calendar customs and rituals in the countries of Non-
Soviet Europe. Winter festivals' ('Kalendarnye obychai i
obryady v strannkh zarubezhnoi Evropy. Zimnie prazdniki'),
1973.
Modern ethnographical science in the Socialist Federal Republic
of Yugoslavia (Sovremennaya etnograficheskaya nauka v
SFRYu), in 'Ethnography in socialist countries' ('Etnografiya
v strannkh sotsializma'), 1975.

L.N. TERENT'EVA   Born 1910 in Barnaul, died 1981, Candi-
date of Historical Sciences, Deputy Director of the USSR Aca-
demy of Sciences Institute of Ethnography in Moscow.   Professor.
Chief publications:
'Questions of the ethnical history of the Baltic peoples'
('Voprosy etnicheskoi istorii narodov Pribaltiki'), Moscow,
1959.
'The   Kolkhoz peasants of Latvia' ('Kholkhoznoe krest'-
yanstvo Latvii'), Moscow, 1960.
'Baltic rural settlements' ('Sel'skoe poseleniya Pribaltiki'),
Moscow, 1964.
'The socialist transformation of the economy, life and culture
of the Latvian peasantry' ('Sotsialisticheskie preobrazovaniya
v khozaistve, bytu i kul'ture latyshskogo krest'yanstva'),
Moscow, 1972.
'Ethnos and family in the USSR' ('Etnos i sem'ya v SSSR'),
Moscow, 1973.

Introduction

Tamara Dragadze

This volume can serve two purposes. On the one hand, people interested in the Soviet Union will have at their disposal translations in English of materials that will demonstrate both the style of Soviet scholars who write in social anthropology, and the richness of living traditions among the diverse nationalities of the country. On the other hand, there has recently been an increasing interest in ethnic relations throughout the various parts of the world. It is of some fascination, at a more general level, to see that despite over half a century of Soviet rule providing a uniform economic and political system, in the sphere of family and marriage the variety of customs is tremendous.

REGIONAL REPRESENTATION

My choice of papers has been governed by several criteria. First, I decided that each of the regions which have been designated by Soviet ethnographic convention should be represented. The Soviet Union is usually divided into the following sectors for study: the Baltic states, the 'European part' of the USSR, the Caucasus, Central Asia and Siberia (including the 'Far North'). The general features of each region I describe separately with the papers, but here I will merely state that their coverage by ethnographers has been uneven. Through historical accident, e.g. the evacuation of the Leningrad ethnographic institute to Tashkent during the war, resulting in an increased interest in Central Asia, or else through native tradition, e.g. Georgia and Armenia have always had an educated intelligentsia interested in national traditions, or for the sake of convenience, e.g. doing fieldwork in the countryside surrounding the capital you live in, some parts of the Soviet Union have engendered intensive ethnographic description at the expense of others. Furthermore the availability of published materials varies considerably, depending on whether the authors work and write for the Moscow and Leningrad branches of the Institute of Ethnography of the USSR Academy of Sciences, in which case they are accessible, or whether the works are printed locally by the publishing houses of the minority republics' institutes, in which case accessibility for all other colleagues, Soviet as well as the even worse-placed faraway Western scholar, is often

1

problematic.   Some republics, e.g. Georgia, publish the majority of their works in the native language, others, e.g.
Tadjikistan, publish more in Russian, their department of
ethnography having less administrative independence from
Moscow.   In the Baltic states, furthermore, after their
absorption into the Soviet Union when Marxist cadres were
sent from Russia to train local scholars, students of ethnography have devoted themselves mostly to the study of material culture, in which they excel, and so local literature on
kinship and marriage is not so readily available (one exception
is the work of Vilve Kalits in S. Dunn (ed.), 'Soviet Ethnography', 1973).

FIELDWORK

Besides regional representation, a criterion governing my
choice of works was that they should be based on ethnographic
fieldwork.   This in fact ruled out many publications since, by
and large, Soviet anthropologists do more historical-documen-
tary studies than in the West, at least in the Anglo-Saxon
schools.   Here also the fieldwork tradition differs considerably
(see Dragadze, Ethnographic Fieldwork in the USSR, 'Journal
of the Anthropological Society of Oxford', 1978).   For example,
rather than spend one or two uninterrupted periods of eighteen
or more months in the field, the Soviet anthropologist usually
goes for short visits, often a couple of months in the summer
over several years to the same area, gathering field data.
This causes a difference in both style and method as exemplified in an entertaining way by Basilov's account of his trip in
this volume.   Using whatever personal information I could
obtain on the authors, I have strictly limited my choice to
works by anthropologists whose study in the given areas is of
long standing and whose knowledge of the local language is
equivalent, if not much better especially if a native himself,
such as Annaklychev, to the best standards we have expected
of social anthropologists in Britain.   It is the case too that
Soviet anthropologists do not believe overwhelmingly in any
advantages of working alone in the field (E. Evans-Pritchard,
'Social Anthropology', 1951).   They often study as members
of a large 'complex expedition' including archaeologists, archi-
tects and others, or as part of a team of anthropologists each
interested in one particular aspect of study: religion, kinship,
material culture and so forth.   I have nevertheless preferred
to choose monographic field studies for this volume, mainly
because of my above-mentioned criterion, since it is those who
have worked alone who have also had to learn the language and
do lengthy work.   Large-scale ethnographic expeditions spon-
sored by the institutes are less likely to be mounted summer
after summer to exactly the same place.

The problem of confidentiality in the Soviet Union is very great for social anthropologists (Dragadze, 'Royal Anthropological Institute Newsletter', June 1980).   Self-censorship is blatantly evident, for example, in Terent'eva's article in this volume, where not only does she have to conform to official ideological views of how things ought to be in Latvia and fit facts accordingly, but it would have been difficult for her to reveal, even orally if not in print, how many religious family ceremonies she had actually witnessed while there was such official pressure against them when she did her work.   The problem of informants' confidentiality presents moral and practical difficulties for most anthropologists working in literate, complex societies, not only confined to totalitarian states (for example, see Ann Sutherland, 'The Hidden Americans; the Gypsies of California', 1976) but of course these problems are exacerbated in a political situation where local officials could be asked to investigate information published in the capital city by an anthropologist.   A problem particular to such a state as the USSR, of course, is that controversial information not reflecting official descriptions of social facts would not get published anyway, except in the form of indignant criticism of the people concerned.

STYLES OF THOUGHT

In my choice of papers I have tried to demonstrate the approaches to the study of kinship and marriage most representative of the Soviet school.   The most dominant feature of Soviet anthropology is that all data is sought, analysed and presented within an historical framework.   As Gellner so aptly put it:

[In British anthropology] one still has the impression that each society trails its own past behind it, as a comet trails its tail.   The tail is studied as this comet's tail, its interest is a function of the interest of the comet, not the other way around.... It is here that the contrast with the instinctive thought-style of a Soviet anthropologist is most marked. One might say that for the Soviet scholar the interest of a comet generally speaking is a function of the interest of its tail, and that all such tails fuse, at least in principle, in an all-embracing history of mankind [E. Gellner, The Soviet and the Savage, 'Current Anthropology', vol. 16, no. 4, 1975].

In the study of kinship and marriage the tendency established by Engels and adopted by Soviet ideologues is to create typologies representing different stages of historical development, notably and notoriously 'matriarchy' and 'patriarchy', the one preceding the other.   Yet this usage has changed considerably in the Soviet Union.   In the late Stalin period, Kosven was reprimanded for not having been sufficiently

'party-minded' because he stressed the importance of avuncular relations among the Caucasian peoples he wrote of. He
defended himself by replying that, on the contrary, his study
of the role of mother's brother was politically important
because it could be used to fight bourgeois foreign anthropologists who denied the relevance of matriarchal survivals.
Recent publications, and they with the sole exception of Popov
form the contents of this volume, have gone a very long way
from there. Butinov has even gone so far as to write - and
actually have published - about his doubts on the whole concept of matriarchy. Fainberg's article here comes closest to
the older Soviet tradition, which is one of the main reasons I
have chosen it to demonstrate the more classical style of Soviet
thought. For a Western anthropologist the approach is almost
quaint, so far back in this century is its equivalent in our
literature. No other comprehensive theoretical model has been
offered to Soviet anthropologists which would have full Party
backing. They tend now to retreat to writing straight descriptions of their ethnographic data, presented as part of a
history of the people concerned, but with little overt analysis.
It would nevertheless be mistaken to view the work of Soviet
anthropologists as unsophisticated because of the apparent
simplicity of presentation. Bardavelidze's paper demonstrates
masterly handling of complex data. The two papers at the
end of the volume, by Kryukov and Girenko, point to thought-
ful reasoning on issues not subject to the restrictions on the
discussion of some other wider theoretical issues. It is
important in this context to remember that in Soviet Marxist
anthropology in recent times, characteristics of kinship and
marriage are presented as 'cultural' features of a society, not
as socio-economic (or structural-functional) factors, that is to
say they are handled more as we would describe a costume or
a sculpture. Semyenov has written (Dragadze, A Meeting of
Minds, 'Current Anthropology', 1978) that kinship relations
have no reality in themselves, are ephemeral reflections of a
society's infra-structure, nothing more.

AMBIVALENT ATTITUDES

As can be noticed in the papers, the authors are reluctant to
be pinned down to actual dates when customs were observed
and, in several cases, the descriptions are accompanied by
such catchphrases as 'but this custom is dying out'. Thus
we are told that the author is referring to 'ancient times' or
else the whole question of time is quietly ignored. There are
indeed tensions between the view that in Soviet times there
should be convergence of thought and custom by all Soviet
peoples, characterised by secularisation, and the view that it
is legitimate that the ways of each of the Soviet nations should
be 'national in form' although, as Stalin also stressed, 'social-

ist in content', and here 'socialist' usually refers to patriotic loyalty to the centralised regime. Anthropologists writing explicitly about the present, such as Terent'eva (in the second half of her article) and Annaklychev, in their anxiety to present their informants in the best possible light, embellish their descriptions with morally biased pronouncements on 'progress' and so on. This ambivalent, almost apologetic attitude is even more obvious in Annaklychev, a non-Russian author, whose keenness to show the discontinuity between pre-Revolutionary and post-Revolutionary Turkmen ways - the latter being characterised by 'progressive' and here this means Europeanised features - dampens his enthusiasm and national pride in the colourful uniqueness of Turkmen custom. In contrast, Shikhareva's article on Russians in the Kuban displays more self-confidence.

ETHNIC DIVERSITY

It would take several volumes to seek actually to explain, in terms acceptable to serious Western scholars in a highly contentious theoretical field, the diversity of customs and their persistence in the USSR. But my intention here has been rather to select materials for the debate itself. In my opinion, anyway, each Soviet nation has its own story to tell as to why and how it kept and developed its particular set of traditions under the regime. These regional cases are intricately linked to the reactions to the nationalities policy of the Soviet government. It must be pointed out that for the minority nationalities Soviet ways have always been associated with Russian culture and have not appeared in the popular eye to represent a supranational Marxist ideology as apparently accepted in sections of Latin America, for example. Non-Russian peoples of the Soviet Union have been incorporated into a highly centralised political regime which, ultimately, is Moscow-dominated.

Reactions at a domestic level vary for different reasons. When Soviet government came to the Baltic state of Latvia where in its capital city, Riga, a higher level of technology was to be found than in most parts of the Soviet Union itself, urban attitudes there to Soviet messages calling for changes in customs and traditions would have been characterised by a very particular form of resistance. Rural experience would differ significantly. In places, including rural Russia, where the Moscow-led Soviets appeared as agents of genuinely improved living conditions through bringing a level of technology which was fascinating and pleasing to unsophisticated people, attitudes towards social change were more ambiguous. At another level this same ambiguity is reflected in the papers presented here. The anthropologists are conscious too, as all

those familiar with the history of Soviet policy will know, that
the 'nationalities question' has always been a very delicate as
well as lively subject of discussion in the USSR.   At a local
level, among the peoples studied themselves, there is constant
discussion of the problem of whether a particular custom
should be viewed as 'religious' or 'folk-traditional' and whether
consistent with some undefined notion of 'progress' or not.
It is in no way my aim to indulge in political commentary at
the expense of anthropological analysis, but it is imperative
that readers be aware of the background in which some of the
papers are written.

ANTHROPOLOGY IN THE USSR

In the mid-nineteenth century an ethnographic society was set
up in St Petersburg by learned scholars and gentlemen of
leisure, many more liberal-minded than some of their counter-
parts in the Royal Anthropological Institute in London, but
they shared an interest in discovering more about the minority
peoples who had now become part of the Russian Empire.   In
the early twentieth century some of the anthropologists who
were also active in opposing the repressive aspects of the
imperial government were exiled to Siberia.   Bogoraz-Tan,
Shternberg and others did excellent fieldwork among the
tribes of the far north, dependent on the natives for their
own survival (in contrast to the superior power-position of
British anthropologists in Africa.   See Talal Asad, 'Anthropology and the Colonial Encounter', 1973), returning as heroes
after the Bolshevik revolution.   With Lenin and other leaders'
interest in minority peoples of the new Soviet fatherland,
anthropologists with officially approved reputations developed
a school of ethnography based on the intense gathering of
ethnographic detail coupled with an evolutionary type of analysis rooted in Marx's, or rather Engels's version of historical
materialism.   At the same time, they were increasingly cut off
from contacts with Western thought (Dragadze, Reply to
Gellner, 'Current Anthropology', vol. 16, no. 4, 1975).   The
so-called Malinowskian revolution passed them by, for example,
and it was only in the Brezhnev period that they were emerg-
ing from their isolation.

It is significant in this context that Kryukov, who is excel-
lently acquainted with Western literature in several languages
and extremely up to date, nevertheless has had to confine
himself in his work included here to old references.   He
alludes to authors such as Rivers because the article was published in 'Sovetskaya Etnografiya' (the main and central ethnographic journal in the USSR) which is destined to a wide
readership among anthropologists throughout the country, some
of whom, unlike many of their colleagues in Moscow and Lenin-

grad, are only now beginning to acquaint themselves with
recent Western literature.

In republics such as Georgia, with its old intellectual and
literary tradition, the heritage of ethnography dates back to
the nineteenth century as well.   Literary men and women pro-
moted scholarly activities to enhance interest in national folklore and custom, and a museum of Caucasian ethnography was
established over a hundred years ago in Tbilissi, which in the
early Soviet period also housed the new school of Georgian
ethnography.   In Central Asia, however, departments of
ethnography were established by the Russians in Soviet times
and still have close links with Moscow and Leningrad, researchers submitting their theses there, for example.

As was the case with other subjects in the social sciences
(E. Weinberg, 'The Development of Sociology in the Soviet
Union', 1974, London, Routledge & Kegan Paul) ethnography
had a chequered history in the early Soviet period, although
it was never abolished as a separate discipline.   It was absorbed into faculties and departments of historical materialism,
then moved to geography and then, finally, to history where
it has stayed.   University departments are in the history
faculty, and Academy departments are either a part of an
Institute of History or, if autonomous, nevertheless closely
linked with that Institute.   Higher degrees are awarded in
'historical science' and the subject is always defined as a
branch of history (S.A. Tokarev, 'Osnovi etnografii', Moscow,
1964).

Undergraduates have to read history, Marxist philosophy, a
foreign language and a series of courses in ethnography as
well as participating in summer expeditions (hence one of the
reasons for the frequency of collective fieldwork).   Not all
those engaging in further research and higher degrees are
graduates from ethnography departments and, having done a
brief survey, I find that leading Soviet scholars in the discipline have usually read straight history, a slightly smaller
number having received an initial training in oriental studies
or philology.

There is a vast network of museums throughout the USSR
and specialists trained not only in material culture studies
(which forms an important part of all courses in ethnography)
but in general aspects of anthropology, too, are employed by
the museums to run them and to write works of specific interest to them.   The main institutes in the USSR employ specialists to do research and to train graduates, the outlying republics specialising mainly in their own nationalities' culture,
whereas Moscow and Leningrad divide their interests between
Soviet and overseas peoples.

These research centres are highly organised, with five-year
and one-year plans of study, ultimately decided by the director.   Such plans are co-ordinated throughout all the sectors,
usually on loosely enough defined themes to be amenable to
the interests of the various specialists, e.g. 'rural life' or
'ethnic process'.   Seminars are held frequently, and it is the
case throughout the Soviet Union that, because of conventional
standards for written presentation as well as official censor-
ship, no published paper ever reflects the versatility and
dynamism of oral discussion.

Each institute and university department has its Communist
Party organisation which participates in most activities, including the editing of their journals and books;   the departments'
chief directors and administrators are usually members so that
there are overlapping, rather than parallel, sets of directives
between party and academic officers.   This not only ensures
that plans for research are acceptable to the policies of the
overall Soviet authorities but also academics receive guidance
on the contemporary official line on ideology and theory and
the degree of flexibility with which discussion will be tolerated
by the government authorities.

ETHNOGRAPHY AND ANTHROPOLOGY

I have alternated loosely with the use of the terms 'anthropology' and 'ethnography'.   The former is the more general term
used in the Anglo-Saxon context for studies of kinship and
marriage, regional custom and so forth.   The latter, etnografia' to give it its Russian form, is the term used in more or
less an equivalent way in the USSR.   It must be pointed out
that these terms are not entirely similar conceptual categories.
Broadly speaking, anthropology, and social anthropology in
particular, although in practice using the same kind of data as
Soviet 'ethnographers', has an overall interest in all broader
implications for understanding humans as social beings in
general.   The Soviet ethnographer gathers data for its own
sake, because his or her job is to record, and, if intended for
wider purposes, then to establish a correct history of a given
people.   The overall history of mankind, not man's social
nature, forms the wider concern (see E. Gellner, op. cit.).
Nowhere is this divergence more clearly visible than in the
Soviet approach to the study of kinship and marriage exemplified in these papers.   There are therefore implications to be
found for our review of anthropology at a general level, while
we have been struggling with its redefinition for over ten
years (see Banaji, Crisis in British Anthropology, 'New Left
Review', no. 64, 1970).   Ultimately, however, because the
theories in our discipline must be rooted in factual evidence,
the availability of ethnographic data on such diverse peoples
as inhabit the USSR is useful in itself.

THE TRANSLATIONS

Wherever possible we have opted for readable English rather than connived literal translation. Joanna Seddon did all the Russian translations while I was engaged in fieldwork, but we checked all texts both together and, when possible, with each Soviet author individually. Kh. A. Argynbayev prepared his text from the Kazakh himself and Katherine Vivien translated the late V. Bardavelidze's paper from the Georgian. It was checked by the author's husband, Academician Giorgi Chitaya, co-founder with her of the ethnography school in Soviet Georgia. V.N. Basilov whose knowledge of English is excellent helped with the final revision of the Central Asian materials which had been the most problematic to translate accurately. The Soviet bibliographies include only those details given by the Soviet scholars themselves.

Part 1
CENTRAL ASIA

INTRODUCTION

Conventionally, Central Asia in Soviet literature refers to the
republics of Tadjikistan, Uzbekistan, Kirghizia, Turkmenistan
and, at least in connection with the ethnography of its indigenous population, the republic of Kazakhstan.

Already in pre-Revolutionary times, Russian orientalists such
as Bartold were fascinated by the ancient history of some of
the Tsarist Empire's recently conquered Asian peoples.
Ancient documents in languages such as Persian and Arabic
have provided a wealth of information as well as architectural
monuments and an unending source of archaeological finds
throughout the territory. When the main Soviet Institute of
Ethnography was evacuated to Tashkent during the Second
World War a further influx of specialists was provided who not
only did their own research but who increasingly since then
have trained local scholars who reside in the Central Asian
capitals.

Each republic has its Academy of Sciences; within the Institute of History, an ethnographic sector whose members engage
in active field research and in documentary analysis, as exemplified by Annaklychev and Argynbaev.

Except for the Tadjiks whose language is Persian, the other
Central Asian republics have languages that are Turkic-based.
They all share, however, the religion of Islam as a defining
feature of their cultures and which provides a partly unifying
link between them even today (see Dragadze, A Muslim way of
life in the Soviet Union, 'New Society', 1980), although this is
not overtly referred to in any of the papers here.

In contrast to Annaklychev and Argynbaev, the late
N. Borozna, L. Monogarova and V. Basilov are Moscow authors
all having spent up to twenty years studying Central Asian
peoples. Borozna deals with a border people, the Uzbek-
Durmen, who, like the Turkmen, Kazakhs and all other Central Asians, are patrilineal. Monogarova with help in statistics from her son A. Kozenko, presents a work of interest to
Soviet scholars studying ethnic integration, very topical at
present (see J. Bromley, 'Etnos i Etnografia', Moscow, 1973).

13

It is a somewhat sensitive issue, but one which nevertheless demonstrates a very different approach to the study of marriage from that of the other papers.   Finally V. Basilov touches on yet another aspect in the study of kinship familiar to anthropologists the world over - legends concerning the genealogies of our ancestors.   These are not only interesting to Basilov in themselves but also as a type of belief which contributes to his overall study of Turkmen beliefs and religious practice which have been his main specialism of research and publications.

1 The wedding ceremonies of the Turkmen workers
*Sh. Annaklychev**

The description of Turkmen wedding ceremonies and customs
occupies an important place in the works of both pre-Revolutionary (1) and Soviet (2) authors, who have studied the
ethnography of the Turkmen people. Judging by information
we have received from a large number of sources, the wedding
ceremonies and customs are noticeably different now from in
the past, although there are some common features.

Under Soviet rule, Turkmen wedding ceremonies and customs
have undergone considerable changes. The marriages of
Turkmen workers today are, with few exceptions, registered
in the ZAGS, and in areas where there are no ZAGS, in the
village Soviets. (ZAGS = Registry Office. ZAGS initials for
Zapisi Aktov Grazhdanskogo Sostayaniya. Records of Civilian
Status Acts. Village Soviets = Village Council Offices. T.D.)
In the industrial centres of the republic the number of young
families whose marriages are attested to by the documents of
the ZAGS is increasing each year. This is favoured above all
by the continued growth in the material well-being of the
workers, in their cultural level, and improvements in living
and other social conditions.

For confirmation of this, let's turn to the facts. In 1958,
321 marriages were registered in Cheleken ZAGS, whereas in
1960 there were over 400. In Kizyl-Arvat, 96 marriages were
registered from 1 January to 1 May 1960 alone, which is more
than in the whole of 1959. During 1959-60, 1,068 marriages
were registered in the ZAGS of the town of Nebit-Dag, 220 in
Kum-Dag, 75 in the village of Vyshka, 255 marriages in the
Serny factory and in Darvaz. About 600 marriages were registered in Krasnovodsk town ZAGS in 1961. Again in Nebit-
Dag 150 marriages were registered in January-February alone
in 1961.

However, some parents insist that not only the contemporary
but also the traditional wedding ceremonies should be observed
on the marriage of their children. Often they are influenced
by the fear that people of the older generation will condemn

* 'Issledovanie po Etnografii Turkmen'('Research in Turkmen
  Ethnography'), eds S.G. Agadzhanov and A. Oyazov,
  Ashkhabad, 1965, pp. 134-63.

them for violating customs of their ancestors.   This reflects
the negative influence of the older and more religious inhabitants.   But even in these cases only parts of the traditional
ceremonies are observed at workers' weddings and these have
undergone considerable changes, especially in recent years.
Parts of the old wedding ceremonies have survived among a
small percentage of the workers of Kizyl-Arvat, Bezmein and
Gaurdak.   However, they are more rarely found among the
industrial workers of Nebit-Dag, Kum-Dag, Krasnovodsk, and
Cheleken.

The Turkmen of the south-east shore of the Caspian Sea
have long had close cultural-economic links with Russia.   Progressive Russian culture penetrated here earlier than in the
central and south-eastern raions of Turkmenistan.   (Raion =
Soviet administrative region or district.   T.D.)   This circumstance naturally had a progressive effect on the development
of the family-social structure and the culture of the Turkmen
of the western raions of the republic.

Almost all marriages in workers' families are concluded in the
traditional way - by negotiations between the parents of those
getting married, although the young men and girls meet quite
freely and themselves decide on the marriage beforehand,
which was not possible in the pre-Revolutionary past. (3)
Negotiations are usually only started with the consent of the
young man and after he has expressed his desire to marry the
girl of his choice.   Parents today do not make arbitrary deci-
sions about the fate of their children.   Girls and young men
marry for love.   The girls usually inform their parents of
their decision to get married through someone close to them,
just as the young men do.   Sometimes, the girl herself warns
her parents of the impending visit of the parents or relatives
of her suitor for marriage.   All this, of course, is a clear
indication of how greatly the position of the Turkmen girl has
changed under Soviet rule and how she now has equal rights
with men.   During the negotiations, which usually take place
in the home of the girl's parents, all questions connected with
the wedding arrangements are decided.   They have to agree
on the date of the wedding, and whether the bridegroom's
parents should contribute towards the meal provided in the
house of the bride's parents on the day of the wedding.   A
large number of people from the bridegroom's side come to take
away the bride, and they have to be given a meal.   Before
the wedding, the bridegroom's parents bring two or three
sheep, several puds (one pud = 16 kg.   T.D.) of rice, flour,
etc., to the bride's house for the wedding meal.   Their close
relatives take some of the burden from them;   they bring
dresses, scarves, necklaces and other gifts as presents for
the bride, her parents, her brothers and their wives.   This
custom of giving presents to the bride, her parents and her

close relatives exists among other Central Asian people. (4)
All this is done with the aim of to some degree lightening the
expenses of the bride's parents. (5)

Until recently, the negotiations with the bride's parents
were carried out by envoys of the bridegroom's parents, who
were called 'elchi' or 'savchy' (matchmakers). There were
usually two or three of them and they were men who were
close relatives of the bridegroom, or other experienced people.
Today matchmakers are still sent (both among the workers and
the village population) when marriage is being conducted in
the traditional way. However, the role of the matchmakers
has lost its former importance in the conclusion of marriage.

On the whole, the matchmakers are now women, usually the
mother or other close relatives of the bridegroom. The ceremonial meetings of the matchmakers with the bride's parents
and relatives are not the same as in the past. Until recently
an 'auspicious' day ('sekhetli gun') was usually chosen for the
negotiations with the bride's parents. This custom is still
occasionally observed today. However, the negotiations are
usually held on Sundays and holidays.

On their arrival in the house of the bride's parents, the
matchmakers usually say 'So and so's son is in love with your
daughter and we have therefore been given full powers to
negotiate with you.' (Planynyn ogly sizing gyzyngyzy
khalapdyr, shonunguchini onung ene-atasy bizi size iberdiler.)
The bride's parents know beforehand why they have come and
only ask the matchmakers questions about the bridegroom for
the sake of the proprieties, traditionally observed on such
occasions. When the matchmakers are the bridegroom's
parents and other male and female relatives, the eldest of them
(usually the bridegroom's mother) announces that they have
come at the bridegroom's request. The matchmakers are
served national dishes. When women come as matchmakers,
they usually bring sweetmeats (sweets, cakes, raisins or wedding doughnuts ('pishme')) with them.

Until recently, the Turkmen girl hid from the matchmakers
when they came to her parents' house. Even after the betrothal she continued to avoid meeting both the matchmaker,
her fiancé's parents and those of his relatives who were older
than him. This still happens today, though rarely. Cases
of it can be found, for example, among workers' families in the
Sernye mines and Bezmein.

This is a result of the fact that some of the youth are still
under the influence of their elders and are afraid of the re-
bukes they will incur if they violate the traditional customs.
Some of the Turkmen workers still hold a so-called 'gengesh-

toi' (feast-meeting). This custom is more solemnly observed
by the western Turkmen, both in towns and country districts,
than by the Turkmen of Kizyl-Arvat and of the central and
south-eastern parts of the republic, where it is only observed by a narrow circle of the bridegroom's relatives. To
give an example: in October 1957, in Dzhebel (in western
Turkmenia where more people are invited. T.D.), a 'gengesh-
toi' was held in the home of a certain Turkmen-railwayman.
About 30 elders from Nebit-Dag, Kum-Dag and Dzhebel, including some who were not related to the bridegroom, took
part in the celebration. Sometimes even representatives of
other nationalities, usually workmates of the bridegroom's
father, are invited to the 'gengesh-toi' - this is particularly
common in the industrial centres of the republic. The feast-
meeting is usually held in the house of the bridegroom's
parents 10-20 days before the wedding. The participants in
the 'gengesh-toi' decide almost everything to do with the forthcoming wedding. A sheep is slaughtered in their honour and
they are served national dishes. After the meal one of the
bridegroom's relatives proposes that they decide the day of
the wedding, they name a day and promise to give all possible
help in arranging the wedding. At this meeting they also
decide how many days the wedding shall last and fix prizes
for the competitions (races, wrestling matches, rifle-shooting,
etc.). They decide which of them shall judge the competition, determine the distance for the races for horses of different ages, determine the responsibilities of each man present at
the wedding, and appoint 'dzharchi' (heralds) to announce the
forthcoming marriage to the inhabitants 2 or 3 days before
the wedding, etc.

In the not so distant past, the herald went around the villages on foot or horseback and in a loud voice announced the
important events to the inhabitants, invited them to weddings
and other celebrations. Today heralds are only used for
weddings. The custom of using a 'dzharchi' to invite people
to a wedding is widespread in raions of western Turkmenia (in
Nebit-Dag and adjacent settlements and villages). In Nebit-
Dag, Kum-Dag and adjacent raions there are heralds specially
appointed by the other inhabitants. (6) They usually take a
taxi and go round the town or village and announce that on
such and such a day there will be a wedding at such and
such a place. Until recently it was usual for only men to be
invited to the wedding, but now the 'dzharchi' announce that
men should bring their wives. Heralds are paid for their
work.

It must be said that in the past the 'gengesh-toi' was held
only by the more well-to-do families, as it made considerable
inroads on the family budget. According to our informers,
rich families in western Turkmenia would sometimes organise

two or even three 'gengesh-toi' to give especial solemnity and magnificence to the forthcoming wedding, which for ordinary families was quite impossible.

Today, the Turkmen workers have other ways of inviting people to a wedding. The most common is the individual invitation. Close male and female relatives of the bridegroom visit the houses of friends and neighbours and invite them to the wedding. Relatives of the bridegroom (both on the mother's and the father's side) who live in other, more distant villages, settlements and towns, are also invited to the wedding beforehand. Sometimes they are visited by one of the bridegroom's relatives, usually a man. He is called a 'chakylykchy' (one who invites, a messenger). In recent years, even newer ways of inviting people to weddings have appeared and are spreading widely among the workers' families, especially in western Turkmenia: after a girl and young man have agreed to get married, special invitations with photographs of the bride and bridegroom are ordered. Photographs of the girl and young man are placed at the top of the invitation and the day and time of the wedding and the names of the bride and bridegroom are written below. Several days before the wedding, the bride and bridegroom send these prepared invitations to their male and female friends, workmates, etc. Ordinary invitations, written on a typewriter are also quite often found. Such invitations are used not only for inviting people to a wedding but also for other family celebrations (moving house, celebration of someone's receiving a decoration, birthdays, etc.). However, these sorts of invitation are not so common among the workers of Kizyl-Arvat, Bezmein and Ashkhabad, as among the workers' families of western Turkmenia.

The registration of the marriage in the ZAGS usually takes place a day or a couple of days before the wedding. (7) On the day of the marriage the bridegroom's close relatives go to the bride's house. They collect the bride and one of her female relatives and usually drive to the ZAGS in a car. The bridegroom is there before them with his friend, the so-called 'musaib' and another of his relatives. The bride and bridegroom usually post an announcement of their marriage in the ZAGS beforehand. After the registration of their marriage in the ZAGS the bride and bridegroom each go back to their separate homes. This is especially common among the Turkmen workers' families of Cheleken.

The day chosen for the wedding is usually not a working day. Several days beforehand, the bridegroom's parents warn the bride's side that they must be prepared on that day to meet the bridegroom's envoys who must take away the bride. As the wedding day approaches their close and dis-

tant relatives, male and female friends, workmates, etc., who
live in other towns, settlements and villages, come to stay in
the houses of the bride and bridegroom.   The women, especially the older ones, bring presents to the wedding.   Usually
they bring cakes, sweets, dried fruit, wedding biscuits and
scarves of different colours and silk, wool and cotton material.

As a rule, they set out to get the bride in the first half of
the day.   All the wedding guests therefore gather in the
bridegroom's house in the morning.   In most cases, the
bridegroom tries not to show himself to the guests until the
wedding starts.   When everything is ready, the wedding procession called the 'gelnalyzhy' (literally: taking the bride),
sets out for the bride's house.   Everyone who wants takes
part in it.   In the past, the bridegroom and his parents were
an exception but now they too sometimes join in the wedding
procession.

Both in western Turkmenia and in the other industrial
centres of the republic, a large number of people - sometimes
as many as fifty to a hundred - take part in the wedding procession. (8)   In the workers' settlements and towns of western Turkmenia many of the older girls can be seen among the
members of the wedding procession, something which didn't
happen in the past.   Under the influence of urban culture
this progressive phenomenon has already spread to the country
population of western Turkmenia.   Girls play the most active
part in the procession among the Turkmen workers (the descendants of Nokhurly) most of whom live in the Geok-Tepe
territorial administration and in a number of industrial towns
and workers' settlements.   Unfortunately, their retrogressive
elders sometimes forbid the girls to take part in the wedding
procession.

The guests who remain behind in the bridegroom's house
until the wedding procession returns with the bride help the
owners of the house to prepare the wedding feast and carry
out other last-minute tasks to do with the wedding arrangements.

In the past, the Turkmens went to get the bride on camels
and horses.   The strongest camel was chosen for the bride
and on its saddle they built a so-called 'kezhebe' (a type of
palanquin.   T.D.).   The 'kezhebe' were decorated with various materials. (9)

Nowadays they go to get the bride in trucks and taxis, on
motor cycles, etc.   The bridegroom's closest friends and some
of his relatives, both on the mother's and on the father's
side, hire taxis at their own expense.   This is one of their
ways of helping the bridegroom and his parents out in the

expenses of the wedding.   Often two or three trucks and
dozens of cars take part.   These are richly decorated in the
traditional way.   For example, the scarves which were in the
past used to decorate the wedding camels are hung from the
radiator of the car in which the bride is to travel ('duebash-
lyk');   a carpet-bag ('due khalyk') usually hangs from the
side of the car and dozens of silk and wollen scarves are
fastened to it.   The trucks are often covered with rugs,
mats and sheepskins.   The cars are decorated with silk
scarves and beautiful materials which are called of old 'at
gulak'.   The most magnificent wedding processions of all are
those of the Turkmen workers of the central raions of the
republic.   Some of the scarves are later given to the bride's
parents and they in turn give them to their close relatives
and neighbours.   There are also some differences among the
wedding processions of the Turkmen workers.   For example,
in western Turkmenia, girls and young men hold a richly
sewn curtain - again called a 'kezhebe' - over the car in
which the bride sits.   This can be traced back to the ancient
custom of conveying the bride in a palanquin ('kezhebe')
attached to the saddle of a camel.

The bridegroom's parents appoint the leaders of the wedding
procession.   These are usually two elderly people - a man
and a woman.   Everyone else taking part has to obey them
unquestioningly.   The leaders are responsible for the safe
return of the members of the wedding procession.   The man
- a trusted friend of the bridegroom's parents - is sometimes
jokingly referred to as 'the commandant'. (10)   The duties of
the leaders of the procession also include the presentation of
gifts to the bride's parents and relatives in the name of the
bridegroom's parents.   The leaders have to be present at the
wedding from beginning to end.

In rare cases, some vigorous young women are unofficially
selected from among the members of the wedding procession.
Their obligations include the staging of a mock battle with the
bride's female friends.   However, this 'battle' has a symbolic
and conventional character which clearly differentiates it from
the old custom, 'dalash'.   These women often wear huge
ornaments called 'bilezik' on their arms.   In the past, the
women's battle for the bride was led by the 'iigit ienge' (the
wife of the bridegroom's elder brother).   Her duties
included winning over the 'ov ienge' (wife of the bride's elder
brother) during the latter's ritual refusal to hand the bride
over to the bridegroom's envoys. (11)

Girls play an active part in the wedding procession of the
Turkmen of the western raions of the republic.   It is usually
the girls who hold the wedding curtain ('kezhebe') mentioned
above.   Each corner of the curtain is held by three girls.

As they go along, the 'kezhebe' is filled by the wind and covers almost all the people in the car.   Often, one of the girls holds a bell in her hand all the way and rings it until the wedding procession reaches the bridegroom's house.   The use of bells at weddings undoubtedly comes from the previous traditions of the wedding caravan.   This is characteristic of the Turkmen of the village raions of western Turkmenia, but it is also sometimes observed in the weddings of the workers of Central Kara-Kum.   Among the inhabitants of Nebit-Dag, Cheleken, Krasnovodsk, Kum-Dag and other workers' settlements the members of the wedding procession give presents to people they meet on the way.   A woman (usually a relative of the bridegroom) sits in the leading car holding scarves ready to give to people they meet.   In some cases the leaders of the wedding procession hand out similar scarves.   The Turkmen workers - those who are descended from Nokhur - give the people they meet little parcels of sweetmeats or fruits. This custom is observed by workers living in Bezmein, Ashkhabad, Kizyl-Arvat, Nebit-Dag, and other towns.   The members of the wedding procession, especially the younger ones, sing songs in different languages as they go.   In the industrial centres, representatives of many other nationalities can often be found at workers' weddings (friends and workmates of the bride and bridegroom).   It is therefore not surprising that the members of the wedding procession sing 'chastushka' (Russian folk-songs), contemporary popular songs in Russian, as well as performing Azerbaidzhanian songs and dances, and so on.   Here it should be noted that the performers of these songs and dances include many young Turkmen, especially in the towns and workers' settlements of western Turkmenia.   The wedding, like other family ceremonies of the Turkmen workers, is gradually assuming an international character.

When the wedding procession reaches the house of the bride's parents, everyone comes out to meet it.   Some of those present, especially the women and girls, go into a specially prepared room.   The men, as a rule, stay outdoors and sit down on sheepskin rugs and mats spread out on the ground.   In cold and rainy weather, they too sit under a canopy slung from the side of the house.   The people who have come for the bride are usually given tea, pilaff, meat, soup, etc.   During the wedding feast in the home of the bride's parents the members of the bride and bridegroom's parties make each other's acquaintance.   They usually sit and eat the wedding meal together.

After they have eaten and handed over the presents they have brought, the bridegroom's envoys go into the house where the bride is sitting in a circle of her female friends. While they are waiting for the wedding procession, the girls

and women dance and make merry.   In some cases the bride's
parents gather in the special room which has been prepared
for the bride, her friends and her female relatives. (12)

When the wedding procession arrives, the female members of
the bridegroom's party, headed by their leader, the 'iigit
ienge', go into the bride's house first.   With the 'iigit
ienge's' help the bride changes her girl's clothes for a new
dress ('chykysh') donated by the bridegroom's parents.   The
bride is also given a new head-dress of scarves brought from
the bridegroom's house ('bashdon').   This way of dressing
the bride is common among the workers' families of Cheleken,
Kum-Dag, Nebit-Dag, Krasnovodsk and, to some extent,
Kizyl-Arvat.   Among the miners of the republic – the
workers' families of Bezmein and Ashkhabad – the bride is
arrayed in a new dress long before the arrival of the bridegroom's party.   In rare cases, instead of a scarf a waistcoat
('kurte'), always red in colour, brought from the bridegroom's
house is placed on the bride's head.

When the bride has been dressed the mock battle between
the bride and bridegroom's parties begins.   In the past, the
battle for the bride was one of the central moments of the
Turkmen wedding ceremony: those who took part in it often
suffered serious injury.   There were cases when the bride's
neighbours sneaked up to the women who had come for the
bride and cut their head-dresses, the hems of their dresses
and the tassels of the scarves with scissors.   P. Ogorodnikov
in the 1870s described how at a wedding he saw in western
Turkmenia the battle ended in a genuine fight: people's
clothes were torn to shreds, their bodies covered in
bruises. (13)

Mock fights between girls and women are still held among
some groups of workers in Turkmenistan, but they are essentially different from the former traditional battle for the bride.
For example, among the workers of Gaurdak, after the guests
have eaten, the leader of the wedding procession divides a
small sum of money among the bride's close relatives, after
which the bridegroom's mother or another of his relatives goes
into the house to the bride.   When she enters the house, the
bride and the friends surrounding her stand up and greet her
with a bow.   She goes up to the bride and pretends that she
wants to look at her face, although as a rule she knows the
bride well before the wedding.   The bride in her turn 'makes
a show of resistance' and hides her face with a scarf.   Meanwhile, the bride's friends jeer at the mother or the female
relatives of the bridegroom.   This fight thus has nothing in
common with the previous custom, when the bride and bridegroom's parties fought in earnest in their 'battle' for the
bride.   Now the battles have taken on a completely new form,

are the occasion of jokes and merrymaking, and have lost
their previous meaning.

One of the most important moments in the wedding ceremony
of the Turkmen workers is when the bride leaves her parents'
house.   In western Turkmenistan the 'ov ienge' usually leads
the bride out and seats her in the car.   Among the workers
of central Kara-Kum, Bezmein, Kizyl-Arvat, Ashkhabad and
Gaurdak, the bride is carried out of the parental home on a
mat or rug.   The bridegroom's male relatives and friends
play an active role in this.   In some cases, the bride's
female relatives sit with her on the mat or carpet.   They will
only let the bride go when they've been given a small sum of
money by the leader of the wedding procession.   After this,
the bridegroom's party sit in the wedding car.   Sometimes
they observe another custom of giving presents to the bride's
party.   For example, among some of the workers of Gaurdak
a female relative of the bride helps the bridegroom's envoys
seat the bride on the mat.   She usually receives a small
present or money for this.   However, the custom described
above, now as previously, is not observed at the weddings of
workers' families who are descendants of the Turkmen-
Nokhurly.

In the past (in the central raions of Turkmenia), there was
a custom by which each of the members of the wedding procession tried to steal something from the house of the bride's
parents.   The guests often took spoons, teapots, bowls and
knives, but if they were caught with the things they had to
take them back.   It was believed that people who got away
with taking something from the bride's home would soon have
a wedding or other celebration.   This custom is no longer
observed at workers' weddings, although traces of it may be
glimpsed on rare occasions among the workers of central
Kara-Kum.

In the past, the majority of the Turkmen believed that the
wedding procession should not set out on its return journey
without first observing another custom.   They used to seat
the bride on a special wedding camel, and when the camel got
up she had to throw herself to the ground.   She was sometimes seriously injured as a result.   If the bride did not
observe this custom, she long remained an object of censure.
It was said that she 'wanted to get married' ('ozi khalap
gitmek') which was considered reprehensible.   Today this
custom has finally died out.

At the beginning of 1960 the author observed an interesting
wedding custom among the Turkmen workers of Gaurdak which
is not found among the workers of the other industrial centres
of the republic.   At this wedding, when the bridegroom's

party had seated the bride in the car and was setting off on
the return journey, two elderly men came out from the crowd
of the bride's relatives gathered on the road with a long cord
with which they roped off the path of the wedding procession. The leader of the wedding procession, who was by
this time in the car, gave each of them a small sum of money,
after which the wedding procession continued on its way. A
similar wedding custom exists in south Kirghizistan, where
children and adolescents stretch a lasso across the road in the
path of the newlyweds. To clear the way, they are given
presents of small sums of money. (14)

Among some of the Turkmen workers, although one now
sees it very rarely, traces have survived of the old custom
by which, when the wedding procession sets off on its return
journey, the bride's party stage an 'unfriendly' sending off
and throw clods of earth and stones after them. This custom
is no longer observed today in western Turkmenia and still
less in the towns and workers' settlements, but it is to some
degree preserved by the workers of Kizyl-Arvat, Bezmein and
central Kara-Kum. (15) In these raions, the female relatives
sometimes throw sticks, stones and bits of mud, and among a
section of the workers at Gaurdak the bride's relatives sprinkle
everyone with flour. However, the content of the custom has
changed and it is now regarded as a game, whereas in the
past people were seriously injured. A. Lomakin described
how the members of the wedding procession usually returned
to the bridegroom's house with bloody noses and broken
teeth. (16) Even about twenty years ago this custom was
comparatively widely observed in some raions of the republic,
especially in villages. There were occasions when unbaked
and fired bricks and jam jars full of black oil were thrown at
the members of the wedding procession. Today this (like
many other) harmful customs of the past has vanished not
only among the workers' families but also among the peasants.
An ethnographical study of the everyday life of Turkmen
families, and of workers in particular, shows that the remnants of this and other customs cannot survive for long, but
that it is necessary to intensify cultural work among the
masses to ensure their final disappearance.

Today when the wedding procession sets off, the bride's
mother sometimes takes a handful of flour and sprinkles the
car in which the bride is to travel, then, turning to her
daughter, says: 'Manlaiy achyk bolsun, yolyak bolsun' ('May
your brow be open; may your road be white'). In addition
the villagers of western Turkmenia, the descendants of the
Nokhurly, many worker and peasant families living in central
Kara-Kum, and the miners of Gaurdak observe a custom by
which the 'ov ienge' or 'ienge' accompanies the bride to the
bridegroom's house and remains there with her for several

days. (17)   However, this custom is not found among the
workers of Bezmein, Ashkhabad and other cities of the
republic.   When the wedding procession arrives at the
bridegroom's house it is met first of all by the bridegroom's
mother who (as in south Kirghizia) sprinkles the bride with
wheat-flour and says 'Ayagyn dushsun agzybir bolun' ('Be
happy, live in peace').   Those present are then sometimes
showered with money.   In addition, elderly women, usually
relatives of the bridegroom, hand out sweets, dried fruit,
wedding doughnuts, etc.   The custom of sprinkling the
bride and the members of the wedding procession exists among
almost all the Turkmen.

After this a whole series of other ceremonies are performed.
At the wedding of the workers of Cheleken, Krasnovodsk,
Nebit-Dag and Kum-Dag, when the sprinkling of the bride and
the guests is over, the car with the bride, the 'ov ienge' and
other members of the wedding procession drives on a few
streets.   Then it stops at the entrance to the house destined
for the newlyweds ('orugoi').   They choose a house not far
from the house of the bridegroom's parents, usually the home
of an elder brother, or neighbour with whom the bridegroom's
parents are on very friendly terms.   In the past, there was
a superstition that one should enter the newlyweds' house only
from the side opposite the side on which the 'unlucky star'
appeared in the sky.   Otherwise unhappiness awaited the
couple.   No such belief exists today among the workers of
Turkmenistan.   Sometimes some young men and women shut
the door of the 'orugoi' from the inside and will only open it
after receiving a present or money.

The Turkmen workers observe a custom by which the 'ienge'
accompanies the bride into the bridegroom's house.   When
they enter the house the 'ienge' asks the bridegroom's parents
what presents (female ornaments) they will give the bride.
After this she allows the bride to sit down and the bridegroom's parents leave the house.   The bride remains in the
house with the 'ienge' and the girls who took part in the wedding procession.

Then the bride is taken to the other house, especially prepared for the newlyweds, and after this the wedding celebrations begin: the songs, dances, wrestling matches, etc.
One interesting wedding custom of the population of both the
towns and villages of western Turkmenia is the performing of
dances called 'zikir' or 'kusht depmek'.   These dances are
accompanied with songs.   The 'zikir' is very widespread
among the Turkmen of today, including the workers.   It is
danced not only at weddings but also at other family celebrations and on popular holidays.   A detailed description and
explanation of the zikir appears in one of our previous publi-

cations, (18) and in part in A. Dzhikiev's monograph. (19)
We will therefore limit ourselves here to a summary of new
materials which we have accumulated in the course of 1959-62.

The 'zikir' is more common in Gazan-Kuli, Cheleken and Krasnovodsk than in Nebit-Dag, Kum-Dag and other settlements,
but all the Turkmen perform it in almost exactly the same
way.   The 'zikir' has four parts 'divana', 'ekedepin' (one
beat), 'uch depin' (three beats), and 'dem-dem' (literally: a
deep breath).   The songs and the movements of the dancers
are very little different in each of these.   The songs for
example have a different number of syllables;   the dances,
beats.

To dance the 'zikir' one needs a special room.   It must be
large, with a wooden floor so that the sound of stamping of
feet can be heard.   Before the 'zikir' begins, a large number
of men and women of various ages gather in the room.   They
stand in a circle and one of them (usually an elderly man)
turns to those around him and says 'bashlalyn' ('let's begin').
After this, someone utters the words 'uaaya uaau', which is
the start of the 'zikir', and is gradually taken up by the
rest.   Meanwhile, the 'gazal' (songs) begin.   In them they
sing about different aspects of their joyless past and their
present happiness.   Some 'gazaly' are dedicated to the heroism of Soviet people in the Great Patriotic War.   Other songs
echo the gratitude of the Turkmen to the Communist Party
and the Soviet government for its concern for ordinary people.
During the 'zikir' they also sing humorous couplets and folk-
songs.   On rare occasions, when there are a lot of religious
old men at the wedding, the 'zikir' starts off with the old
songs, sometimes religious ones.   But there are very few
such songs and they are sung only to please the older people
present.

While on a study trip to Cheleken, Krasnovodsk, Nebit-Dag,
Kum-Dag and other towns and settlements, the author wrote
down over 500 verses of songs sung in the wedding 'zikir'.
They are all the fruit of national creativity.   We therefore
consider it necessary to include some of these songs and
verses here.

Samarvaryn misi bar,
Tussesinin isi bar,
Tshchilerin oiynde,
Radiolan besi bar.

There is a brass samovar
There is a smell of smoke
From the houses of the workers
comes the sounds of the radio-
gramophone.

Sary sandyk ne gerek,
Sabyn salmaga gerek
Kakan ishden gelende
Elin yuvmaga gerek

What's the yellow box for?
It's for putting soap in;
When my father comes from work,
It's for washing his hands.

Suit gerek, gaimak gerek
Gaimagy yaimak gerek,
Gyzyn pula stanyn,
Gozuni oimak gerek

A man needs milk and cream;
One shouldn't beat cream
But the man who sells his
daughter (gives her for kalym)
Should have his eyes put out.

Kusht depishme, yaryshma
Yaryhanda galyshma,
Nebitdagly, Chelekenchi
Bir-birinden galushma.

It's better not to fight during
the songs and dances of the zikir,
But if you fight, it's better
not to be beaten
The Nebitdagsi and the Chelekins
are as good as each other in a fight.

Sometimes in the 'zikir' they sing 'gazal' describing the evils
of pre-Revolutionary life:

Khiva gitdim at bilen,
Boinym doly khat bilen,
Eser menin manlaiym
Yazylypdyr yat bilen.

I went by horse to Khiva,
I had many letters with me,
Unlucky fate condemned me,
To be taken for a stranger.

Songs about the overthrow of the feudal and capitalist yoke,
and the struggles of the workers against their class-enemies
occupy an important place in the repertoire of songs sung
during the 'zikir':

Kapitalisti iykdyk biz,
Lykyp ustun chykdyk biz,
Azatlygyn urunda
Kop zekhmetler chekdik biz

We overthrew the power of the
capitalists,
We were the conquerors
The road to freedom wasn't easy.

Beiik-beiik ak zhailar,
Tezeden dogan ailar,
Garyplaryn zoryndan
Yok bolun gitdi bailar

Big huge white houses
(Above them) - a new moon shines
Thanks to the strength of the poor
The beys have vanished for ever.

Ekin ekier kolkhozlar,
Dokundokier kolkhozlar,
Bai, suitkhor kulaklaryn
Kokun gyryar kolkhozlar.

The Kolkhoz plough and sow,
They fertilise their fields
The kolkhozniks pull the beys
and the kulak parasites up
by the roots.

Agach-agazha bakar,
Arasyndan suv akar,
Teze yoly gorenler,
Kone yola kim bakar?

Two trees stand together,
Between them water flows,
Can he who has seen the new road
Turn back on the old?

As everyone knows, in the first days of the Great Patriotic
War of the Soviet Union against Hitler's Germany, the Communist Party called on the whole Soviet people to hasten the
defeat of the enemy by all means possible.   The party adopted the slogan 'All for the front, all for victory'.   The
party's call to the people was repeated in the songs sung in
the 'zikir':

I
Guvandyryp ilimiz,
Berkidelin tylymyz,
Fronta kop zat berin,
Pugta gushap biliniz

To bring joy to our people
Let's strengthen the home front!
Tie your belt tightly
Help the front in every way.

II
Agach-agazha bakar,
Arasyndan suv akar,
Gakhryman sovet khalky
Dushmandan ustun chykar.

Two trees stand together
Between them water flows
The heroic Soviet people
Will all the same defeat its enemy.

III
Biz ileri iorieris,
Ganym leshin serieris,
Fashistleri dargadyp
Gyzyl baidak gerieris

We are moving forward,
We will destroy our enemies
We will rout the fascists,
And see the red flag flying.

IV
Gyzlar, zekhmet chekelin,
Nebiti kop alalyn,
Ummasyz bailyk alyp,
Batany berkidelin

Girls, let us work
Extract more oil!
We will strengthen our motherland
With the extraction of incalculable wealth.

We also took down many songs and verses glorifying the
Communist Party:

Duralyna, duralyn,
Kaspide torlar guralyn,
Partiyan sayasynda,
Biz kommunizm guralyn

Stand up, stand up,
We will throw the net into the Caspian
We will build communism
Under the banner of the party.

Sovetlerde gul bitdi,
Lal dillere dil bitdi,
Yashasyn kompartiya!
Medeniet osdi gitdi

Under Soviet power flowers bloomed,
The dumb began to speak
Our culture grew beyond all recognition
Long live the Communist Party.

In 1962 a canal was built to carry the water of the great
mid-Asian river, Amu-Dar'ya, through Kara-Kum to the capital
of our republic.   This artificial Kara-Kum river, as the
people called it, was more than 800 kilometres long.   The
construction of the canal was reflected in the popular songs
which were sung at weddings and other celebrations:

Garaguma suv geler,
Suv ustune guv geler,
Chanap yatan boz-meidan
Goie gulzara doner

Suv geler aka-aka,
Daglardan boke-boke,
Garagumda bag ekeres,
Zhoyalar cheke-cheke

The first verse says that a great water will come to the sands
of Kara-Kum, and swans will come with it.   The last two lines
speak of the people's conviction that the water brought from
the Amu-Dar'ya will transform the desert and the steppe into
a flowering land.   The second verse is also dedicated to the
canal, which will irrigate the barren desert.   It says that
with the coming of water, Kara-Kum will turn into a beautiful
garden.

Sometimes the songs sung in the 'zikir' include satirical and
humorous verse, like the Russian Chastushka.

Moskviche munerin,
Pobeda mashyn bolmasa
Ol oglana barmaryn,
Goluma sagat almasa

Khellik bize, khellik biz,
Gumdagyndan geldik biz,
Nebitdagyn gyzlaryn,
Dalashmany aldyk biz.

Almanyn agyna bak,
Sagadyn bagyna bak,
Meni goresin gelse
Kaspin boyna bak,

Krasnovodskin ak dashy,
Zhailar salmaga yagshy,
Krasnovodskin gyzlary,
Kino barmaga yagshy

Agach agachsyz bolmas
Agach mivesiz bolmas
Nebitdagyn gyzlarnyn
Goly sagatsyz bolmas

Ak bilek atly bolar,
Gyz soen bagtly bolar,
Soen gyzyn almasa
Iuregi otly bolar

A short summary of the contents of each verse gives us the following: (1) A girl turns to her girlfriends and says that if she can't ride in a 'Pobeda' car she'll go in a 'Moscvitch', but in no case will she marry her beloved unless he gives her a wristwatch. (20)   (2) The girls participating in a wedding procession are proud that they have come from Kum-Dag and are taking the bride to Nebit-Dag without the traditional battle between women and girls.   (3) The girl advises the young man to turn his attention to the white apples and that if he wants to see her, he must come to the shore of the Caspian Sea.   (4) The girl praises Krasnovodsk, and sings of how good the white stone quarried near the town is for building houses with, and how good it is to go to the cinema with the girls of Krasnovodsk.   (5) Says that barren and fruitful trees don't look the same but a girl from Nebit-Dag can't do without a wristwatch.   (6) Is in praise of a girl's tender white hands, the strength of love and stresses that if a boy can't marry his love, he will always carry a fire in his heart.

These songs are sometimes sung to the accompaniment of an accordion at Turkmen weddings in the towns.   However, this phenomenon has not yet assumed a mass character.

The wedding 'zikir' (dance. T.D.) performed by the population of western Turkmenia today has appeared in the last

20-30 years.   The so-called 'zikir' that existed before had a
completely different meaning and was performed at the 'healing' of the sick.   This was really nothing more than a
shaman ('porkhan') ritual, in which the 'porkhan' twirled
round and round in ecstasy.   During this ritual, the
'porkhan' shouted various magic incantations.   The aim of
the shaman 'zikir' was to 'drive the evil spirits' out of the
body of the sick man.   The modern 'zikir' has nothing in
common with the previous 'zikir' except the name.

The 'zikir' organised during the wedding in the bridegroom's
house usually continues with breaks for 3 days.   The 'zikir'
is performed even in cases when the bride is a representative
of another nationality.   In workers' families Azerbaidzhanian
songs and dances are performed as well as the 'zikir' during
the wedding (and also other) ceremonies.   The workers of
Krasnovodsk and Cheleken are especially noted for this.

In some places, for example in Gaurdak, girls and women
(especially the younger ones) assemble in the house appointed
for the bride, sing songs, play tambourines and perform
Uzbek dances.   The men invite professional singers ('bagshy')
to sing to them to the accompaniment of a 'dutar' (two-stringed
instrument.   T.D.).   Many of the women and girls come here
from their separate part of the house.   They, together with
the men, listen with rapt attention to the merry, joyful old
and new songs.   At workers' weddings (especially in Krasnovodsk) it is often Azerbaidzhanian singers who sing and
dance.   In this case they play their national musical instru-
ments, on which one can also play the Turkmen melodies.

The games and sports begin on the day the bride is brought
to the bridegroom's house.   The wedding ceremonies of the
workers of Cheleken, Nebit-Dag, Kum-Dag and Krasnovodsk,
and also of the rural districts of western Turkmenia, are distinguished by the fact that national wrestling ('goresh') occupies one of the most important places in the games held in
honour of the marriage.   Among the other Turkmen it plays
a secondary role. (21)   The games of 'yaglyga tobusmak'
(jumping in the air to reach a scarf) and 'cheke-cheke' 'iuzuk'
(the ring) are immensely popular among the workers of Kizyl-
Arvat, Bezmein, central Kara-Kum, Ashkhabad and a number
of other towns and settlements, while they are almost unknown
to the population of western Turkmenia.

The last game is the most popular wedding entertainment of
all among the population of central Turkmenia.   Men and boys
of all ages take part in it.   The players (of whom there are
sometimes as many as 70-80) are divided into two groups, each
of which has two or three leaders chosen from those most experienced in the game.   They sit on the ground and form a

wide circle, divided into two halves. A leader of one of the
contending groups takes some small object in his hand, usually
a penknife, and shows it to everybody. Then he goes up to
each of the players in his group in turn, and tries to hide
the object on one of them without the players of the opposing
group seeing. After this, the leaders of the other group
search for the hidden object. According to the rules of the
game, nobody has the right to touch a player's throat. If
they find the hidden knife, they are the winners, and if not,
the losers. A prize of 80-100 or more roubles, goes to the
winning group.

In some cases, the marriage is concluded in the presence of
two witnesses ('opiyadakazy'). The witnesses chosen are
often elderly people. Cases have been observed among the
workers of western Turkmenia where, after the conclusion of
the marriage, the bridegroom and his friend ('musaib') go into
the house where the bride is sitting in a circle of women and
girls. The 'ov ienge' and the 'iigit ienge' sit next to the
bride and join the bride and bridegroom by their little fingers
('kulen barmak'). Meanwhile, the young men who came with
the bridegroom remain outside on the street, and divide themselves into two groups. One group goes into the room to
defend the bridegroom and the 'musaib' from the others who
are waiting in the streets to 'attack' them. The young men
surround the bridegroom and go outside where the second
group falls on them. A mock battle ensues, during the
course of which the group of young men who are defending
the bridegroom have to remain outside the bride's house.

Sometime later, the 'musaib' and the bridegroom return to
the room where the bride and both 'ienge' are. Turning to
the bridegroom, the 'ov ienge' says 'Gotur due iitdirme, arpa
chorek iidirme' ('Don't let your bride take the reins and drive
a camel, covered with ringworm; don't let her eat cakes made
from barley flour'). After this both 'ienge' go away leaving
only the 'musaib', the bridegroom and the bride in the room.
The bridegroom asks the bride to show her face to the
'musaib', although the latter has usually seen her before the
wedding. The bridegroom takes the scarf from her face, or,
with the bridegroom's permission, the 'musaib' does this, after
which he goes out leaving the newlyweds alone.

Among the workers of Gaurdak one of the 'ienge' takes the
bridegroom to the bride. When they arrive the bride's relatives (the other 'ienge') leave the house. The moment the
bridegroom enters the house, the bride stands up. The
bridegroom's 'ienge' joins their hands. Sometimes when this
happens, the bride tries to stand on the bridegroom's foot
without being noticed. Some of the girls believe that a bride
who stands on the bridegroom's foot will have the upper hand

in married life. After the 'enne' goes, the bridegroom throws sweetmeats about the room and sprinkles the bride with them (sweets, cakes, currants, etc.).

Among the workers of western Turkmenia, when the 'ov ienge' and the 'iigit' go, the 'musaib' asks the latter to bring teapots, sugar bowls and a boiling samovar. The young men present then jokingly test how well the bride can boil, pour and serve tea. Then they all go, leaving the bride and bridegroom alone. The 'musaib' stays outside and guards the house ('oi goram') from the curious far into the night.

As has already been said, the workers of western Turkmenia have a custom by which a young man in order to get married has to obtain the services of a trustworthy and usually single workmate, called the 'musaib' (the equivalent of the best man in an English marriage. T.D.). The 'musaib' helps the bridegroom in every way and the bridegroom will perform the same services for him if he gets married. The bridegroom and his best man remain close friends for the rest of their lives. The 'musaib' provides refreshments at his own expense for those who come to congratulate the bridegroom, while he is in the 'musaib''s house. The bridegroom goes to the 'musaib''s house on the first day of the wedding and stays there until his meeting with the bride. The 'musaib' himself hires and pays for a car for the wedding procession and is one of the leaders of the procession; if any of the bride's party makes a claim on the bride when the bridegroom's envoys come for her, he gives them various presents. Among the Turkmen of other raions, instead of a workmate, the bridegroom has a close friend who accompanies him everywhere for several days before and after the wedding; he has no special name to distinguish him from his other friends, but he carries out some of the functions of the 'musaib' - for example he 'guards' the house in which the bride and bridegroom stay on their wedding night. Some of our informants told us that this guarding of the young couple was the most important of the 'musaib''s duties.

We could not find any information about the rights and duties of the 'musaib' in ethnographical literature. None the less, the appointment of a 'musaib' at weddings appears to be an ancient custom. In the distant past, the 'musaib' probably had the right of the first night. It is also interesting that in the past when the young men surrounding the bridegroom expressed a wish to see the bride's face and she resisted, the 'musaib', with the bridegroom's permission, tore the veil from her face and displayed the bride to those around them. However, the custom of appointing a 'musaib' today has lost its former meaning. The 'musaib' as we said earlier, is now usually a close friend of the bridegroom and his family.

On the second day after the wedding the Turkmen workers
observe a series of other customs.   The women and girls
take the bride to the house of the bridegroom's parents,
where her clothes are changed for those of a married woman
and the bridegroom's sister or the daughter of one of his
close relatives gives her a new skull-cap.   Among the descendants of Nokhurly the girl is dressed in women's clothes
in her father's house.

In several raions (among the workers of Kizyl-Arvat and
Bezmein) a mock battle between the girls and the women sometimes takes place when the bride discards her girl's clothes.
The girls surround the bride and refuse to let the women
dress her in women's clothes.   The battle usually ends with
the victory of the women.   A woman's head-dress ('alyndany
topby') is placed on the bride's head.   The bride's hair is
plaited in two tresses which hang down her back.   Among
the workers of Gaurdak, during the three days after she discards her girl's clothes the bride goes with her 'ienge' to the
bridegroom's house and greets his parents with a bow.   However, this custom does not exist among the Turkmen of other
areas of Turkmenia.

As recently as 20 years ago most of the Turkmen still preserved an old custom which was observed when the bride's
face was shown to those around her.   The bridegroom took a
long cord and went up to the bride, who sat on a sheepskin
carpet or mat with a headscarf tied tightly over her face.
The bridegroom wound the cord round her neck.   Then he
stepped back and violently pulled the cord towards him.
This operation, which often caused injury, was repeated until
the scarf fell from the bride's head.   Today this custom no
longer exists either among the workers or in the rural districts of the republic.

In the past, one of the customs observed strictly by almost
all the Turkmen groups was 'gaitarma' (the return of the
bride to her parents' home).   This custom common to many
peoples has now practically disappeared among the Turkmen
workers.   Traces of this harmful tradition are found - sometimes, but very rarely.   But even then this custom is very
different from the old 'gaitarma'.   Previously, the bride remained in her parents' house for 10-15 years.   She was often
allowed to return to her husband only after full payment of
the 'kalym' (bridewealth. T.D.).   Now, for example among
some of the workers of western Turkmenia (Cheleken, Krasnovodsk, Nebit-Dag, Kum-Dag), the young woman goes back
to her parents three or four days after the wedding.   However, if she wishes she can return to her husband on the
following day.   The young woman never stays in her parents'
house (where the custom of returning is observed) for more
than 5-10 days.

This contemporary custom has nothing in common with the
compulsory seclusion of the young woman.   It is preserved
by a few workers as a formal survival of the past.   Even so,
a decisive battle must be waged against such survivals in
whatever form they appear.   Young people and public opinion
should take an active part in this.

We must note that this battle has already commenced.   In
July 1960 the members of the Komsomol (Young Communists.
T.D.) of Maryisk raion carried out a special raid to check up
on cases of 'gaitarma'.   As a result of this raid, thirteen
young women were restored to their husbands.   All this took
place without any pressure being brought to bear and with the
full agreement of the bride's parents, after a heart-to-heart
talk with them.   Similar initiatives ought to be taken to root
out traces of the old ways wherever they are found.

An ethnographical study of the weddings of Turkmen workers today shows that socialist construction has led to great
changes in the spiritual aspects of Turkmen culture.   The
harmful ceremonies still observed in some places are quickly
vanishing and are being relegated to the sphere of tradition.
Many of the harmful traditional wedding ceremonies and customs have gone for good.   New and progressive wedding
ceremonies and customs have appeared: the participation of
girls and representatives of other nationalities in the wedding
procession, new wedding songs and dances, the registration of
marriage in the ZAGS.   The life of contemporary Turkmen
workers' families shows that the harmful wedding ceremonies
and customs which have survived from the past have lost their
former social importance.

The Komsomol wedding is one example of the new wedding
ceremony.   The description of a Komsomol wedding among
either the Turkmen of the country districts or the towns and
workers' settlements is a theme for a separate article.   The
Komsomol wedding is therefore not examined in the present
work.   The author hopes that a special article by him on this
theme will be published in the near future.

NOTES

1   K.K. Bode, Essays on the Turkmen Areas of the South-
East Shore of the Caspian Sea, 'Notes of the Fatherland',
no. 8, 1856, pp. 287-9;   A. Vamberi, 'A Journey Through
Central Asia', Moscow, 1874, pp. 278-80;   P. Ogorodnikov,
'Travels in the Caspian Provinces of Persia', 2nd ed.,
St Petersburg, 1878, pp. 217-20;   A. Lomakin, 'The Cus-
tomary Law of the Turkmen (Adat)', Ashkhabad, 1897,
pp. 3-4;   and others.

2   D.G. Yomudskaya-Burunova, 'The Women of Old Turk-
    menia', Moscow-Leningrad, 1931, pp. 26-7; G.P. Vasileva,
    The Turkmen-Nokhurl, 'Central Asian Ethnographic
    Papers', Moscow, 1954, pp. 196-9; D. Ovesov, The Turk-
    men-Murchal, 'Works of YuTAKE', vol. 9, Ashkhabad,
    1959, pp. 260-7; A. Dzhikiev, 'The Turkmen of the
    South-East Shore of the Caspian Sea', Ashkhabad, 1961,
    pp. 125-31; A. Orzov, 'The Balkan Turkmen in the late
    Nineteenth and early Twentieth Century', unpublished
    Candidat Thesis, Moscow, 1961, pp. 294-305; K. Ovezber-
    dyev, Materials on the Ethnography of the Turkmen-Saryk
    of the Pendin Oasis, 'Works of the Institute of History,
    Archeology and Ethnography of the Academy of Sciences
    of the Turkmen SSR', vol. 6, Ethnographical Series,
    Ashkhabad, 1962, pp. 159-65; and others.
3   P.P. Ogorodnikov, op. cit., p. 218.
4   On this, see the sections Uzbeks and Tadzhiks in the
    book, 'The Peoples of Central Asia and Kazakhstan', vol.
    1, Moscow, 1962, pp. 328, 616.
5   In modern weddings, between 100 and 300 people from
    both sides gather in the house of the bride's parents.
    No celebration makes as great an inroad on the family's
    budget as weddings.
6   These heralds do not exist in Kizyl-Arvat, Bezmein, the
    Sern factory, Darvaz, Ashkhabad, Gaurdak and a number
    of other industrial centres of the republic.
7   Unfortunately, there are still some cases when the mar-
    riage is registered a long time after the wedding.
8   Among the Turkmen workers of Gaurdak, between twenty
    and twenty-five people go to get the bride; they are
    mainly close relatives of the bridegroom.
9   See P.P. Ogorodnikov, op. cit., p. 218; Count Sholle,
    Bulate, Bonvalo et al., 'From Paris to the Farthest
    Bounds of India', Moscow, 1890, p. 108.
10 The Turkmen of the industrial centres of the republic
    usually call them this.
11 The terms 'iigit ienge' and 'ov ienge' were found mainly
    among the population of western Turkmenia; in other dis-
    tricts they are simply called 'enne'.   Their functions in
    the wedding ceremony were almost identical.   The role of
    the 'iigit ienge' and the 'ov ienge' could be fulfilled by
    any close female relatives of the bridegroom and bride.
12 The bride and her friends are usually in the house of one
    of their neighbours.   Similar customs have been observed
    among other peoples.   See, for example, O.A. Sukhareva,
    Aspects of the Marriage and Wedding Customs of the Tadz-
    hiks of Shakhristan Village, 'Papers of the Scientific Sec-
    tion at the Eastern Faculty of the Central Asian State Uni-
    versity', no. 1, Tashkent, 1928, p. 79.
13 P.P. Ogorodnikov, op. cit., p. 219.
14 'The Peoples of Central Asia and Kazakhstan', vol. 2,
    Moscow, 1963, p. 273.

15 D. Ovesov, op. cit., p. 3.
16 A. Lomakin, op. cit., p. 3.
17 G.P. Vasileva, op. cit., p. 199.
18 For a detailed account of the wedding zikir, see Sh.
    Annaklychev, 'The Daily Life of the Oil-Workers of Nebit-
    Daga and Kum-Daga', 1961, pp. 126-32; V.N. Basilov,
    The Origins of the Turkmen-Ata, 'Premuslim Beliefs and
    Rituals in Central Asia', Moscow, 1975.
19 A. Dzhikiev, op. cit., pp. 142-5.
20 In western Turkmenia, the bridegroom gives his fiancée
    watches and other presents.
21 See Sh. Annaklychev, op. cit., pp. 135-7.

2 The kinship system and customs connected with the ban on pronouncing the personal names of elder relatives among the Kazakhs
Kh.A. Argynbaev, 1975*

Many traces of kinship ties, connected with patriarchal kinship relations, can be found in Kazakh life. In the first place, the extent of Kazakh kinship relations is limited by the exogamic prohibition, observed to this day to the seventh generation. Patrilineal kinship relations are usually maintained within these limits up to the seventh generation of descendants from one ancestor. This also affects the laws of inheritance. Thus, where there was no direct heir, all the movable property and even the widow of the dead man were inherited by his relatives according to their degree of kinship in the father's line. These include siblings, first cousins, second cousins, and, in the absence of these, even more distant kinsmen. All this indicates that kinship ties were comparatively persistent and widespread among the pre-Revolutionary Kazakhs.

Close kinship ties were also strictly maintained in everyday life in the form of mutual moral and material aid. Thus, at the time of marriages of sons and daughters, the apportionment of property among married sons, the organisation of burial and funeral ceremonies, or in the case of natural calamities (such as fires, death by starvation of cattle during winter fodder shortages), relatives would help each other in accordance with the degree of their kinship and their wealth. The Kazakhs call this family solidarity - 'zhylu', 'nemeurin', and 'ume'. 'Zhylu' is the most ancient and palpable of these forms of aid. The other varieties are the product of later periods and are of more modest dimensions. These mutually beneficial ties between relatives gave rise to the Kazakh proverb - 'Kop zhiylsa kol' ('Collective aid is the guarantee of plenty').

This mutual aid among relatives started centuries ago in the period of the tribal system. At that time the members of the kin group enjoyed equal social status. Later, as a result of the emergence of property, material inequality, and classes, the mutual kinship ties and mutual material support gradually assumed a class character. 'Zhylu' was still widespread among the Kazakhs in the late-nineteenth to early-twentieth century, but by this time it chiefly answered the interests of

* A translation from the original Kazakh by personal courtesy of the author. See Appendix, p. 58 below, Chapter I, 3.

the propertied classes of the population. Thus, large quan-
tities of cattle and money were collected from almost the whole
of the kin group as so-called mutual aid for powerful beys and
other influential people, while only a narrow circle of close
relatives contributed to help members of the non-propertied
strata of the population. In this way, material aid among
the kin lost its former disinterested character. Further evidence of this is provided by such popular sayings as
'Almaktyn da salmagy bar' ('To be a brother means to feel
responsibility') or 'Bai baiga, sai saiga kuyady' ('Riches flow
to the rich man, but the little brook becomes a still smaller
brook').

The existence of some traces of kinship relations must
therefore not be taken to mean that the previous stable social
relations within the kin group were preserved among the pre-
Revolutionary Kazakhs. The development of class contradictions and the intensive introduction of commodity-money relations in Kazakh society led to the weakening of kinship and
the strengthening of local ties. This is confirmed by the
popular saying 'Tuystan zhurs zhakyn' ('Friendship is
stronger than kinship'), or 'Atalastyn aty ozgansha, auldastyn
zhaiy ozsyn' ('Better your neighbour's horse win the races
than your kinsman's horse').

From the second half of the nineteenth century the Tsarist
administration began to define the boundaries of 'oblast',
'uezd', 'volost' and 'aul' administrative units in accordance
with geographical considerations, instead of the kinship and
tribal affiliations of the Kazakh population. These administrative measures were designed to help liquidate the kinship
and tribal ties of the Kazakh population not only within the
boundaries of the 'oblasts' and 'uezds', but also within those
of the 'volost' and administrative 'auls'. But the local authorities sometimes allowed Kazakhs of one or the other kin
group to move from one 'volost' to their kinsmen in another.
This, in the opinion of General Grodekov, (1) was a deliberate
undermining of the foundations of a true Tsarist colonial
policy.

The Kazakhs maintain kinship ties in the female as well as
the male line. They call children of married daughters and
sisters 'zhien' in relationship to their mother's relatives, and
the 'zhien''s mother's relatives are called 'nagashy'. According to centuries-old customs the 'nagashy' would try not to
offend and, as far as possible, not to refuse their 'zhiens'
anything. They believed that if close relatives of the mother
chastised their 'zhiens', their arms would twitch ever afterwards. In the past, people had to give their grandchildren
by their daughters forty yearling goats ('serkesh'). But
during the last century this custom fell into disuse. 'Zhiens'

could therefore ask their mother's relatives for anything they
pleased - good fast horses, birds of prey, hunting dogs, etc.
If they were refused they had the right to take what they
wanted without asking and had to answer to no one for this.
They could always say that they had not yet received the
forty yearling goats allotted by law.   The customary law
demanded that 'zhiens' could take goods of any value from
their mother's relatives on up to three occasions. (2)

The mother's relatives always favoured their 'zhiens', pro-
tected them, and were indulgent towards their pranks and
whims.   This is explained by the fact that there was no
ordinary, everyday rivalry between them, since, according to
the exogamy law, they were representatives of different kins
or subkins in the father's line.   Their interests therefore
hardly ever clashed, and especially not on the question of
their mother's father's inheritance.   In addition, the girls,
who would be sold when the time came for bride-money
('kalym'), were regarded by their relatives as delicate creat-
ures, victims of fate forced willynilly to leave the family nest
for ever.   As a result, they always took the part of the
children of their daughters, and sisters treated them well and
wished them nothing but good.

In the customs defining the relations between the 'zhiens'
and the 'nagashy' one can glimpse shadows of more ancient
social institutions, especially if it is considered that 'zhiens'
behave much more freely with their uncles in the mother's
line.   Their mutual relations almost always bear a very touching character, evidently a survival of avuncular relations. (3)
It is well known that the ancient Greeks and Germans treated
the children of their daughters and sisters with great respect.
... (The author refers to F. Engels, 'The Origins of the
Family, Private Property and the State', Russian text,
'K. Marx and F. Engels Collected Works', tome II, Moscow,
1949, p. 273.   T.D.)   This shows that the Kazakhs like
other peoples of the world lived at one time in their history
in a matriarchal kinship system.

Since the Kazakhs only maintain blood relationships in the
male line, the children of brothers and those of sisters can
marry each other without this being considered a violation of
the exogamy ban.   The mother's relations joke that 'zhien el
bolmas, zhelke as bolmas' ('a zhien cannot be kin, a horse
cannot be food'):   a pun on the words 'zhien' and 'zhilo'.

This emphasises that the 'zhiens' are representatives of
another kin or tribe.   But the 'zhiens' in their turn, with no
less irony, would reply 'zhien nege el bolmas yn maly bolsa,
zhelke nege as blomasyn maiy bolsa' ('why can't a zhien be kin if
he has lots of cattle, why can't a horse be food if it is fat'),

clearly hinting at the importance of the economic connections
in relations between relatives in the female line.

   Matchmaking and marriage unions concluded between different kin and tribal groups also lead to the formulation of
affinal ties which are of great interest for science.   One must
first consider the relationship of the son-in-law with his wife's
relatives - 'kaiyn zhurt'.   Not only the parents, but also the
near relatives of his wife would treat him with great respect,
especially if the son-in-law lived on friendly terms with his
wife and did not treat her badly.   The son-in-law, for his
part, also behaved very politely towards his wife's relatives.
He would treat those older than him as his elder relatives,
and show a particular, almost fatherly, concern for the
younger ones, and friendly relationships often developed
between them.   Not to mention his mother-in-law, even the
wives of his wife's elder brothers would show particular concern for the son-in-law, fulfilling all his wishes.   They would
keep a store of breast of mutton with which to regale him
every time he came.   Usually the son-in-law would take
mutton from the dish and share it with his wife's relatives.
If no breast of mutton appeared on the dish, he had the full
right, jokingly, to remind the wives of his wife's elder
brothers about this.   His wife's younger relatives were also
supposed to regale the son-in-law with breast of mutton; as a
rule he did not nag the wives of the younger brothers about
it, but, on the contrary, treated them very kindly.   However, the Kazakhs considered it a mark of disrespect to the
son-in-law and his wife if the son-in-law was not given the
breast of mutton.   In south Kazakhstan, especially in
Semirech'ye, in return for the mutton the son-in-law was
obliged to place a sum of money on the dish for the master of
the house.   However, this does not seem to have been the
general custom: in the northern oblasts of Kazakhstan, none
of our informants could remember it.

   The duration and intensiveness of the son-in-law's relationship with his wife's relatives depends on the length of their
conjugal life and his wife's treatment by her husband's relatives.   In the case of his wife's premature death, especially
if she had no children and he did not make a sororate (i.e.
husband marries his wife's sister.   T.D.) marriage with his
dead wife's younger sister, all ties between them were gradually broken.   But affinal ties between the two kin groups
could of course be continued, if they so wished, through the
conclusion of other marriage unions.   This is evidently the
source of the popular saying 'Kuieu zhuz zhyldyk, kuda myn
zhylgyk' ('sons-in-law for 100 years but father-in-law for
1,000 years').   As a result, affinal ties (i.e. mutual relations
on the sides of the fathers-in-law), could survive for quite a
long time and were frequently renewed ('suiek zhangyrtu) in

the course of several generations.   The fathers-in-law were
therefore joined by ties of friendship and mutual respect.

The children of sisters, and of first and of second female
cousins, who had married representatives of different kinship
groups regarded each other as cousins, 'bole'.   Close kinship
relations were formed between them in accordance with the
degree of kinship of their mothers.   This is the reason for
the popular saying 'Tort ayaktyda bota, ekI ayaktyda bole
tatu' ('Among the animals, camels, among people cousins are
friends').   Since the Kazakhs maintained the blood relationship only in the male line, the children of sisters, and of first
and second female cousins could marry each other, if the kinship relations of their fathers didn't fall under the exogamy
barrier.   In the first place, their mothers had an interest in
this - they knew each other well and hoped that their children
would get on together and each treated the other with particular tenderness.   One popular saying refers to this possibility: 'Ayagin korIp asyn Ish, anasyn korIp kyzyn al' ('See
the cup and take the food, see the mother and take the
daughter to wife').   In addition, it was easier for these
parents to agree on the questions of 'kalym', the trousseau,
mutual presents, wedding arrangements, etc.

There used to be many different kinship and affinal relations
found among the Kazakhs.   These mutual relations were based
on the obligations and responsibilities imposed by various customs and traditions.   Every Kazakh knew them well and would
always try to avoid breaking these customary laws.

The Kazakh custom of friendship between peers ('kurdas')
is also of interest.   Such friendship would last for their
whole life.   They would usually talk to each other freely
about anything, joke without embarrassment, laugh, play silly
tricks on each other, and neither of them ever took offence at
this.   They would even entertain ideas of communality of wives
and children.   Knowing this tradition, their wives and children too would joke and make merry together.   This is the
reason for a popular saying that 'EkesI kurdastyn balasy da
kurdas' ('The children of peers are peers').   Sometimes
strangers meeting by chance and discovering that they were
peers would at once find a common language and express their
thoughts without embarrassment, permit themselves to make
various jokes, etc., appropriate to the relationship of peers.
Such relationships between peers, in particular the idea of the
communality of wives and children, might well be a survival of
group marriage, an element coming up to the present day from
primitive times.

Before the Revolution the ancient tradition of adopted
brothers ('tamyr') was widespread among the Kazakhs.   These

were strong friendships between men, formed irrespective of
their ages.   Some were brought together by their parents,
others in the struggle against a common enemy, and others
met simply in everyday life, for example through their shared
taste ('kalau') for a good horse, a bird of prey, a hunting
dog, etc.   Earlier, men would officially announce their
friendship before witnesses, kissing a sabre or dagger and
declaring, 'From this day forth let only death divide us!'   At
the end of the nineteenth and the beginning of the twentieth
century they began to practise rites of a more peaceful
character.   Now the friends had only to embrace three times,
pressing each other to their bared chests.   However, the
ritual force and meaning of the ceremony was in no way dimin-
ished, since neither of them, with rare exceptions, would
betray the 'tamyr' and each stayed true to his oath to the end
of his life.   They would not offend each other under any
circumstances, would always be the first to go to the other's
aid, shared good and bad times.   And, finally, the two men's
friendship could be further strengthened by the marriage of
their children.

The Kazakhs have a large number of terms defining the different degrees of kinship and affinal relationships and classifying the kinship system.   Evidence of this is provided both
by literary sources and by our field work.   For instance, the
term 'aga' (elder brother) is used to refer to a brother or
first or second male cousin, and also to more distantly related
elder men and the younger brothers of the father of Ego.
The term 'zhien' (grandson, nephew in the female line) is
used to refer to the children of daughters, sisters, and female
cousins of various degrees of kinship.   The term 'kaiyn ata'
(husband's father or wife's father) is also used to refer to the
father and the elder brothers of the father of the husband of
the wife (or the wife of the husband) in question.   The
Kazakhs have a large number of general terms, defining categories of kinship and affinal relations.

As this brief description shows, the terms for kinship and
affinal relations used by the Kazakhs are grouped in accordance with the age of the relatives in the father's and in the
mother's line, and with affinal ties in relation to Ego.

The Kazakhs are formed from three 'zhuz', scattered over a
huge territory.   Their language has been shown to include
three main dialects (west, northeast and south).   But no dia-
lectal disparities have been discovered in the kinship and affinal terms used.   Therefore, the general terms for the affinal
and kinship system mentioned above are common to the
Kazakhs as a whole and witness the system's extreme stability.
... (The author refers to H.L. Morgan's confirmation that
kinship systems are more passive and less adaptive than the

family.   He quotes H.L. Morgan, 'Ancient Society', Russian
text, 'Drevneye Obshestvo', Leningrad, 1934, p. 250. T.D.)

The scheme we have constructed of kinship and affinal relations in the father's line embraces seven generations.   Thus,
the first group includes the generation of the grandfather and
grandmother of Ego;   the second, the generation of his father
and mother;   the fourth, the generation of his children;   the
fifth, the generation of his grandchildren;   the sixth, the
generation of his greatgrandchildren;   and the seventh, the
generation of the great-great-grandchildren of Ego.   It is
understood that Ego can be a man or a woman, and that the
terms for the Kazakh kinship and affinal system relating to
him or her have some special features.

We have as far as possible reflected these special features
in our schema.   In addition, for convenience sake, we have
separated the terms of the kinship and affinal systems into
four independent schema (see end of article).

The first schema includes the kinship and affinal terms for
the father's line of the male or female Ego concerned ('oz
zhurty');   the second includes the terms for the mother's line
('nagashy zhurty');   the third includes the terms for the line
of the wife's father ('kaiyn zhurty');   and in the fourth we
put the terms for the line of the husband's father ('kaiyn
zhurty').   As the first schema shows, there are seven generations from the grandfather of Ego to his great-great-grandchildren, in the father's line.   The Kazakhs have kinship
terms for these seven generations.   They have no special
terms for the eighth generation either in the ascending or the
descending line.   Thus, in the ascending line from the
grandfather ('ata', 'baba') of Ego, all ancestors are called by
the names 'ata', 'baba', which mean 'grandfather'.   In daily
life there is no great distinction between these terms.   None
the less, the term 'baba' refers particularly to the grandfather,
the greatgrandfather or other ancestors in the direct line of
blood relationship, while the term 'ata' has a wider meaning,
and embraces collateral lines of kinship as well.   Therefore,
when they say 'argy atalarymuz' (greatgrandfather), grandfathers both in the direct line and in the collateral line are
included in this, but when they say 'babalarymyz' (great-
grandfather, ancestor), they mean only ancestors in the direct
line of blood relationship.   And in the descending line, the
terms 'nemene' or 'shopshek' are used for the seventh generation in the male line and 'tuazhat' for the female line.
According to our schema, this would refer to the great-great-
grandsons of Ego.   There are no corresponding kinship terms
for the eighth generation in the descending line, either in the
male or the female line.   In connection with this it should be
mentioned that the term 'nemene' comes from the (interroga-

tory. T.D.) word 'nemene?', which in other languages is
translated by the indefinite 'what's this?' The reason for
the term 'shopshek' is even clearer, its ordinary meaning is
'the broken-off twigs of ancient trees'. The term 'tuazhat'
means 'one who is already foreign for his kin'. In the
eighth generation, in the male and in the female line, all real
kinship ties are therefore finally broken. This makes quite
clear the real importance of the Kazakhs' exogamy ban, which
exists, in particular, to the seventh generation. Some differences in the observation of the exogamy ban have been noted
in different districts of the vast territory of Kazakhstan.
These are linked to the differences in the development of
social-economic relations. Thus, in the northern districts of
pre-Revolutionary Kazakhstan, exogamous marriages were concluded, though not often, by members of the fifth generation
in the male line. It was another matter in the south of
Kazakhstan, where the representatives of some Kazakh kin
groups, although they had already long ago crossed the limit
of seven generations, still preserved the exogamy ban.
There were in all twelve such kin groups in Semirech'ye
('Andas', 'Kelpe', 'Siyrshy', 'Myrza', 'Akbuiym', 'Aryktynym',
'Kushik', 'Balgaly', 'Kaishyiy', 'BaishegIr', 'Spatai', 'Orakty')
of the tribe of Zhalair, (4) and the kin group 'sary' of the
tribe of Alban, (5) in Chimkent oblast, the kin groups of
'Zhetimder' and 'Bozhban' of the tribe of Konrat. (6) At the
present time, according to the Kazakh 'shezhre' (genealogy),
each of these kin groups consists of 10-13 generations, but
they still strictly observe the exogamy ban. This does not
mean that real kinship ties continue beyond the seventh generation, or that they have kinship terms for thirteen generations, just that they preserve the ancient traditions.

We will now list the basic kinship and affinal terms used by
the Kazakhs.

Table 2.1

Category of terms	Kazakh terms	Translation
In the father's line	'baba', 'ata'	grandfather
('oz zhurty')	'ana', 'ezhe'	grandmother
	'eke'	father
	'sheshe'	mother
	'aga'	elder brother
	'InI'	younger brother
	'apa'	elder sister
	'karyndas' (Ego husband)	younger sister

Category of terms	Kazakh terms	Translation
	'inii' (Ego wife)	younger sister
	'ul'	son
	'kyz'	daughter
	'nemere'	grandson, granddaughter
	'shobere'	great-grandson, great-granddaughter
	'nemene', 'shopshek'	great-great-grandson great-great-granddaughter
	'nemere aga'	elder male cousin
	'nemere ini'	younger male cousin
	'nemere apa'	elder female cousin
	'nemere karyndas' (Ego man)	younger female cousin
	'nemere sinii' (Ego woman)	younger female cousin
	'shobere aga'	elder male second cousin
	'shobere ini'	younger male second cousin
	'shobere apa'	elder female second cousin
	'shobere karyndas' (Ego man)	younger female second cousin
	'shobere sinii' (Ego woman)	younger female second cousin
	'zhenge'	wife of elder brother
	'kelin'	wife of younger brother
	'katyn', 'eiel', 'zaiyp'	wife
	'beibishe'	first wife
	'tokal'	second wife

Category of terms	Kazakh terms	Translation
	'er', 'bai' 'kuiei', 'zhubai'	husband
In the mother's line ('nagashy zhurt')	'nagashy ata'	mother's father
	'nagashy ezhe'	mother's mother
	'nagashy'	all men in the mother's line
	'nagashy aga'	elder brother in mother's line
	'nagashy ini'	younger brother in mother's line
	'nagashy apa'	elder sister in mother's line
	'nagashy karyndas' (Ego man)	younger sister in mother's line
	'nagashy sinii' (Ego woman)	younger sister in mother's line
	'nagashy zhenge'	elder brother's wife in mother's line
	'nagashy kelin'	younger brother's wife in mother's line
In the female line ('kiz ugrady')	'zhien'	daughter's or sister's children
	'zhienshar'	grandchildren of daughter or sister
	'tuazhat'	great-grandchildren of daughter or sister
	'zhien kelin'	daughter's son's wife or sister's son's wife
	'zhien kuieu'	daughter's daughter's husband or sister's daughter's husband
	'bele'	children of sisters (in relationship to each other)
	'bazha'	husbands of sisters
In the line of wife's relatives ('kaiyn zhurt')	'kaiyn ata'	wife's father
	'kaiyn ene'	wife's mother

Category of terms	Kazakh terms	Translation
	'kaiyn aga'	wife's elder brother
	'kaiyn bike'	wife's elder sister
	'baldyz'	wife's younger sister
	'kaiyn'	wife's younger brother
	'zhenge'	wife's elder brother's wife
	'kelin'	wife's younger brother's wife
In the affinal line	'kuda'	father of son-in-law
('kudandalylyk')	'kudagi'	mother of son-in-law
	'kudasha'	husband's or wife's sister
	'kuda bala'	husband's or wife's younger brothers

Of course, not all the Kazakh kinship and affinal terms were
brought into everyday use. The older members of the kin
usually addressed the younger by their proper names.   And
the younger members, in particular the women, depending on
their sex and age, and degree of kinship and affinal relationship, avoided pronouncing proper names when they addressed
their elders.   Instead they used many kinship terms as
proper names or altered them slightly and they often gave
them special nicknames.   This tradition survives to this day,
especially in country districts.   Before the Revolution, the
Kazakhs usually married off their sons at the age of 17-18.
As a result their children never called their fathers 'Father'
('eke'), but addressed them as elder brothers ('aga').   On
the same principle they addressed their mothers as elder sisters ('apa').   And they usually called their grandfathers
('ata', 'baba') 'eke' (father).   They called the elder brothers
of their grandfather 'uliken ata' (elder grandfather), the
younger 'kishi ata' (younger grandfather).   They addressed
the elder brothers of their father as 'kishi aga' (younger
elder brother) or as a term of endearment 'keke' (dear uncle),
'agatai' (little elder brother).   In most cases they followed
their mother's example and gave their father's younger
brothers individual nicknames.   Thus, if she called her husband's younger brothers 'shyrak' (little light), 'inishegim' (my
little younger brother), or 'kenzhe' (kid), in the same way,
her son could call his uncles 'shyrak agatai', 'inshegim agatai'

or 'kenzhe agatai', i.e. he addressed them by adding the word
'agatai' (elder brother) to their nicknames.   When he addressed his father's younger brothers, he sometimes called them
by their own names, adding the word 'agatai' or alternatively
he himself chose some endearment for them and added to it
the term 'aga' (elder brother).   Thus, one often meets with
the nickname 'Tetti aga' (sweet elder brother), etc.   He
addressed his father's sisters or his own elder sisters respectfully as 'apai', 'apatai' or 'tete'.   'Apa' and 'tete' mean
elder sister, and the endings 'i' and 'tai' are a sign of a particular preference.

   Kazakh women did not pronounce the proper names of those
of their husband's relatives born before their marriage, independent of their sex and age.   The first literary documenta-
tion of this comes from N.I. Il'minsky, who wrote that 'the
wife never calls her husband's relatives by their names.   They
thought up special nicknames for their husband's brothers and
sisters.'   It was considered a great sin to break this ancient
tradition.   Even the names of deceased relatives were never
pronounced aloud.   On her arrival in the village, the young
bride would carefully inspect her husband's relatives and
choose nicknames for them to correspond to their various
sexes and ages.   She was helped in this, in the first place
by her powers of observation, her ability to notice the particular personal qualities of her husband's different relatives.
Her husband's parents regarded her as their own child, so
she could call her father-in-law simply 'ata' or 'eke' (grandfather, father), her mother-in-law 'ezhe' (grandmother).
She could call her father-in-law's brothers 'uliken ata' (elder
grandfather), 'kishi ata' (younger grandfather);   her husband's elder brothers 'ulken aga' (elder elder brother),
'zhaksy aga' (good elder brother), 'agakem' (my respected
elder brother);   her other brothers-in-law 'sal zhigit'
(dandy boy), 'myrza zhigit' (generous boy), 'ortanshy' (the
middle one), 'teteles' (the next to her husband in age),
'inishegim' (my little younger brother), 'kenzhe' (kid),
'kenzhem' (my kid);   her husband's younger sisters
'shireilim' (my beauty), 'erke zhan' (dear soul), 'kek-ildim'
(my curly locks), 'erkem' (my naughty one);   the wives of
her husband's elder brothers 'ulken apa' (elder elder sister),
'kishi apa' (younger elder sister), 'zhaksy apa' (good elder
sister), 'zheneshe' (from the word 'zhenge' - bride, but
'zheneshe' is more of a term of endearment), etc.   This
tradition was also extended to first cousins, second cousins
and more distant relatives of her husband, their wives and
children, born before her marriage.   In connection with this
one should note that the children of her husband's relatives,
especially those who were born after her marriage addressed
her respectfully as 'zheneshe' or 'tete', etc.

It was easier for the young bride to find other names for those of her husband's relatives who held official posts or were people of influence. Thus she would call the volost administrator 'bolys aga', 'bolys ata', 'bolys kainym'; the people's judges ('biev'), 'bii ata', 'bii aga'; people who had made a pilgrimage to Mecca ('kazhi'), 'kazhi ata', 'kazhi', etc.

This tradition was so strong that Kazakh women would re-frain from pronouncing the proper names of complete strangers where these were the same as the names of their respected elder relatives. In this respect, it is worth mentioning the following example: in the Bayan-Aul region of Pavlodar oblast in the second half of the nineteenth to the beginning of the twentieth century, there lived a powerful bey, my grand-father's elder cousin, Kulatai by name (1850-1931). He was also a 'kazhi' since he had been on pilgrimage to Mecca. My grandmother (1861-1957) called him simply 'kazhi', and my mother (1892-1963), 'kazhi ata'. In 1939-57 when we were living in Taldy-Kurgan oblast, I was a witness to the fact that my grandmother addressed a young neighbour called Kulatai (born 1926) as 'kazhi attas' ('kazhi''s namesake), and my mother addressed him as 'kazhi atam attas' (grandfather 'kazhi''s namesake).

Before the Revolution, male Kazakh names were very often taken from those of rivers, mountains, or wild or domestic animals. Because of this the women would even alter the names of rivers, places and animals if they were the same as those of people they respected. (7) Thus, if the names of people she respected were Sarybai, Sulushash, Burkitbai and Bieke, the young bride would change the name of the river 'Sary-Su' to 'Shikie-Su' ('sary' - yellow, 'shikil' - a synonym of that word, 'su' -water); the hill 'Sulu tobe' to 'edemi tobe' ('sulu' - beauty, 'edemi' - a synonym of that word, 'tobe' - hill); the bird of prey 'berkut' (eagle) to 'kyran' (the hunter); the domestic animal 'bie' (mare) to 'sauar' (milk-cow), etc.

When they had to pronounce the names of complete strangers which were the same as those of their respected relatives, Kazakh women resorted to deliberately mispronouncing the names. For example for the proper name Mambet, they would say 'Sambet'; for Ell, 'Sell'; for Tursyn, 'Mursyn', for Akhmed, 'Sakhmed'; and for Zhakyp, 'Makhyp', etc. (8)

Before the Revolution, Kazakh women as a rule did not call their husbands by their proper names. They usually addres-sed them as the head of the household - 'otagasy' - or added the word 'agasy' (elder brother in the sense of father) to the names of his elder son or daughter. This resulted in: 'Zaleldyn agasy' (father of Zalela), 'Shamshiyanyn agasy'

(father of Shamshin), etc.   A large number of examples of
similar usages, connected with the tradition which forbade a
wife to pronounce the proper name of her elder relatives and
her husband's relatives, can be found among the Kazakh
people.   To emphasise the resourcefulness of Kazakh women
in observing this tradition, I will relate an interesting anec-
dote which comes from literary sources: one wife was not
allowed to name a stream ('bulak'), a lake ('kol'), a reed
('kamys'), a sheep ('koi'), a wolf ('kaskyr'), a knife
('pyshak'), or a whetstone ('kairak') as these words were
also used as the proper names of her husband's relatives.
The young woman, coming to the stream for water, noticed
that beyond the stream, on the shore of the lake, in the
reeds, a wolf was attacking a sheep.   She shouted to her
father-in-law 'Master, Master!   On the other side of the
babbling (stream), on the shore of the shining (lake), in
among the rustling (reeds), a ferocious (wolf) is carrying off
a bleating (sheep).   Quick, bring a sharpened (knife) honed
on a sharpener (whetstone)!'   This is of course, a legend,
but such anecdotal situations must have occurred in the daily
life of the Kazakhs.   Such resourceful women were regarded
as very wise and were objects of great popular esteem.

As we have seen, Kazakh kinship relations usually continued
to the seventh generation and there were also affinal ties.
Evidence of this is provided by the exogamic prohibition which
survives to this day, and the widespread nature of the kinship terms (Schema 1) which also refer to seven generations
inclusively.

Affinal relations were also important, but, as our materials
and the extent of the affinal terms (Schemas 2 and 3) show,
they were only maintained for three to four generations.

Our materials show that many different sorts of nicknames
were commonly used and that the tradition of respect for
elder relatives was strictly observed by the Kazakh youth and
especially by the women.   This tradition is alive today, but
the majority of the previous versions of common names and
nicknames used by Kazakh women for their husband's relatives
have fallen out of use, so that at the present time young
women call everyone except their husband's close elder relatives by their proper names.   This is in no way regarded as
a mark of disrespect, still less as a violation of tradition.

And, finally, it must be noted that our report is written
largely on the basis of field material.   More specialised research is needed to explore the more complex aspects of the
Kazakh kinship and affinal system.

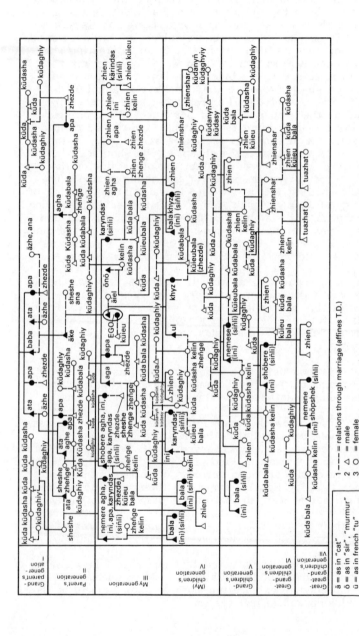

Schema 1   *Terms of kinship and affinity in the father's line in relation to Ego who is male or female*

1 – – – = relations through marriage (affines T.D.)
2 △ = male
3 ○ = female
4 ● ▲ = 'blood relation' through the male line (agnates T.D.)
5 ( ) = in brackets are kinship terms for when Ego is female and some kinship terms particular to specific age - group

ä = as in "cat"
ö = as in "sir", "murmur"
ü = as in french "tu"
ñ = as in sonya

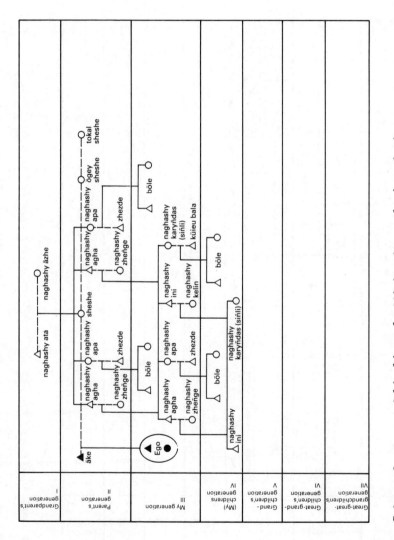

Schema 2 *Terms of kinship and affinity for mother's relatives when Ego is a man or a woman*

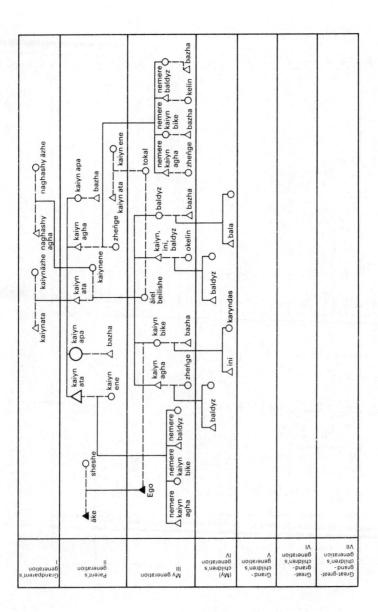

Schema 3 *Terms of kinship for wife's relatives when Ego is a man*

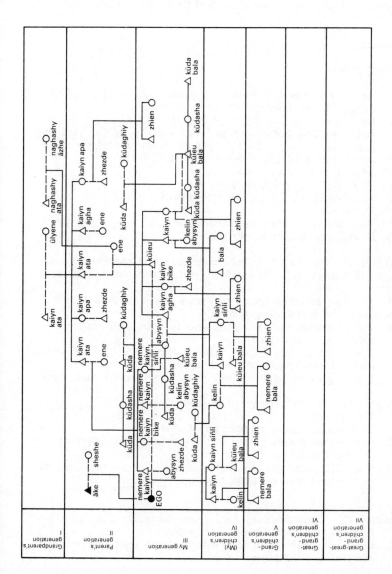

Schema 4 *Terms of kinship and affinity for husband's relatives when Ego is a woman*

APPENDIX

Kh. A. Argynbaev, 'Family and Marriage among the Kazakh
People (a Historical-Ethnographical Survey)', Nauka, Alma-Ata,
1973.

Contents

Introduction

Chapter I   The pre-Revolutionary family and family relations
1   Forms of the family.
2   Patrimony and the right of inheritance.
3   Relationships between relatives; kinship system and cus-
    toms, connected with the ban on pronouncing the per-
    sonal names of the elder relatives.
4   The custom of adoption.
5   The customs of hospitality.
6   The position of women in the family.
7   Polygamy.
8   The customs connected with childbirth and education.
9   Burial and memorial rituals.

Chapter II   The pre-Revolutionary forms of concluding marriage. Weddings and the customs and rituals connected with
them
1   The age of marriage, exogamous and religious taboos.
2   Forms of concluding marriage.
3   Matchmaking and betrothal and the customs and rituals
    connected with them.
4   The bride-groom's first visit to the bride - the feasts and
    and customs connected with them.
5   Weddings and customs and rituals connected with them.

Chapter III   Bride-money and dowry
1   The amount and composition of bride-money.
2   The amount and composition of dowry.
3   Bride-money and dowry among the peoples neighbouring
    on the Kazakhs.
4   The formation and character of customs surrounding the
    payment of bride-money and the preparation of the
    dowry.

Chapter IV   Contemporary family and marriage relations
1   Forms of the family and family relations
2   Forms of concluding marriage and the customs and rituals
    connected with them.

Conclusion

NOTES

1 N.I. Grodekov, 'The Kirgiz and Kara-Kirgiz of Syrdarin Region', Tashkent, 1889, p. 13.
2 L.F. Ballyuzek, Popular Customs, which formerly had, and in part still have, the Force of Law in the Lesser Kirgiz Horde, 'Proceedings of the Orenburg Section of the Russian Geographical Society', vol. 2, Kazan, 1871, p. 109.
3 Evidence of this is provided by our field work and by the 'Dialectological Dictionary of the Kazakh Language', Alma-Ata, 1961 (in the Kazakh language).
4 Field work in Tald-Kurgan Region (1960).
5 Field work in Alma-Atin Region (1968).
6 Field work in Chimkent Region (1958).
7 A. Samoilovich, Taboo Words in the Speech of the Married Kazakh-Kirgiz Women, 'The Living Past', vols 1-2, 1915, pp. 166-70.
8 Ibid., p. 165.

3 Some features of the traditional wedding ceremony of the Uzbek-Durmen of the southern raions of Tadzhikistan and Uzbekistan
N.G. Borozna*

The weddings of the Uzbek-Durmen (1) have undergone a number of changes in recent years - some of the old elements of the ritual have been lost and new ones gained. However, even today the wedding ritual basically preserves its traditional form, and a few of its features are archaic with roots going back to the epoch of the communal kinship system.

The Durmen wedding contains traces of features which come from the former nomad and semi-nomad peoples of Central Asia and Kazakhstan - the Kazakhstan, the Kirgiz, the Karakalpaks and the Turkmen. It reflects the previous kinship-tribal divisions and exogamy which are based on , in the opinion of T.A. Zhdanko, 'one of the most persistent survivals of the communal kinship system of peoples with a semi-nomadic life.' (2)

It is generally considered that the Dashtikipchak Uzbeks long ago discarded the practice of exogamy. The custom of marriages between cousins who are the children of two brothers is cited as evidence of this. (3) However, as well as marriage between parallel cousins who are the children of two brothers, marriages between the children of two sisters, and between cross-cousins - the children of a brother and a sister - has survived almost up to this day and is witness to the exogamous nature of kinship among the Durmens in the past. (4) The Durmen prefer a marriage between cousins who are the son and daughter of two sisters to the marriage of children of two brothers, which dates from a much later time - the time of the decay of the kinship-tribal system.

According to our informants, mutual marriage connections between particular kin groups still existed at the end of the nineteenth/beginning of the twentieth century. Until recently, there were four large kinship groups among the Durmen of the Babatag mountains: the Saksan, the Nogai, the Churdak and the Charchur. This type of division is undoubtedly a survival of dual exogamy and has also been observed among other peoples. (5) Even at the present time, when the division of the Babatag Durmen into kin

* First published in 'Sovetskaya Etnografiya', 1969, no. 2, pp. 80-6.

groups has no longer any real significance, marriages between people from the groups which intermarried in the past are still preferred.

The custom of marriage between parallel cousins is preserved by the Durmen to some degree even today. Cases have been observed of a woman from the Nogai kin group, married to a man from the Saksan kin group, trying to marry her son to a girl from the Nogai kin group, preferably her sister's daughter. This again confirms that exogamy was practised in the time of Durmen patriarchal kin.

Today young people sometimes don't even know what kinship subdivisions they belong to, and even for many of the older people the kinship-tribal division has passed into the realm of history. Marriages are for the most part concluded as the result of the mutual attachment of the young man and girl, regardless of what kin group they belong to. The semi-nomad Uzbek tribes were endogamous; as among the Durmen, marriages were concluded only within the framework of one's tribe. The same phenomenon has been observed among the Lokaits and the Kungrat. However, with time, the ban on marrying girls from other tribes began to break down, both among the Durmen and other Uzbek groups. At the end of the nineteenth century the Durmen sometimes married Tadzhiks. In the Zeravshan valley, as A.D. Grebenkin informs us, the Ming, Katagan, Karakalpak and men from other Uzbek groups only married within the framework of their tribe. (6) The Durmen were thus not unusual in this.

The forms of marriage of the former semi-nomad Uzbeks have much in common with those of other peoples of Central Asia and Kazakhstan, and we will therefore give a brief description of some of them.

The cradle betrothal ('etak dzhirtish') was widespread among the Uzbeks of Dashtikipchak origin and also among the Uzbeks of Khorezm, the Kazakhs, the Kirgiz, the Karakalpaks and the settled populations of Central Asia. (7) The betrothal usually took place between parents whose children were cousins.

The customs of levirate and sororate formerly observed by the Durmen are now extremely rarely met with, although they are encouraged by the old people. M.O. Kosven thinks that levirate and sororate are survivals of group marriage in a period of dual exogamy. (8) We were told of one case of levirate where a younger brother married the widow of his deceased elder brother in the village of Tarypaya in 1963. A man of 26, who had only just come back from the army, he gave in to the persuasion of his parents and married brothers

and married the 36-year-old widow of his elder brother, who
had been left with two children.   The brothers and the
parents of the man who married were governed by purely
economic considerations;   they didn't want to have to give any
of their common property to the widow.   It should be added
that levirate and sororate as forms of marriage also existed in
Central Asia among peoples whose economy was based on
cattle-rearing and among the settled farmers. (9)   This confirms that the stages of development of the family and family
relations were identical among the settled and nomadic peoples.

Marriage by abduction took place among the Durmen only in
exceptional circumstances.   The young man took the girl to
his 'kishlak' (village).   Only in the course of time, when the
girls' parents recognised him as her husband, did the official
wedding ceremony take place.   Such forms of marriage are
hardly ever encountered today.

There is little literary information directly about the wedding
rituals of the semi-nomad Uzbeks and the Durmen in particular. (10)   Our description of the Durmen wedding will therefore be based on materials from the field work carried out by
the author in the southern raions of Uzbekistan and Tadzhikistan (1958, 1959, 1961, 1964). (11)

The wedding ceremony was earlier, and to a considerable
degree still is, an affair which concerns the whole village,
and above all, all the bride and bridegroom's relatives.
Among the Durmen of Kabadian, Babatag, and the Kafirnigan
valley, like many other peoples, (12) the bride and bridegroom's fellow-villagers take a very active part in the wedding.

Today, although marriage is concluded by the mutual agreement of the young man and girl, the basic wedding rituals are
still performed during the wedding period - the 'council' of
elders, the matchmaking, the betrothal, and the marriage
ceremony.

Before the wedding arrangements are settled, a council of
elders ('maslakhat') meets several times on both the bride and
bridegroom's sides.   Today the elders, the relatives and the
most highly respected members of the kolkhoz, sovkhoz, and
village, regardless of age, participate in the 'maslakhat'.
This usually includes the leaders of the brigade in which the
young man and girl work, the managers of the farm, accoun-
tants, leading members of the collective farm, etc.   No wedding ever takes place without a 'maslakhat'.   The first meeting is held in the house of the young man's parents.   There
they decide who to send to the girl's house as matchmakers,
and discuss questions connected with the organisation of the

wedding. On the bride's side, the 'maslakhat' is held only after the matchmaking has begun. The merits of the bride-groom and his relatives are discussed, and details of the arrangements of the wedding celebration.

After the 'maslakhat' on the bridegroom's side has decided the question of matchmakers, the ceremony of matchmaking ('kudalyk') is performed. Both men and women can be matchmakers ('sauchi'). In Kabadian they usually choose a woman, who must not only be eloquent and respected by her fellow-villagers, but also have healthy children. In the Kafirnigan valley and among the Ozbaks of Babatonga two or three men are usually chosen as the matchmakers.

It is customary for the male matchmakers to loosen the belts of their trousers before going into the house of the girl's parents. It is thought that this will make the girl's parents more compliant. Then they break up a 'kizlak' (brick of manure used for heating) and scatter the bits round the yard and over the threshold of the house. This symbolises their wish for the prosperity and well-being of the family (i.e. that they may have many cattle). The matchmakers are received by the girl's father, but her mother and often some of her close relatives have to be present as well. If the girl's parents agree at once, they perform the ritual of breaking bread which symbolises their wish that the young wife will live happily and have plenty of bread. This custom also exists among the settled population of the Tadzhiks and Uzbeks who do not preserve kinship-tribal divisions. The semi-nomad Uzbeks probably borrowed it from them.

The matchmakers are then served food. In the past, if the matchmakers' offer was turned down, they would not get any-thing to eat or even be offered tea. The matchmakers usual-ly come to the girl's house three times, and the answer re-ceived on the third occasion is considered final. However, cases have been known in which the matchmaker came up to ten times. If they reached agreement on the marriage, the wedding preparations were begun.

The Durmen always hold the main wedding celebrations, the betrothal ('patiya-toi') and the marriage ceremony ('nika-toi') in the bride's house. The wedding is also celebrated in the bride's house among other groups of former semi-nomadic Uzbeks, (13) and also the Kazakhs and the Kirgiz, (14) the Karakalpaks and the Tadzhiks. (15) Only among the Turk-men was it formerly and occasionally still today held in the house of the bridegroom's parents. (16)

The 'patiya-toi' is the first stage of the wedding ceremony of the Durmen, Kungrat and other Dashtikipchak Uzbeks.

Betrothal was previously considered obligatory if the bride
was a girl of 9-13.   If a widow or a girl over 20 got married, the 'patiya-toi' was not held.   Now that the marriage
age for girls has changed (they usually get married at 18-24),
the 'patiya-toi' is often not celebrated.

The bride and bridegroom wear their wedding clothes for
the 'patiya-toi'.   These are not radically different from their
ordinary clothes, but there are some particular stipulations.
The wedding clothes have to be new.   The bridegroom wears
a new coat ('chapan') of a silky material ('bekasab'), belted
round with a silk or a cotton scarf, sewn by the bride for
the wedding day.   Although today most young and middle-
aged men wear hats or caps on their heads, the bridegroom
has to appear in a turban at his wedding (it is wound round
his head by his elder brother, or if he doesn't have one, by
one of his close friends).   The bridegroom puts a new skull
cap, especially sewn for the occasion by the bride, under his
turban.   The bridegroom's footwear are the traditional boots
('etik').   Earlier the bridegroom could not always afford new
clothes for his wedding, in which case he could borrow a
smart coat and boots from any inhabitant of the village.   No
payment was required for this.

The bride used to wear a new dress, coat ('chapan') and
scarf.   The bottom of her dress was not hemmed, which was
a symbol of her wish for a happy married life.   Today a
fashionable dress with embroidered sleeves with a yoke and a
stand-up collar and trimmed with ruches ('parnar') is made
for the bride, but, just as in the past, the bottom is not
hemmed.   On her feet the bride used to wear soft boots with
leather soles; today she usually has new shoes with low
heels.   The complicated woman's head-dress - turban in
style ('sallya') - is wound round the bride's head in her husband's house by an expert in this or by one of her husband's
female friends.

The matchmakers buy food for the 'patiya-toi' and take it to
the house of the girl's father.   A large number of guests are
invited to the party, where they are served pilaff and roast
meat and the forthcoming wedding is announced.   After the
betrothal the bridegroom's relatives, according to custom, give
the bride's relatives scarves, coats and other presents.   A
similar custom of present-giving is widespread throughout
Central Asia. (17)

In the period between the betrothal and the marriage ceremony, the bridegroom visits the bride in secret.   This custom survives today.   Thus, one young man from the settlement of Dugab in Babataya was engaged to be married to a
girl from the village of Tarypaya in the Kafirnigan valley.

For a year before the wedding, every day after work, he rowed across the Kafirnigan on a raft made of reeds to see his bride in Tarypaya. It is approximately 40 km from Dugab to Tarypaya by road.

In the past, the bride's father was paid half of the 'kalym' (bridewealth. T.D.) in the period between the betrothal and the marriage. The second half was paid later, but always before the marriage ceremony was performed. Before the establishment of Soviet power, 'kalym' was widespread among all the peoples of Central Asia and Kazakhstan. (18) Both its amount and the composition of the dowry were settled on the advice of the elders when the matchmakers came to the house of the girl's parents to receive their final answer. The whole of the 'kalym' went to the bride's father, her elder brother or, if she had neither a father or brother, to her uncle on her mother's side.

At the end of the nineteenth century, according to A.D. Grebenkin's information, the nomad Uzbek Yus 'paid' 5-10 sheep, the Kutchi 60-80 roubles, and the Mingi 40-200 roubles for the bride. A.D. Grebenkin notes that the Uzbeks rarely paid the 'kalym' in money, the sum stipulated was usually met in cattle and grain. (19)

Our oldest informants claim that there were no norms for the amount of 'kalym' before the Revolution. Among the Kungrats the 'kalym' usually consisted of 50-100 sheep or 1,000 roubles in money, among the inhabitants of Babatag, it was 100 head of sheep and 10 head of big-horned cattle and 4 horses. Durmen men rarely married before the age of 40, since they couldn't afford the 'kalym' before then.

An in-depth analysis of the origin of the institution of 'kalym' is given in the work of N.A. Kislyakov. In his opinion the 'kalym' of the peoples of Central Asia and Kazakhstan is a particular way of buying women from another kin group. The custom of buying a wife, writes N.A. Kislyakov, is inseparably connected with the large patriarchal family. (20) Thus, the custom of paying 'kalym' is connected with the large patriarchal family and, it would seem, should have totally disappeared when this type of family died out. As is known, such a family is already a thing of the past among the peoples of Central Asia and Kazakhstan and only its transitional form, the undivided family, survives. However, cases when 'kalym' is paid for a bride still occur today, sometimes even when there is no undivided family involved. 'Kalym' is one of the most persistent and slow to disappear of the harmful survivals of feudal-patriarchal relations among the peoples of Central Asia and Kazakhstan. However, the nature of this custom has changed under Soviet

rule, under the influence of the development of socialist econ-
omics and culture and changes in the structure of society and
everyday life.　If before the October Revolution the Durmen
included cattle and money in the 'kalym' they paid for the
bride, now the 'kalym' mostly consists of presents for the
bride's relatives:　cloth, coats, dresses, shoes.　Sometimes,
the bride's father is also given money with which to buy
things for his daughter's dowry.　The girl's family itself
provides the major part of the dowry.

They begin to amass the dowry from the time the girl is
eight or nine.　It includes various articles of clothing, and
household goods, always an even number of each item, e.g.
4 dresses, 6 scarves, 2 'chapan', etc.　Carpet bags
('mapramach') and rugs, which must be woven by the girl,
are also an essential part of the dowry.　Today the rugs are
sometimes replaced by piled carpets, bought in a shop.　All
the soft coverings needed for a 'yurt' (tent.　T.D.) are also
included in the bride's dowry (they are packed in the
'mapramach').　The different straps with which the wooden
poles of the yurt-frame ('kerege') and the curved poles
('nukozy') are tied together are also woven by the bride herself.　Her mother or her aunt usually helps the girl in this
work.

Now, when they no longer live in 'yurts', the girl is usually
given a set of yurt-coverings by her mother or her grandmother on her mother's side.　The inclusion of yurt-coverings in the dowry is evidence of the persistence of nomad and
semi-nomad traditions among the Durmen.　Earlier the 'yurt'
or 'lochik' (a dwelling of a semi-nomad type) which the bride's
father either made or bought for her was taken to the bridegroom's village as part of the dowry.

A similar custom existed among other nomad and semi-nomad
peoples - the Kazakhs, the Kirgiz, the Karakalpaks and the
Turkmen.　Both the semi-nomad Uzbeks and the Kazakhs
called the wedding 'yurt' the 'otau', (21)　The custom of
giving a 'yurt' as dowry is still preserved by the Durmen of
the Babatag mountains.　However, it no longer exists in
Kabadian and in the valley of the middle course of the Kafirnigan River;　and instead a room in the house of the girl's
parents is set aside for the young couple.

The contents of the dowry are hung up for inspection in the
'yurt' or room (in the husband's house) by the long woven
straps with which the 'kerege' and the curved poles are tied
together.　If the dowry is displayed in a 'yurt', the contents
are hung from the 'kerege'.　We managed to observe this
custom in the village of Sarylka (Babatag mountains).　There
the young wife came to her husband's settlement with a young

child and brought a 'yurt' as part of her dowry. The dowry
was displayed in the 'yurt' (22) and the young woman sat
behind the curtain ('chemyldyk') according to the custom of
her mother with her child in her arms.

As has already been said, in the period between the
'patiya-toi' (betrothal feast) and the 'nika-toi' (wedding feast)
the bridegroom visits the bride in secret, but he cannot take
her to his house until the second half of the 'kalym' has been
paid.

When the whole of the 'kalym' has been paid the 'nika-toi'
is held. Today this ritual is performed after an agreed
number of presents, and sometimes money as well, have been
given to the bride's parents and relatives. On the eve of
the 'nika-toi' a party is given for the bridegroom's male
friends. This custom is still observed. The bride and her
girlfriends bake cakes of puff pastry ('katlama') in her house,
which her parents, brothers and sisters vacate for the purpose. The bride's girlfriends place the cakes in twenty
wooden dishes ('tabak') and take them into the neighbouring
house where the bridegroom's friends are. The young men
take the cakes and fill the empty dishes with pieces of cloth
as presents for the girls. The girls take the dishes of
presents and run and hide in another house - preferably that
of the bride's uncle on her mother's side, where the bride is
waiting for them. (23) The young men give the master of
the house a present and he lets them in to where the girls
are. The young people then play games and generally enjoy
themselves. Often in the past it was at these parties that
boys and girls met for the first time and fell in love.

The root of this interesting custom seems to go back to the
time of the original communal system. The present-giving
took place between particular age sets, between young men
and girls of approximately the same age. In the past,
according to the stories of the old men, intimate relations
were permitted between the young men and the girls on these
occasions. This should probably be seen as a survival of
group marriages.

The 'nika-toi' of the Durmen and all the peoples of Central
Asia, is a communal type of marriage ritual. It is always
held in the house of the girl's parents at midnight, in the
presence of the bride and bridegroom's male relatives. The
mullah places a cake in a cup of water and covers it with a
piece of gauze. Then he reads the marriage prayer over
the cup. The bride and groom are not present at the ceremony. The bride and her girlfriends sit in the yard of the
house, and the bridegroom also waits nearby. Two or three
of the men of the highest standing go to ask for the bride's

consent to the marriage, and convey her answer to the mullah
and the men present at the prayers.   The mullah himself
asks the bridegroom for his consent to the marriage.   Even
today, although the civil registration of marriage is now
common, the Durmen still perform this old Moslem ritual.
However, like other old customs, its significance has changed
and it is performed mainly out of habit, by force of tradition,
to please the older generation of relatives.

After the 'nika-toi', the bride's girlfriends carry her on a
piece of white sheepskin (and now sometimes a rug or blanket)
into the wedding 'yurt' or house.   On the threshold sits an
old woman ('kampyr') brought there by the bride's mother.
The bridegroom's closest friend has to give this old woman a
sum of money before she will allow the bridegroom into the
wedding 'yurt' (or house).   A similar system exists among
many of the peoples of Central Asia and among the
Kazakhs. (24)   N.A. Kislyakov considers it one of the survivals of a matrilocal system of society. (25)

The bridegroom goes up to the bride, covering his face with
the skirt of his coat.   He is given a mirror to look in so that
he will be 'as pure as a mirror'.   The bride's friends produce
a bowl of butter or jam, and they smear the bridegroom's lips
with it.   This is a magic act which symbolises the wish that
they may be happy and have many children.   Then one of
the bride's married sisters sews a couple of stitches onto the
bridegroom's outer clothing to protect him from the evil eye.
The young couple's bed is made by one of the bride's female
relatives.   The bride's mother or aunt presides over all these
preparations.

Among the Uzbeks of the southern raions of Tadzhikistan
and Uzbekistan, the bride's journey to her husband's house
(already as wife and bride - 'kelin') takes place late in the
afternoon, always before dark.   Among the Uzbeks and
Tadzhiks of other raions of Tadzhikistan, on the other hand,
the bride is brought to her husband's house in the evening.
The way is lighted with torches and ritual bonfires are lit in
the yards of her and her husband's house. (26)   The ritual
bonfires occupy an important place in the wedding ceremonies
of the Uzbeks of Dashtikipchak origin. (27)   Today a bonfire
is lit only at the bridegroom's house just before the bride's
arrival, although not so long ago, as we were told in
Kabadian, a bonfire was lit in the yard of the girl's house as
well.   The wood for the bonfire is prepared and lit by the
bride's sponsor mother.

The institution of a sponsor mother and father, who wel-
come the bride into her husband's house and act as her
guardians, is highly characteristic of the groups of former

semi-nomad Uzbeks. Before the bride comes to his house,
her husband asks one of his close friends and his wife to act
as her sponsor (adopted) father and mother. (28) The
adopted father has to provide mutton in honour of the bride's
arrival and cook pilaff for her and the guests. When the
bride approaches the house, the adopted mother takes her
horse by the bridle and leads it three times round the bonfire. (29) Then she gives the horse a dish of barley.

If the bride comes in a car, as often happens now, the
adopted mother helps her out, takes her by the arm and they
walk together three times round the bonfire. The husband's
mother then announces her gift of a cow or sheep to his
bride. The 'kelin' and her adopted mother bow. After
this a sheepskin is spread out on the threshold and the bride
steps onto it. She is handed a cup of butter or sheep fat
and a spoon. She goes up to the bonfire with her adopted
mother, and throws three spoonfuls of butter onto the fire.
This symbolises her wish for the future prosperity of the life
of the family.

Then the adopted mother takes the 'kelin' by the hand and
leads her into the house where they sit together behind the
curtain ('chimyldyk') for three days. In the past, after
these three days had elapsed the girl went back to her
parents' house and stayed there for a week or more. Now
the custom of returning home is hardly ever observed. After
three days, during which she talks only to her adopted
mother, and avoids her husband's relatives, the bride comes
out from behind the curtain. Her mother-in-law organises
the inspection of the bride ('kelin korsatar').

A universally respected old man is specially invited to the
inspection to uncover the bride's face. (30) He lifts up her
veil with his stick and says 'Don't run round the village,
don't speak evil.' After this the visitors give presents to
the father and mother and everyone drinks milk soup ('ak
bulamyk'). The adopted parents have to treat the young
woman as their daughter on her arrival at her husband's
house and thereafter. This interesting custom is most
common among the former cattle-raising population of Central
Asia. Like some of the other wedding customs and rituals,
it probably originated in the period of the break-up of the
matriarchal kinship system and the consolidation of the patri-
local type of settlement, and reflects the wish of the husband's kin to adopt the girl, as if to assert their right over
her.

The analysis of the Durmen wedding rituals reveals that
they have much in common with those of peoples who led a
nomadic and semi-nomadic existence in the past, in particular

with those of the Kazakhs and also the Kirgiz, the Karakalpaks, and, to a certain extent, the Turkmen.   Among their
common features are the persistence of kinship-tribal divisions
and the tribal endogamy and kinship exogamy connected with
this, and a series of customs and rituals to do with the conduct of the wedding (e.g. the custom of giving a 'yurt' as
dowry).   The former semi-nomad Uzbeks borrowed some of
their other wedding rituals too from the surrounding settled
population, in particular the Tadzhiks (e.g. the custom of
breaking bread, etc.).   In addition, the traditional Uzbek
wedding has undergone great changes.   Under Soviet rule
new customs and rituals have formed, the content of the old
rituals has changed and many of them have disappeared entirely.   This applies to the wedding ritual among others.
The centuries-old custom of matchmaking is now performed in
a purely formal way, since the young people themselves agree
on the wedding beforehand.   Earlier the bride was taken to
her husband's house on horseback and various magic rituals
were performed on the way.   Now the bride and her dowry
usually come by car, and many of the magic rituals formerly
connected with the wedding procession have died out.

The material presented here shows that the traditional wedding of the Dashtikipchak Uzbeks preserves some attributes of
communal kinship relations, features such as the holding of
the main wedding celebration in the house of the bride's
parents, the survivals of such forms of marriage as levirate
and sororate, the custom of avoidance, the preservation of
magic rituals, etc.   All these features, however, have lost
their original meaning, and if they are encountered today, it
is in a changed form and purely as tradition.

NOTES

1   The Durmen are one of the ethnographical groups of
    Uzbeks of Dashtikipchak origin, the descendants of the
    tribes of Dashtikipchak Uzbeks who came to Central Asia
    in the sixteenth century.   In distinction from the main
    groupings of the Uzbeks, they led a semi-nomad life and
    preserved their kin and tribal divisions until quite recent-
    ly.   The Uzbeks of Dashtikipchak origin include the
    Katagan, the Durmen, the Kungrat, the Lokaits, the
    Naiman and others.   The materials used in this article
    mainly relate to the Durmen who live in the valley of the
    river Kafirnigan (Tadzhikistan) and the Babatag moun-
    tains (Uzbekistan).   For more detail on the ethnographi-
    cal group of Uzbeks of Dashtikipchak origin, see B.K.
    Karmysheva, Findings on the Ethnogenesis of the Popula-
    tion of the Southern and Western Districts of Uzbekistan,
    'Transactions of the Institute of Ethnography of the

Academy of Sciences of the USSR', vol. 27, Moscow, 1957;
B.K. Karmysheva, Ethnic and Territorial Groups of the
Population of the North-Eastern Part of the Kashka-Darin
Region of the Uzbek SSR, ibid., vol. 33, Moscow, 1960.
2   T.A. Zhdanko, Essays on the Historical Ethnography of
the Karakalpak. Kin and Tribal Structure and Resettlement in the Nineteenth and early Twentieth Century,
'Works of the Institute of Ethnography of the Academy of
Sciences of the USSR', vol. 9, Moscow-Leningrad, 1950,
p. 70.
3   See 'The Peoples of Central Asia and Kazakhstan', vol. 1,
Moscow, 1962, p. 315.
4   It should be remarked that, in Central Asia, survivals of
exogamy can be traced most clearly among the Karakalpak.   See T.A. Zhdanko, The Daily Life of the Karakalpak Kolkhoz Village, 'Soviet Ethnography', 1949, no. 2,
p. 13.
5   Survivals of dual organisation among the Turkmen were
discovered by S.P. Tolstov; see S.P. Tolstov, Survivals
of Totemism and Dual Organisation among the Turkmen,
'Problems of the History of Pre-Capitalist Societies', 1935,
nos 9-10.
6   A.D. Grebenkin, The Uzbeks, 'Papers on Russian Turkestan', vol. 2, Moscow, 1872, pp. 76, 86, 98.
7   K.L. Zadykhina, The Uzbeks of the Amu-Dar Delta,
'Works of the Khorezm Archeological-Ethnographical Expedition', vol. 1, Moscow, 1952, p. 399; A. Dzhumagulov,
'Family and Marriage among the Kirgiz of the Chu Valley',
Frunze, 1962. pp. 30, 32; T.A. Zhdanko, op. cit., pp.
70-1.   The cradle betrothal also existed among the
peoples of Siberia. see N.P. Dvrenkova, Survivals of the
Maternal Kin among the Altai Turks. 'Soviet Ethnography'.
1937, no. 4, p. 19; I.D. Starynkevich, Forms of the
Conclusion of Marriage among the Turkic Tribes of Siberia
and the Nomads of Central Asia, 'Papers of MAE', vol. 9,
Leningrad, 1930.
8   M.O. Kosven, On the Problem of Group Marriage, 'Transactions of the Institute of Ethnography', vol. 1, 1946,
pp. 19-22.
9   'The Peoples of Central Asia and Kazakhstan', vol. 1,
Moscow, 1962, vol. 2, Moscow, 1963 (see the sections on
the family and the organisation of marriage within the
family).
10 Information about the weddings of the semi-nomad Uzbeks,
including the Durmen, can be found in A.D. Grebenkin,
op. cit., pp. 64-8.   Soviet ethnographers K.L. Zadykhina, N.P. Lobacheva, K. Shaniyazov and T. Faiziev have
described the wedding ritual of the northern Uzbeks of
Khorez, the Uzbek-Karluk and the Kuram; see K.L.
Zadykhina, op. cit., pp. 402-5; N.P. Lobacheva, The
Wedding Rituals of the Khorez Uzbeks, 'Transactions of the

Institute of Ethnography', vol. 34, 1960; K. Shaniyazov,
'The Uzbek-Karluk (A Historical-Ethnographical Essay)',
Tashkent, 1964, pp. 140-52; T. Faiziev, 'The Uzbek-
Kuram (in the Past and Present)', Synopsis of a Candidat
Thesis, Tashkent, 1963, p. 21.

11 I will take the opportunity of thanking Ternash Nurman-
tov, accountant of the Kalinin Sovkhoz, and many others,
who helped me in collecting materials.

12 L.Ya. Shternberg remarked on the essential part played by
the collective in the weddings of the peoples of N.E.
Siberia.   'Marriage', he wrote, 'is a social act, sanctioned
by the collective, the kin among peoples with a kinship
organisation and, among our peasantry, the group of relatives and indeed the whole society.' L.Ya. Shternberg,
'Family and Kinship among the Peoples of North-Eastern
Siberia', Leningrad, 1933, p. 182.

13 A.D. Grebenkin, op. cit., p. 66.

14 Kh. Kustanaev, 'Ethnographical Essays on the Kirgiz of
Perov and Kazalin Districts', Tashkent, 1894, pp. 27, 82;
R. Karutts, 'Among the Kirgiz and Turkmen on Mangy-
shlak', St Petersburg, 1910, p. 98.

15 N.A. Kislyakov, Family and Marriage among the Tadzhiks,
'Works of the Institute of Ethnography', New Series, vol.
43, Moscow-Leningrad, 1959, pp. 95-6; N.A. Kislyakov,
Survivals of Matriarchy in the Marriage Rituals of Central
Asia, 'Transactions of the Institute of Ethnography', vol.
28, 1958, p. 24.

16 A. Dzhikiev, Wedding Rituals of the Turkmen-Salyr in the
late Nineteenth and early Twentieth Century, 'Works of
the Institute of History, Archeology and Ethnography of
the Academy of Sciences of the Turkmen SSR', vol. 7,
Ethnographical Series, Ashkhabad, 1963.

17 See N.A. Kislyakov, 'Family and Marriage among the
Tadzhiks', pp. 80-4, 123-6.

18 See R. Karutts, op. cit., p. 10; N.I. Grodekov, 'The
Kirgiz and the Karakalpak of Syr-Dar Region', vol. 1,
Tashkent, 1883, pp. 48, 60, 61, 77; A. Podarkova,
Marriage and Divorce among the Kirgiz, 'Central Asia. A
Monthly Literary-Historical Publication', vol. 2, Tashkent,
1910; N.A. Kislyakov, 'Family and Marriage among the
Tadzhiks', pp. 136-80.

19 A.D. Grebenkin, op. cit., pp. 76, 85, 92, 109.

20 N.A. Kislyakov, 'Family and Marriage among the Tadzhiks',
p. 177.   See also M.O. Kosven, Bride Purchase and
Matriarchy, 'Proceedings of Moscow State University', vol.
61, History, no. 2, Moscow, 1940, pp. 103, 105, 109, 114.

21 F. Fielstrup, The Wedding Tents of the Turkic Peoples,
'Materials on Ethnography. Ethnographic Section of the
State Russian Museum', vol. 3, no. 1, Leningrad, pp.
111-12.

22 An inspection of the dowry, hung up in the 'yurt', was

also organised by the Kazakhs and Kirgiz, ibid., pp. 114-15.

23 At the end of the nineteenth century, a similar custom existed among the Kazakhs.   See F. L.-y, The Wedding Customs of the Kirgiz of Orenburg Department, 'Moscow Gazette', 1862, no. 151; Altysarin, An Essay on the Betrothal and Wedding Customs of the Kirgiz of Orenburg Department, 'Proceedings of the Orenburg Section of the Russian Geographical Society', 1870, no. 1; I.I. Ibragimov, Ethnographical Essays on the Kirgiz People, 'Russian Turkestan', no. 2, 1872; and others.

24 N.I. Grodekov, op. cit., p. 21.

25 N.A. Kislyakov, Survivals of Matriarchy in the Wedding Rituals of the Peoples of Central Asia, 'Transactions of the Institute of Ethnography', no. 27, 1957.

26 See N.A. Kislyakov, Some Materials on the Question of the Ethnogenesis of the Tadzhiks, ibid., no. 30, 1958, pp. 130-4.

27 In the past, a bonfire was lit in the yard of the house or in front of the 'yurt', by the Uzbeks, the Uzbek-Karluk and others.   See K.L. Zadykhina, op. cit., p. 403; K. Shaniyazov, 'The Uzbek-Karluk', p. 149.

28 The bride calls her adopted mother 'ina' (mother), her adopted father 'ata' (father) and her husband correspondingly calls them 'kainina' (mother-in-law) and 'kainata' (father-in-law).   Among the northern groups of Khorez Uzbeks, the bride calls her adopted mother 'murundukene'.   See K.L. Zadykhina, op. cit., p. 403; N.P. Lobacheva, op. cit., p. 43.

29 The Tadzhiks had a similar custom.   See N.A. Kislyakov. 'Family and Marriage among the Tadzhiks' p. 112.

30 The Tadzhiks held similar inspections.   See N.A. Kislyakov, 'Family and Marriage among the Tadzhiks', pp. 116-17.

4 A statistical study of indices of single- nationality and mixed-nationality marriages in Dushanbe

*A.V. Kozenko and L.F. Monogarova**

The problem of ethnic development embraces a large number of questions which come into the field not only of ethnographers, but also of specialists from related disciplines: historians, sociologists, philosophers, linguists and others.

Ethnic processes of consolidation and assimilation are really the concrete expression of contacts between peoples of different groups within them. The study of an important aspect of ethnic contacts - the dynamics of mixed marriages between members of different nationalities - is of particular interest in this connection.

The town, and especially the capital, is a focus of ethnic processes. Towns always have a more variegated ethnic composition than the surrounding villages: 'the population of towns everywhere - in Poland, in Latvia, in the Ukraine, in Belorussia, etc. - is distinguished by its highly variegated national composition.' (1) Processes of linguistic and ethnic assimilation and consolidation can be seen more clearly in the town. As a result, questions of contacts between nationalities are mainly studied in the town.

In 1969 one of the authors of this article, L.F. Monogarova, gathered statistical material on single-nationality and mixed marriages concluded in the period 1946-66 inclusive, in the archive of the town ZAGS in Dushanbe, the capital of the Tadzhik Soviet Socialist Republic. In this multinational town, as in the towns of other republics of the USSR, as a result of particular historical and social causes, (2) the proportion of the indigenous population, Tadzhiks and Uzbeks, is smaller than the proportion of other nationalities (see Table 4.1) which has led to a large number of nationally mixed marriages of various types. Out of 55,000 marriages concluded in the town in 1946-66, over 22,000 were nationally mixed.

The numerically largest group of peoples of other nationalities in Dushanbe is the Russians; the most numerous of the indigenous peoples are the Tadzhiks and the Uzbeks. Therefore, taking the quantitative factor into account, i.e. the

* First published in 'Sovetskaya Etnografiya', 1971, no. 6, pp. 112-18.

Table **4.1** *The numerical and national composition of the population of Dushanbe**

Nationality	Both sexes	Men	Women
Tadzhiks	43,008	24,508	18,500
Russians	108,236	45,538	62,698
Uzbeks	23,178	12,587	10,591
Tatars	12,506	5,363	7,143
Ukrainians	9,912	4,536	5,376
Jews	8,720	4,161	4,559
Mordovians	3,194	1,187	2,007
Osetins	1,721	867	854
Other nationalities	16,662	8,128	8,534
Total	227,137	108,875+	120,262

* The table uses the data of the all-union census of 1959, see 'Itogi Vsecoyuznoi perepisi naseleniya 1959 g. Tadzhikskaya SSR', M 1963, pp. 122-3.   A settlement of a suburban type - Verzobsk GES (population equals 2,895, of which 1,388 are men and 1,507 women) which comes under the Dushanbe town soviet - was included in the Dushanbe figures.
+ Incorrectly printed in Russian text;   total should be 106,875 (T.D.).

absolute number of Tadzhiks, Uzbeks and Russians, in Dushanbe, we chose these peoples for a study of the frequency of single-nationality and mixed marriages and their theoretical probability for the whole period examined.   O.A. Gantskaya and G.F. Debets, (3) and also Yu. I. Pershits (4) have shown that the frequency of single-nationality and mixed marriages P_{jk} with their theoretical probability P^*_{jk} (the probability that in the arbitrarily chosen couple the nationality of the husband will be j and that of the wife k), (5) characterises the degree of endogamy of the ethnos.

The fact that the study covers all marriages in Dushanbe for over two decades made it possible to examine the trend of development of the frequency of single-nationality and mixed marriages in their theoretical probability, in Dushanbe.

In our article, all the indices are regarded not statistically, but as functions of time.   For example: $P^*_{jk} = P^*_{jk}(t)$.

The actual frequency of single-nationality and mixed marriages among the three numerically predominant peoples in
Dushanbe, and also in the theoretical probability of these
marriages is presented in the form of graphs to make the
trends clearer.   In each of the graphs the frequencies of
marriages of a particular kind are given $P_{jk}(t)$ and the
theoretical probability $P^*_{jk}(t)$ in percentages.

In our work the indices j and k represent 1, 2, and 3
where 1 is for Tadzhiks, 2 is for Uzbeks and 3 stands for
Russians.

Each graph gives the frequency of single-nationality marriages among the Tadzhiks, Uzbeks, and Russians as greater
than their theoretical probability (Graphs 1-3).   During this

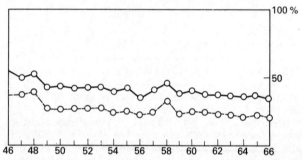

Graph 1 *Marriages of Russian men with Russian women (here
and in the following graphs the unbroken lines represent
observed data and the broken lines represent theoretical
possibilities.   Dates on the horizontal scale and percentages
on the vertical scale)*

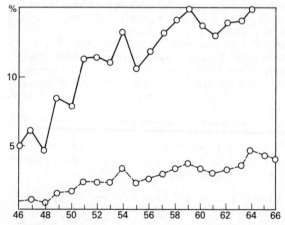

Graph 2 *Marriages of Tadzhik men with Tadzhik women*

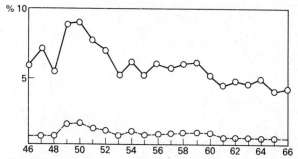

Graph 3 *Marriages of Uzbek men with Uzbek women*

20-year period, a stable picture emerges.   The frequency of single-nationality marriages among the Tadzhiks grows more quickly than the theoretical probability.   This can be seen as evidence of the relative stability of the Tadzhik ethnos in the nationality mixed environment (see Graph 2);   even though in the town, and especially in the capital, the possibility of contacts between the nationalities, among their marriages, is surely greater than in other parts of the republic. Our materials confirm Yu. I. Bromley's theory that 'a permanent attribute of ethnic communities in a stable situation, i.e. typical for them, is endogamy in the wide sense of the word, i.e. understood as the preference for marrying within one's community.' (6)

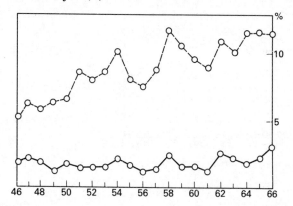

Graph 4 *Marriages of Tadzhik men with Russian women*

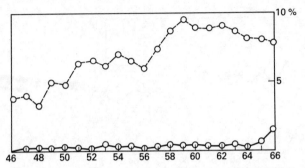

Graph 5   *Marriages of Russian men with Tadzhik women*

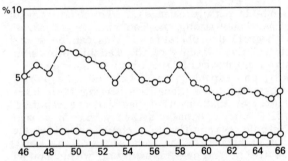

Graph 6   *Marriages of Uzbek men with Russian women*

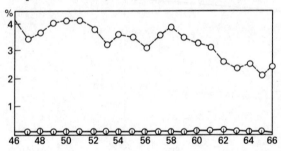

Graph 7   *Marriages of Russian men with Uzbek women*

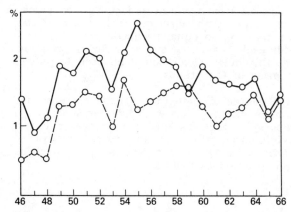

Graph 8   *Marriages of Uzbek men with Tadzhik women*

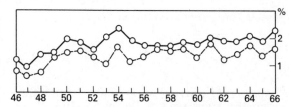

Graph 9   *Marriages of Tadzhik men with Uzbek women*

An examination of mixed Tadzhik-Uzbek and Uzbek-Tadzhik marriages (Graphs 8 and 9) reveals an almost total coincidence of the observed frequency of marriages with their theoretical probability: the difference is nowhere over 1 per cent for the whole 20 years.

A comparison of the observed frequency of the nationally mixed marriages of Tadzhiks and Uzbeks with Russians and their theoretical probability (Graphs 4-7) shows that the theoretical probability is significantly greater than the observed frequency. This proves that the national factor has real influence in the choice of spouse in these types of mixed marriages.

As we saw above, the graphs make it possible to judge the degree of endogamy of the different ethnoses represented in Dushanbe. However, special indices are needed to compare the degree of endogamy of different ethnoses. In the study mentioned above, Yu. I. Pershits introduces a series of indices characterising the structure of nationally mixed marriages. Thus, the coefficient

$$\lambda_{jk} = \frac{(P_{jj})}{(P^*_{jj})} : \frac{(P_{jk})}{(P^*_{jk})}$$

shows how much more often men of the nationality j conclude single-nationality marriages than marriages with women of the nationality k, when there is an equal proportion of each in the total number for each year.   A similar index is used for women.   However, this index alone cannot be used to judge the degree of endogamy of the ethnos.

For comparing the degree of endogamy of different ethnoses, it is much more convenient in our view to have an index giving the preference for single-nationality marriages over mixed, without dividing the latter according to nationality. This index qj is defined by Yu. I. Pershits as $q_j = \lambda_{jk}$ where all $j \neq k$ and qj is expressed as follows:

$$q_j = \frac{n_{jj} (n - f_j)}{f_j (m_j - n_{jj})}$$

For women we calculated the indices in the same way:

$$q'_j = \frac{n_{jj} (n - m_j)}{m_j (f_j - n_{jj})}$$

Where n = the total number of marriages examined; n_{jj} = the number of single-nationality marriages of the nationality j; m_j = the number of men of nationality j marrying; f_j = the number of women of nationality j marrying.

Table 4.2 gives the incidence of q_i, q_i' and q_2, q_2' for 1946, 1956 and 1966.   An examination of Table 4.2 shows that the Tadzhik men more willingly conclude mixed-nationality marriages than Uzbeks.   The reverse is true of women: Uzbeks more willingly marry representatives of other nationalities than Tadzhiks.

Table 4.2 *Index of a preference for single-nationality marriages over nationally mixed marriages (without dividing the latter by nationality)*

| Index | Year | | |
	1946	1956	1966
q_i	17.5	16.6	9.6
q_i'	37	25.4	22.8
q_2	21.7	16.2	16.3
q_2'	22.4	25.5	19.2

The information given in Table 4.2 also shows the significant predominance of single-nationality marriages over nationality mixed *in toto*.

It is interesting to compare the number of marriages of men and women of any given nationality with those of people of other nationalities.   Thus, it seems useful to introduce an index which will allow us to compare the frequency of marriages of men of nationality j and women of the same nationality j with representatives of other nationalities.

$$\eta_j = \frac{q'_j}{q_j} = \frac{f_j \ (h - m_j) \ (m_j - n_{jj})}{m_j \ (n - f_j) \ (f_j - n_{jj})}$$

Table 4.3 gives the incidence of n_j for 1946, 1956 and 1966. This table shows that twice the number of Tadzhik men marry women of other nationalities as Tadzhik women marry men of other nationalities.   There is not such a great difference among the Uzbeks.   It is true that one should remember at this point that single-nationality marriages predominate among these peoples.

Table 4.3 *Index showing how much more often men of a particular nationality conclude nationally mixed marriages than women of the same nationality*

Index		Year	
	1946	1956	1966
η_1	2.1	1.6	2.4
η_2	1.03	1.57	1.18

From the above material it is clear that the percentage of nationally mixed marriages over the 20-year period examined is of a considerable size.   However, by itself the percentage of nationally mixed marriages does not define the degree of stability of the endogamy of a certain ethnos.   This can only be judged on the results of a comparison of the true proportion of nationally mixed marriages with their theoretical probability.

Our materials showed the strong stability of the endogamy of the Tadzhiks and Uzbeks.

Yu. I. Bromley remarks that the factors which contribute to endogamy of an ethnos 'may include both natural and social phenomena'. (7)   In the town only social factors are of importance, language is not an obstacle since the population of the towns of the Union republics is as a rule bi-lingual and

multi-lingual.   (The authors mean non-Russian republics.
T.D.)   The main social factors influencing the endogamy of
the ethnos seem to be elements of traditional culture and customs, especially religious survivals.   This theory is confirmed
by the fact that the Tadzhiks and Uzbeks, whose family relations have been considerably influenced by Islam, and whose
traditional culture and customs have much in common, conclude mixed marriages with each other more often than with
Russians.

The stability of the Tadzhik ethnos is also confirmed by the
data on the nationality chosen by teenagers in nationally mixed
families.   For example, according to L.F. Monogarova's
material, (8) in families where the father is a Tadzhik and the
mother Russian, more than 82 per cent of teenagers adopt the
father's (Tadzhik) nationality;   and in cases where the father
is a Tadzhik and the mother an Uzbek, over 74 per cent adopt
the father's (Tadzhik) nationality.

This circumstance, in turn, is evidence of the definite
stability of the ethnos of the Tadzhiks, Uzbeks and Russians
living in Dushanbe, in spite of the various contacts between
the nationalities, which include marriage.

NOTES

1   V.I. Lenin, 'Collected Works', 4th ed., vol. 24, p. 149.
2   On this, see V.V. Pokshishevsky, Some Problems in the
    Study of Ethnic Processes in the Towns of the USSR,
    'Soviet Ethnography', 1969, no. 5;   V.I. Kozlov, Ethno-
    geographical Aspects of Urbanisation in the USSR, 'Geo-
    graphical Aspects of Urbanisation', 1971, nos 5-6, pp. 62-
    72.
3   O.A. Gantskaya, G.F. Debets, The Graphic Depiction of
    the Results of Statistical Investigation of Interracial
    Marriage, 'Soviet Ethnography', 1966, no. 3.
4   Yu. I. Pershits, The Methodology of Comparing the Indices
    of Single-Nationality and Mixed Marriage, 'Soviet Ethnog-
    raphy', 1967, no. 4.
5   Ibid., p. 129.
6   Yu. I. Bromley, Ethnos and Endogamy, 'Soviet Ethnog-
    raphy', 1969, no. 6, p. 84.
7   Ibid., p. 87.
8   L.F. Monogarova, 'Statistical Materials, Collected in the
    Police Department of the Central District of the City of
    Dushanbe', manuscript, Archive of the Institute of
    Ethnography.

5   Legend: to believe or not to believe?

*V.N.Basilov**

In 1965 while I was gathering material on the survivals of
ancestor worship in the Serakh raion of Turkmenistan, I
asked the older inhabitants about the legendary ancestor of
the Salyr 'tribe', Salyr-Gazan (as the Turkmen pronounce
this name).   I wanted to find out whether any traces of the
worship of Salyr-Gazan survived and, if so, in what form,
and so I got various people to write down the legends of this
proud and mighty hero.   Salyr-Gazan or Salor-Kazan, the
ancestor of many Turkmen 'tribes', is well known from medieval sources based on popular traditions, and from the epic
tales of the Oguz. (1)   However, what I heard differed considerably from previously published legends, and prompted me
to make a more detailed study of this Turkmen version.

Many of the older inhabitants claimed that a book of the
adventures and deeds of Salyr-Gazan existed in Takhta-Bazar
raion.   They gave me the name and the address of the book's
owner.   Taking a ticket for the mail plane, I flew out to
Takhta-Bazar, wondering how to spend the day that was just
beginning: it was Sunday, everything was closed.

I got out of the aeroplane and walked along the smooth clay
surface of the aerodrome.   The sun was hot, quite unlike
December.   What should I do?   Waste a whole day just for
the sake of organising my work on an official basis?   It would
be a pity, my study trip was coming to an end.   I looked
around.   In the distance I could see the neat white houses of
a village, right on the ridges of the steep hills, which rose
beyond Murgab.   'It's part of the Lenin Kolkhoz,' someone
explained, and I set out there on foot through the steppe,
battling with the dusty, dry grass, which clung to my
trousers.

An hour and a half later I was resting in the large hall of
the village school.   Teachers, agronomists and kolkhoz workers lay in picturesque poses on the floor on sheepskins and
rugs.   These were the ones who hadn't hurried home after
the feast held to celebrate the successful ending of the agricultural year.   Many of them were still drinking tea.   They

* First published in 'Sovetskaya Etnografiya', 1974, no. 1,
  pp. 163-72.

listened to my story, gave me something to eat, and then sat
me down next to a middle-aged man in a tall kubanka-cap,
who had been watching me with a grin.   He told me his name
'Amanmukhammed Berdyev, kolkhoz worker.'   It was obvious
from his face that he was well aware he had been pointed out
by his fellow-villagers as the expert on customs and traditions.   He filled two bowls with green tea – one for me and
one for him – and began to talk.

Here is the legend as he told it to me or rather, my summary of it.

"Salyr-Gazan is our ancestor.   Many years ago he lived
among the Uzbeks and took an Uzbek girl as his wife.   She
bore him three sons: the eldest was called Utamysh, the
middle one, Tokhtamysh, the youngest, Yalkamysh.   The
Padishah of the Uzbeks feared that Salyr-Gazan coveted his
throne.   He decided to get rid of him, summoned him and
said, 'The Padishah of Iran has a heroine for a daughter.
Go, take her for your wife.   Your son by her will become a
famous hero.'

Salyr-Gazan set out.   After travelling far and wide he came
at last to Iran.   A poor lonely old woman took him under her
roof.   He commanded her: 'Tell the Padishah that I intend
to marry his daughter.'   The old woman tried to talk him out
of it: 'Don't go to the Padishah's daughter, she's stronger
than you, she'll chop off your head.   Several men have
already lost their heads this way.' (2)   However, Salyr-
Gazan was firm in his resolution: 'Either I die or I marry
her!'   He stubbornly repeated his order to the old woman.
'Go tomorrow morning and sweep at the Padishah's doors.' (3)
On the morning of the following day the sovereign of Iran saw
the old woman sweeping at the doors of his court, 'Why are
you sweeping?' he asked.   'You haven't got a son.'   'I
gained a son today,' answered the old woman.   'He's in love
with your daughter.'   The Padishah reminded her of the conditions which his daughter laid down for all her suitors: her
husband would be the man who vanquished her in combat.
The old woman repeated this to Salyr-Gazan.

On the appointed day, Salyr-Gazan met the Iranian prin-
cess and vanquished her.   Soon after the wedding, which
was held in the palace and lasted for three days, Salyr-Gazan
went back to Uzbekistan, leaving his young wife alone.

As soon as the hero returned, the Padishah of the Uzbeks
treacherously murdered him.   He invited Salyr-Gazan to visit
him, on a carefully chosen day.   It was winter.   He ordered
his army to stand on the shore of the frozen lake and throw
their sabres along the ice to meet the hero on his way to the

castle, thereby cutting off his legs.   Salyr-Gazan fell onto
the ice in a pool of blood.   The soldiers cut off his head and
took it to the wicked Tsar.

Meanwhile, the daughter of the Padishah of Iran gave birth
to a son, who was called Salyr.   The boy grew up stronger
than all the other boys of his age.   One day the boys he'd
beaten in wrestling began to taunt him: 'You have not got a
father!'   Salyr thought about it, went home and asked his
mother to make him some hot roasted grains of wheat.   His
mother got the food ready, and held a spoon out to him.
'No, give me the grains in your palm' said Salyr.   His mother
put the hot grains into the hollow of her hand and the boy
grabbed her fingers hard in his fist.   'Who is my father?' he
asked.   His mother couldn't bear the burning pain and told
him, 'Your father is the hero Salyr-Gazan.   He was treacherously murdered by the Padishah of the Uzbeks.'   'Then I will
go and avenge my father's blood,' Salyr resolved.

The boy set out for Uzbekistan and there he found three of
his brothers whose mother was the Uzbek woman.   They also
saw it as their duty to kill the Uzbek Padishah and went with
Salyr to the royal palace.   On the way, the brothers met a
traveller, who proposed that they should try their strength
with him.   The brothers fought him in turn, but no one
emerged the winner, their strengths were equal.   When they
were all exhausted, the brothers asked the stranger, 'Who are
you?'   'Sary' (i.e. the yellow).   'No, you're Ersary' (er =
man, hero).   Then they asked each other what kins and
tribes they belonged to.   It turned out that they had the
same grandfather.   'Where are you going?' inquired Ersary.
'The Padishah of the Uzbeks killed our father.   We want to
avenge him,' was the answer.   Ersary decided to go with the
brothers and the five of them continued on their way.

They came to the castle of the Uzbek Padishah.   The fort-
ress was surrounded by a moat, filled with water from the
river, and armed guards were posted everywhere.   The
brothers strolled around the town and tried to find out how
they could penetrate the Padishah's stronghold.   At last, one
old woman whispered, 'Once a year the garrison is relieved.
On that day you can get into the castle.'   The brothers
waited for that day, mixed in with the crowd of soldiers,
entered the palace and killed the Uzbek Padishah who was
known by the name of It-Emdzhek-Uzbek (Uzbek Dog Chest)
because his chest was like a dog's. (4)

After this, Salyr returned to Iran, Ersary settled on the
banks of Amudar'ya, and the three brothers went to Mangyshlak.   Bad news was waiting for them: while they were
away their sister had been carried off by the Tatar Padishah.

The brothers told their grandfather, the father of Salyr-
Gazan, that they wanted to do battle with the offender, kill
him and take their sister back. 'Don't do that,' said their
grandfather, 'The Tatar Padishah is powerful, and there are
only three of you. It would be better to invite him and your
sister to stay. Give them presents, and above all, don't
forget to lead three of our mares to his stallion, so that they
will bear fine foals for you.' The brothers did as he said.
Soon the mares foaled and their grandfather reared three
valiant steeds. One day their sister came home for a visit.
The brothers didn't want to let her go back, but their sister
said, 'Don't keep me. It would be better to carry off the
daughter of one of the Tatar Padishah's other wives.'

Some time after her departure the brothers set out on
horseback. The way was long, over hills and plains, but at
last they saw the dwelling of the Tatar Padishah. His
daughter was washing clothes, and the sister of the Turkmen
brothers was also busy working. The riders greeted their
sister, but called her 'Aunt', as if this were the first time
they had met her. She answered them with the traditional
greeting. 'Give us some water to drink, Aunt,' asked the
brothers. 'Give the djigits something to drink,' their sister
told the girl. She handed Utamysh a bowl of water. He
drank and gave the cup back to her. Tokhtamysh also drank
and gave the cup back. But Yalkamysh flung the cup down
without drinking from it. He grabbed the girl by the arm,
hoisted her into his saddle and rode away like the wind.
Soon the pursuers, led by the Tatar Padishah himself, began
to catch up with him. 'Should I shoot at your father or at
his horse?' Yalkamysh asked the girl. 'Don't shoot at my
father or at his horse,' the girl replied. 'Then I will split
his saddle with my arrow,' Yalkamysh decided. Bending his
yellow bow, he aimed at the saddle; the shot was so accurate
that the saddle fell to pieces. 'Stop!' shouted the Tatar
Padishah. 'I won't touch you now. Let me give you some
advice: never let your stallion go with other people's mares.'
With these words he turned his horse round and galloped back.

When Yalkamysh's brothers caught up with him, they
stopped to rest. Tokhtamysh said to the girl: 'Yalkamysh
and I will sit on one sheepskin, you sit with Utamysh, he's
the eldest brother.' But the girl refused: 'I won't be
passed from hand to hand. Yalkamysh carried me off, and
I'll stay with him to the end of my days.' The brothers
started to quarrel, but Yalkamysh said: 'Let our grandfather
decide how it shall be.' They went home and told their
grandfather everything. 'Whose wife will you be my child?'
the old man asked the girl. 'I will marry no one but Yalkamysh,' the girl declared. Thereupon their grandfather sent
matchmakers to families with marriageable daughters and the

weddings of all three brothers were celebrated with great
magnificence on the same night.   The descendants of Utamysh
and Tokhtamysh are the Teke Turkmen.   The tribe Teke is
divided into two main branches - Otamysh and Tokhtamysh;
the descendants of Yalkamysh are we, the Saryk, and since
the wife of Yalkamysh was a Tatar girl, we may address the
Tatars as 'Uncle'." (5)

I repeat, I have only given a condensed version of the legend.
I couldn't keep pace with the story-teller, although Amanmukhammed-aga, seeing me scribbling furiously, spoke slowly,
with pauses, took sips of tea from the bowl and threw in
jokes for the benefit of those gathered round.   Judging by
the attention with which about thirty people were listening to
Amanmukhammed-aga (and probably not for the first time
either), he was a famous story-teller.   But all the same, I
didn't manage to write the legend down word for word in
Turkmen, and my version naturally doesn't convey all the
stylistic peculiarities of the genre.

However, the content of the legend is not distorted (I read
my version through to the story-teller and he approved it).
The above account can therefore be used as a source, especially since I couldn't find the book: its owner had died and
the manuscript, according to his sons, had been lost 40 years
before.

What is there of interest in the legend of these hero-
ancestors?

First, it is difficult to accept that the events it describes
really happened.   From the first word, a fairy-tale atmosphere surrounds us.   Enemies want the hero's death and
send him on a dangerous journey.   This is a common element
in fairy-stories.   Both the heroine who kills her vanquished
suitors and the old woman who helps the hero are found in
the fairy-tales of other peoples.   The son born in his
father's absence is also common in world folklore.   It is
interesting that Salyr, the son of Salyr-Gazan, behaves just
like a fairy-tale hero in his efforts to discover who his father
is.   Let us compare this episode with an extract from the
Altai fairy-tales.   A certain Eki-Moos killed the hero Arslan.
Arslan's wife was pregnant at the time and soon afterwards
gave birth to a son.   The boy grew up and asked his mother
where his father was.   His mother refused to say.   But one
day when the boy was playing with other children, they began
to fight, first in play and then in earnest.   Arslan's son
overpowered all his friends and pulled their coats off them.
They reproached him: 'You're good at robbing us of our
coats, but if you're such a hero, why don't you go and look
for your father?'   'I will give you your coats back if you tell

me where my father is.'   And the boy received the reply
'Your father was killed by Eki-Moos.'   He decided to avenge
his father's death.   His mother tried to talk him out of it
but he went to meet his enemy, engaged in single combat with
him, and vanquished him. (6)

   In Amanmukhammed Berdyev's version the Uzbek Padishah
is called Dog Chest.   This name reflects the former importance of the dog in the myths of the Turkish-speaking tribes.
They at one time regarded the dog as a sacred animal (and
the wolf, too).   The Kirgiz preserve a tradition that they
are descended from a big red dog and forty girls.   The
migration of the Turks to Central Asia was also said to have
been led by a beast-like dog.   'When the time came to go he
called them, saying in their language: "Get up!"'... When he
stopped, they stopped too, until they reached the districts
over which they later ruled.' (7)   Some traditions connect
the origin of the Turkmen tribe Yomud with a dog.   In one
version, one of Salyr-Gazan's wives, who had no children of
her own removed the newborn son of another wife out of
jealousy, gave him to a bitch in pup, and put a puppy in the
cradle.   The boy was given the name 'Yovm It' (suckled by
a dog), which was later changed to 'Yomut'. (8)   Dogs also
play a part in the Turkmen legend about their migration from
Syrdar'ya. (9)   With time, the mythical dog in the Turkmen
tales underwent the same changes as fabulous animal-patrons
in the traditions of other peoples.   It was remembered that
dogs had played a part in ancient history, but their exact
role was forgotten.   Since then the cult of the dog has died
out.   When the old beliefs perished, other meanings began to
be attached to the role of the dog in the legends, and the dog
even came to be seen as the enemy of the Turkmen.

   The legend of Salyr-Gazan is, therefore, essentially an epic
fairy-tale rather than an account of real historical events.
This confirms the theory that the legends of the Turkish-
speaking peoples about the founders of their tribes are closely
related to epic tales, that the genealogical legends at one time
formed part of the epics, and that the traditions about the
origin of peoples are based on myths which grew out of
ancient religious cults. (10)

   If this is so, then how well-off are we for historical information about the distant past?   Can one agree with authors who
look in legends for evidence of wars and migrations which
really happened and seem to find it there?   This question
takes us far beyond the limits of Turkmen ethnography.
Every people has its historical traditions but a scientific
approach to information preserved in the popular memory has
not yet been fully worked out.   Some researchers are inclined
to believe the traditions, others are more sceptical.   It would

be naive to think that an analysis of one Turkmen legend
could decide the question, but it is worth undertaking as it
will provide one side with a new argument.

Can historical facts be found in the legend of Salyr-Gazan?
Yes, they can. In Amanmukhammed Berdyev's version, the
Uzbek Padishah is called It-Emdzhek, but many other story-
tellers pronounce the name slightly differently: It-Bedzhen
(Dog Bedzhen). The word 'bedzhen' tells us a lot by itself.
This is the name of the Turkish-speaking people (the Bechene,
Bidzhine, are the Pechenegs of the Russian chronicles, anni-
hilated by the Oguz at the end of the ninth century).
After a long and bloody war its surviving members joined the
Oguz union of tribes. It is quite possible that the death of
Salyr-Gazan at the hands of Dog Bedzhen in the legend is
connected with some big military defeat of the Salyrs, who
took an active part in the struggle against the Pechenegs.
In addition, Salyr-Gazan's enemy is an Uzbek, and some versions say that his castle was in Samarkand. These details
evidently come from later events - and are connected with the
migration of the Turkmen between the tenth and twelfth centuries from the shores of Syrdar'ya to the area around Samarkand and Bukhara.

But the central idea of the legend we have been examining
is surely to set up a genealogical schema which establishes a
close relationship between the Salyr, Teke, Saryk and Ersari
tribes; the first three being descended from Salyr-Gazan and
the Ersary from his nephew. To ascertain the value of the
legend as a historical source we must therefore find out
whether conceptions concerning the kinship of these groups
remained unchanged throughout the centuries.

Detailed accounts of the historical (and that means the
genealogical) traditions of the Turkmen have come down to us
through the works of medieval historians, of whom the best
known are Rashid-ad-Din (fourteenth century) and the Khan
of Khiva (seventeenth-century). These works name the
ancestors of the Turkmen as the Oguz.

There the founder of the Oguz was the mythical Oguz-Khan,
a descendant of Adam ('Yes, if it please Allah!'). The
twenty-four Oguz tribes were descended from the twenty-four
grandchildren of Oguz by his legal wives, and some of the
other tribes were founded by the grandchildren of Oguz by
his concubines.

Although towards the thirteenth century, the name 'Turkmen'
had already ousted the name 'Oguz' and historical works no
longer mentioned the Oguz people, the name 'Oguz-Khan' was
evidently still part of the Turkmen traditions in the time of

Abulghazi.   This is clear from one version of the genealogical
legends, which the Khan historian considered incorrect, in
which the founder of the Turkmen is called Oguz.

However, the traditional genealogical schema was highly sus-
ceptible to innovations.   Many of the versions of the historical traditions, written down in the nineteenth century no
longer derive the Turkmen from Oguz.   Instead there are
two ancestors and part of the tribe is seen as the descendants
of Sayin-Khan, part as the descendants of Esen-Khan.   Who
Esen-Khan was, is not explained.   But Sayin-Khan (or
Soyun-Khan) is another name for Batu.   This shows
how the Mongol invasion brought about changes in the genealogical legends.   There was no clear idea about which of the
Turkmen tribes belonged to which of the two groups.   One
history lists the 'tribes and kins' of the Okhla, Gyoklen,
Eimur and Salyr who lived on the banks of the river Atrek,
and Gyurgen as the members of the 'Sainkhani' group; (11)
while other sources say that the 'Sainkhani' group is made up
of the Teke and the Yomud tribes.   According to the research I carried out among the Gyoklens, Soyun-Khan had six
sons: Gyoklen, Yomud, Teke, Ersary, Salyr and Saryk,
whereas Esen-Khan had three: Garadahly, Emreli and
Chovdur.   However, N.N. Yomudsky knew a tradition in
which the Gyoklen regarded themselves as the children of
Esen-Khan. (12)   Some of the Turkmen tribes were included
in neither group.   Today the people retain a very confused
idea of the two groups. (13)

Only a very few of the legends taken down from the elders
of the Turkmen last century mention Oguz-Khan.   There is
no Oguz in our legend- the history of the first four Turkmen
tribes begins with Salyr-Gazan.   The father of Salyr-Gazan
who appears in the middle of the story, does not play a very
important role and is not even given a name.   But most
interesting of all is the question of which Turkmen tribes are
regarded as ancient.   There are four such tribes: the
Salyr, Teke, Saryk (descendants of Salyr-Gazan) and the
Ersari (descendants of his nephew).   Some versions add the
Yomud.   Of these the Salyr are known to be one of the Oguz
tribes.   The four other groups entered the historical arena
later, and seem to have been formed from the remnants of a
number of different tribes.   They may have existed in the
Oguz era as minor kins of some larger tribes, but they only
became independent and numerous later, after the Mongol invasion.   Therefore, the legends of Salyr-Gazan contain no
genealogical traditions surviving from the pre-Mongol era.

In addition, it diverges from the accounts of the Turkmen
genealogical traditions written in the later Middle Ages.
Abulghazi's work, for example, accepts that the Salyr are

connected with the Teke, Saryk, Yomud and Ersari but adds
that these four tribes are descended from people of 'the
Salyr il' (il = 'people' in Turkmen), i.e. they are regarded as
younger than the Salyr.   This schema of kinship ties undoubtedly represents a memory of the tribal union of the
'external' salyrs (fourteenth-sixteenth century),into which
five tribes are listed as entering.   The chief place in this
tribal union seems to have been occupied by the Salyr who
gave their name to the whole grouping.(14)   This is why the
version of the tradition reproduced in Abulghazi's work gives
priority to the Salyr.   However, in our legend this schema is
disrupted.   The ancestors of the tribes of the post-Mongol
epoch are placed on an equal footing with the Salyr.

But one must examine all the versions of a given legend.
Do the other versions which A. Dzhikiev has taken down give
a different picture?   No.   Moreover a comparison of the versions given by the different story-tellers, convinces us that
the legends do not reflect a single view of the relationship
between the three tribes.   Salyr does not always occupy an
important role.   Many versions say that Teke-Mukhammed,
the legendary founder of the Teke, is Salyr-Gazan's eldest
son, and give him the chief role in the murder of the Uzbek
Padishah.   Others place the avenging knife in the hands of
the hero Ersary. (15)

There are also versions of the legend which mention all the
founders of the five tribes listed and one in which the founders of other tribes appear.   Thus, in one of the accounts
written down by A. Dzhikiev, there is a sixth brother called
Emreli. (16)   Finally, not all the legends say that the founders of the tribes were brothers.   For example, one tradition
calls Ersary Salyr-Gazan's younger brother. (17)   Another
version says that Yomud was the adopted son of Ersary-baba,
the legendary founder of the Ersari 'tribe', and married his
daughter. (18)   Different genealogical traditions refer to different people as the founder brothers.   Thus, A. Borns in
the first half of the last century wrote down what the Turk-
men-Gyoklen said: 'They maintain that the three great tribes:
Yamud, Goklan and Taka (Teke V.B) are descended from the
three brothers; but the third is less well born than the first
two, for he was the son of a Persian slave.' (19)   It would
be easy to find many other such examples, confirming that
the genealogical information contained in the legend cannot be
accepted as trustworthy evidence of the close relationship of
the different Turkmen groups in the past.

However strange this may seem, it is the fairy-tale and
mythological elements that persist in the genealogical legends
rather than historical facts about the mutual relations of the
different tribes several centuries ago.   Political changes (if

one can so describe the rise and fall of various tribes) lead to changes in a people's view of its history.   The Teke became one of the leading Turkmen tribes so many versions depict the founder of the Teke as the main hero, and Salyr is faceless and pushed into the background.   In some versions of the legend, which I took down from the Turkmen-Salyr, even they say that their ancestor Salyr was Salyr-Gazan's youngest son.

Such 'modernisation' is not typical only of the legend of Salyr-Gazan.   Here is another example: the oral tradition of the Turkmen-Chovdur, written down by K. Niyazklychev.   A certain hero engaged in combat with other adventurers in the vicinity of Tashkent, and emerged the winner.   According to the custom of the times, those vanquished in combat were put to death.   But the hero made peace with his rival and, when he returned home, took him along.   On the way they met a Kazakh girl, a girl-champion, who had already overpowered many young men in combat; however, the hero defeated her and made her his wife.   Some time later, when she was pregnant, he set off on his travels again, and was lost without news.   After a long search, his adopted brother learnt that the hero was no longer among the living.   And, since a custom which has survived almost to our days prescribed that the younger brother should marry the widow of his eldest brother, the adopted brother of the dead hero became the husband of the Kazakh girl.

This legend bears a faint resemblance to the story of Salyr-Gazan and his sons: there is a contest with a girl-champion and the fact that the action takes place in the vicinity of Tashkent may be construed as a memory of the time when the Turkmen tribes lived within the borders of present-day Uzbekistan.   But the most interesting part of it is the list of the offspring of the Kazakh girl.   The son of the dead hero was named Teke, and her sons by her second husband Yomud, Gyoklen, Saryk and Chovdur.   Thus Teke is here the eldest son, and Chovdur (the founder of the Chovdurs, one of the most ancient Oguz tribes) is the youngest, although the legend also recognises his especial resourcefulness and quick-wittedness (he was the one who thought up the plan to rescue their father from prison). (20)

The analysis of such legends leads us to conclude that the main importance of the genealogical traditions is that they reflect the conceptions of a people about its origin.   These conceptions were reshaped under the influence of the most recent changes in events.   The past was looked at in the light of a later balance of forces, and memories of ancient times were adapted to the interests of the present day. Cases of the conscious distortion of genealogical tradition are also known.   As long ago as the time of the Oguz, when the

Sel'dzhuks came to power, they declared themselves to be descendants of the mythical hero Afrosiab (Abulghazi mentions this with disgust), (21) and although the popular genealogical legends were usually modified by a spontaneous unconscious process, this does not affect the main issue: the information contained in them must be used with extreme caution.

In defence of the legends, one can say that they faithfully reflect the fact that more than one people participated in the formation of the Turkmen, which gives them an advantage over the versions transcribed and touched upon by the medieval historians. Rashid-ad-Din and Abulghazi, for example, depicted the Oguz as almost the only ancestors of the Turkmen and essentially equated the Oguz and the Turkmen. Even the alteration in the features of the Turkmen from Mongoloid to European took place, in Abulghazi's opinion, 'under the influence of the climate.' (22) In fact the Oguz tribes became merged with different peoples, and the Turkmen were not formed on the basis of the Oguz tribes alone; the popular traditions provide clear evidence of this.

Our legend of Salyr-Gazan, in which one of the hero's wives is an Uzbek girl and the Saryk are kin of the Tatars, also provides evidence of connections with other peoples. In the legends of the Turkmen-Ata and the Turkmen-Chovdur, the wife of the founder of the tribe was a Kazakh girl. (23) The genealogical traditions also admit the participation of the Persians in the formation of the Turkmen people: the girl-champion, whom Salyr-Gazan vanquished in combat, is usually the daughter of the Padishah of Iran.

However, the legends do not provide grounds for saying that the Teke and the Saryk are more closely related to the Uzbeks than other Turkmen groups, for example. The genealogical schema is reproduced in different ways in the different versions of the legend of Salyr-Gazan. In some of them, Salyr-Gazan has only one son by his Uzbek wife - Ersary (this is obviously connected with the migration of the Turkmen-Ersari in the seventeenth century to the banks of the Amudar'ya, where they were neighbours of the Uzbeks). However, other versions say that the founder of the Teke was not the son of the Uzbek girl but of the daughter of the Iranian Padishah: and the Chovdur legend derives the Teke from the son of the Kazakh heroine. A. Dzhikiev took down a legend about the marriage of Salyr-Gazan to a Karakalpak girl. (24) Therefore, by the end of the last century, the legends only preserved the most general idea of the kinship connections of the Turkmen with other peoples, and one can hardly agree with the opinion that the reference to other peoples in the legends 'are a fact of no small importance in the study of the ethno-genetical connections [of the Turkmen] with the other peoples of Central Asia.' (25)

Perhaps several centuries ago, memories of ancient times survived in a fuller and more reliable form in the popular memory? In a fuller form - yes - but their reliability remains in question. Already in the seventeenth century there were discrepancies between the different historical traditions, even those set down in writing. Abulghazi openly admits that there were glaring contradictions between the different records of genealogical traditions which he encountered.

Thus, there is a grain of truth in the historical traditions of the Turkmen about their distant past. They refer to separate historical events. However, the facts enshrined in the legends have received a highly individual gloss and one must know how to interpret them. This is the main problem in our research. It has to be admitted that there are at this time no reliable criteria to enable us to separate the historical materials in the legends from the folklore patterns and subjects. Essentially, we can regard details in a legend as evidence of a historical nature only in cases where we have written evidence of contemporaries or archeological findings which confirm the legend. Thus, in our legend about Salyr-Gazan, the historical data about the Pechenegs already available allowed us to see their name in the name of the wicked Padishah It-Bedzhen. But if we hadn't known anything about the Pechenegs it would have been more correct to think that It-Bedzhen was a corrupted form of the name It-Emdzhen, which is a name we can make sense of. We look at the mention of Samarkand as a memory of the time when the Turkmen tribes lived in the vicinity of Zeravshan because we know this fact from historical sources. On the same principle, the journey of Salyr-Gazan to the capital of the Iranian Padishah could also be regarded as a memory of the migration of part of the tribe right into the heart of Iran, but it is wiser to refrain from such an interpretation. Iran and the Golden Horde at various times extended their rule over many of the Turkmen tribes and their lands were naturally regarded as enemy territory. As a result, they became associated with the ancient mythological theme of the hero's marriage which involved his journeying to far-distant lands to meet dangers and more journeying. For example, in a whole number of stories the sister of the Turkmen heroes is carried off not by the Tatar Padishah but by the Uzbek or the Kazakh Khan. (26)

It would seem appropriate to conclude the critical examination of this legend by admitting that the information contained in legends may be useful not only where their ethnographical material is fully confirmed by other sources. For, at times, the legends simply contradict more objective evidence. The legend of Salyr-Gazan and his sons is one example of this. On the basis of ethnographical features and differences in

dialects, A. Dzhikiev correctly considers that among the
tribes of the Salyr union the Teke are most closely related to
the Yomud and the Salyr, and that the Saryk and the Ersari
form another group. (27)   But the legends give another picture.   Usually, the story-tellers forget to mention Yomud as
one of the brothers or deny that he was a blood relation.
Ersary is also said to be merely a cousin of the chief charac-
ters.   The Saryks, however, as in A. Berdyev's version,
are said to be especially closely connected to the Teke.   This
is how far you can trust legends.

When Amanmukhammed-aga finished his story of Salyr-Gazan
and his sons, silence reigned in the crowded school hall, all
eyes were turned on the story-teller;   his listeners seemed to
be reliving the stirring events of legendary times.   Seemed.
... But isn't it better to check upon one's first impression?
I asked Amanmukhammed-aga whether he thought that the
legend described the adventures of Salyr-Gazan as they really
happened.

Amanmukhammed-aga thought a little.   He filled his bowl
with tea, stroked his beard with his hand and then announced:
'Perhaps there are mistakes in some of the details, but in
general it's correct.   I believe.'   And he addes as proof:
'After all, there was a book.'

I didn't find this answer unexpected.   I had already been
given reason to be convinced that many of the older Turkmen
believed the historical traditions were completely true.   One
old man in Serakhs confirmed this: 'You Russians are also
descended from Salyr-Gazan, indeed you're more closely related to the Salyr than the Teke are.   We call the Teke
"Garyndash" (relative), but we should call the Russians
"Gardash" (brother).'   The legends have obviously been preserved in the popular memory because they are taken seriously.   This is why I haven't attempted to determine the genre
to which the story of Salyr-Gazan belongs.   For me, it's a
legend with obvious fairy-tale elements.   But the story-teller
and some of his listeners regarded it as history.

Two teachers disagreed with Amanmukhammed-aga.   They
called the legend a fairy-tale and turned his attention to the
absurdities and contradictions it contained.   Part of the
audience greeted this with approval, and some of them helped
the questioners to formulate their ideas more coherently.
Amanmukhammed-aga stared at the young people, but said
nothing.   Then he nodded his head in the direction of my
open diary and asked: 'And what do you say, my guest?   If
this is all a fable, why have you come to write it down?'

I remember, I carefully replied that there is a grain of truth

in the legends.   And although in many cases it is not easy to
find the key to the allegorical language of a legend, although
the real order of events is sometimes disregarded in an extra-
ordinary manner, the historian has to turn to legend when he
lacks other, more reliable and comprehensible documents.

Amanmukhammed-aga seemed to be satisfied.

However, I've now become even more convinced that the
value of the legend lies not in the scanty reference to real
historical events, frequently expressed in an allegorical way
which admits of arbitrary and consequently dubious interpretation.   As I see it, the importance of the legend as a historical source does not lie in the fact that similar subjects are
found among the folklore of other peoples, and that they may
serve as evidence of their distant kinship or their former contacts with the Turkmen.   No, the legend of Salyr-Gazan is
important for the historian above all because it reflects the
traditional conceptions of a people about its own past, its
worldview, and also traces the beliefs and myths of deep
antiquity.

NOTES

1   For a summary of information about Salyr-Gazan, see V.M.
    Shirmunsky, The Heroic Epos of the Oguz and the 'Book
    of Korkut', in 'The Book of my Fore-Father Korkut',
    Moscow-Leningrad, 1962, pp. 174-90.
2   Sometimes this part prompts story-tellers to enter into
    terrifying details.   For example, as he came up to the
    town wall, Salyr-Gazan sees a gloomy soldier casting a
    severed head down from the ramparts.   The people ex-
    plain to the stranger that the daughter of the Iranian
    Tsar has just disposed of the latest suitor to her hand.
    But Amanmukhammed Berdyev for some reason missed out
    this popular detail.
3   The custom according to which the matchmaker sweeps at
    the doors of the girl's parents existed in Central Asia
    among the Uzbeks and Tadzhiks.   See, for example,
    'Ethnographical Essays on the Uzbek Rural Population',
    Moscow, 1969, p. 227.   Only one Turkmen group has
    been so far discovered to observe this custom, 'On the
    birth of a daughter to the family, a neighbour who has a
    son, comes to the yard of the family with the new-born
    baby and "sweeps" the yard with his tall hat (papakha),
    which is an expression of his wish to take the baby to his
    son.'   It is unclear from the text whether this description
    relates to the sub-kin of the Olam, who are included among
    the Salyr (Serakh District), or to the independent group
    of the Ulam (Khodzhambas District).   See A. Bakhtiarov,

Remnants of the 'vanished' Alan, 'Turkmen Studies', 1930, nos 8-9, p. 39.

4 In one of the versions of the legend, the rule of Samarkand is called It-Emen (suckled by a dog), since his mother, being married, had entered into an illegal relationship (noted by me in Serakh District of the Turkmen SSR).

5 The Turkmen-Ata call the Kazakhs uncles, since, according to legend, the wife of their ancestor was a Kazakh girl. The Turkmen-Shikh call the Turkmen-Garadash uncles, as their ancestor, Pakyr-Shikh, seems to have married the daughter of the Garadash Yazyr-Khan (K. Ataev, Some Details on the Ethnography of the Turkmen-Shikh, 'Works of the Institute of History, Archeology and Ethnography of the Academy of Sciences of the Turkmen SSR', vol. 7, Ashkhabad, 1963, p. 76). Usually the Turkmen use the term 'daiy' for all representatives of their mothers' kin (tire, tapia), irrespective of their age. Such terminological usage should probably be regarded as a survival of an extinct exogamy law.

6 V.I. Verbitsky, 'The Altai Settlers', Moscow, 1893, pp. 149-50. Parallels to the Altai case are found among other peoples of Central Asia and in the Caucasus.

7 A. Dzhikiev, Materials on the Ethnography of the Mangyshlak Turkmen, 'Works of the Institute of History, Archeology and Ethnography of the Academy of Sciences of the Turkmen SSR', vol. 7, Ashkhabad, 1963, p. 200.

8 I also took this legend down in the Lenin kolkhoz in Takhtabazar District. G.P. Vasileva and A. Dzhikiev heard similar stories about the founder of the Yomud 'tribe' being suckled by a dog in other regions of Turkmenia; these versions were not connected with the legend of Salyr-Gazan. See G.P. Vasileva, Some Common Elements in the Culture of the Turkmen and Bashkirs relating to their Ethnogenesis, 'The Archeology and Ethnography of the Bashkirs', vol. 4, Ufa, 1971, pp. 202-3; A. Dzhikiev, 'An Ethnographic Essay on the Population of South-East Turkmenistan', Ashkhabad, 1972, pp. 17, 21. Survivals of a legend which calls to mind the Roman story of Romulus and Remus have been observed among the Bashkirs and Kirgiz. See R.G. Kuzeev, N.V. Bikbulatov, S.N. Shitova, The Trans-Ural Bashkirs, 'The Archeology and Ethnography of the Bashkirs', vol. 1, Ufa, 1962, p. 197; S.M. Abramzon, 'The Kirgiz and their Ethnogenetical and Historical-Cultural Ties', Moscow, 1971, p. 287.

9 See S.G. Agadzhanov, 'Essays on the History of the Oguz and the Turkmen of Central Asia', vols 9-13, Ashkhabad, 1969, pp. 227-9. This includes references to other works.

10 For more details, see V.N. Basilov, 'The Cult of Holy Men in Islam'. Moscow, 1970, pp. 43-5.

11 'Materials on the History of the Turkmen and Turkmenia', vol. 2, 1938, p. 94.

12   N.N. Yomudsky, Karash-Khan Ogly. From the Popular
     Tradition of the Turkmen. The Genealogy of the Turkmen-
     Yomud, 'Papers Dedicated to V.V. Bartold', Tashkent,
     1927, p. 318.
13   See, for example, K. Ataev, 'The Economy and Economic
     Life of the Turkmen Population of Atek in the late Nine-
     teenth and early Twentieth Century', Candidat Thesis,
     Moscow, 1966, p. 41.
14   For more details, see A. Dzhikiev, 'An Ethnographic
     Essay on the Population of South-East Turkmenistan', pp.
     8-11, 33.
15   Ibid., pp. 15, 28, 31.
16   Ibid., pp. 14-15.
17   A. Dzhikiev, Ethnographic Findings on the Ethnogenesis
     of the Turkmen-Salyr, 'Speech at the Seventh Internation-
     al Congress of Anthropological and Ethnographic Sciences',
     Moscow, 1964, p. 3.
18   N.N. Yomudsky, op. cit., p. 322.
19   A. Borns, 'A Journey to Bokhara', vol. 3, Moscow, 1849,
     p. 350.
20   K. Niyazklychev, 'The Turkmen-Chovdur', Candidat
     Thesis, Moscow, 1968, pp. 36-8.
21   A.N. Kononov, 'The Genealogy of the Turkmen. A work
     by Abulghazi, the Khan of Khiva', Moscow-Leningrad,
     1958, p. 70.
22   Ibid., p. 57.
23   N. Niyazklychev, op. cit., p. 49.   Similar legends about
     kinship with the Turkmen are found among the neighbour-
     ing peoples, in particular, the Karakalpak.   See T.A.
     Zhdanko, The Karakalpak of the Khorez Oasis, 'Works of
     the Khorez Archeological-Ethnographical Expedition', vol.
     1, Moscow, 1952, pp. 484-50.
24   A. Dzhikiev, Ethnographic Findings on the Ethnogenesis
     of the Turkmen-Salyr, p. 2.
25   A. Dzhikiev, 'An Ethnographic Essay on the Population of
     South-East Turkmenistan', p. 16.
26   Ibid., pp. 21-2, 26-7, 29-31.   The Kazakh is also named
     as the enemy of Salyr-Gazan in one of G.P. Vasileva's
     notes.
27   A. Dzhikiev, 'An Ethnographic Essay on the Population of
     South-East Turkmenistan', pp. 34-5.

Part II
EUROPEAN RUSSIA

INTRODUCTION

The regional name of 'European Russia' is misleading, referring as it does to the western part of the Russian Soviet
Federation of Socialist Republics, i.e. west of the Urals; on
the whole, 'European Soviet Union' is the more accurate, if
less familiar, term to designate the region included by those
who study it.   The republics of Byelorussia, Ukraine,
Moldavia, as well as the autonomous republics and regions of
the RSFSR all come under this rubric.   They share a background of Christian religion, long domination by the Russian
Empire and early membership of the Soviet Union (as compared
to the Baltic states).   The three Union republics have, in
their capitals, departments of ethnography whose staff write
more in their native language than in Russian.   The autonomous regions of the RSFSR include non-Russian minorities
such as the Mordvians.   Local ethnographers do research
under the auspices of the pedagogical institutes there as well
as in history departments of the universities, some of which
are large and prestigious (e.g. Kharkov) and publish in
Russian.

The two papers here represent the most typical approach to
studying the region since they are emulated by local scholars,
and are published in the leading central journal 'Sovetskaya
Etnografiya'.   They also give a more comprehensive picture of
regional customs and history than other works I examined
which, in comparison, tend to be descriptions of field data
given in bulletin style.   Both are about Russian cases which,
in comparison with the wealth of work on, say, Central Asia
or the Caucasus, are less studied by anthropologists whether
themselves Russian or not.

101

6   The weddings of the rural population of the Kuban (1)

*M.S. Shikhareva, 1967**

The weddings of the rural population of the Kuban have many
features which derive primarily from the traditional Ukranian
and southern Great Russian wedding ceremony which has existed here since last century.   Although views on marriage and
wedding rituals have changed radically, much of the former
structure of the conduct of the wedding has been preserved.
As is known, the Kuban Cossacks were not the original inhabitants of the area.   The annexation of these lands by the
Russian government and their settlement by Russians and
Ukranians began at the end of the eighteenth century.
Catherine II granted Tamansk peninsula and the right bank of
the Kuban (up to the mouth of the river Laba) to the Cossacks
of the Black Sea Host, founded in 1787-8, and they began to
settle there from the beginning of the 1790s.   The majority of
the Black Sea Host were Ukranians.   Throughout the whole
of the nineteenth century the Black Sea Host grew continually
as a result of government resettlement, primarily of people
from Ukranian provinces (Novorossisk, Chernigovsk, Kharkov,
Poltava and Kiev).   At almost the same time, the Kuban lands
to the east of the river Laba began to be settled by Cossacks
from the regions of the Don Host, as well as settlers from the
Central Russian provinces - Voronezh, Kursk, Orlov, Tambov
- and in particular, from the Ukraine.   The distribution of
the settlers was organised in such a way that their outposts
formed a distinct system of fortifications, called the Old Line.

In the 1840s outposts grew up along the river Laba, forming
the New Line.   The population of these settlements was
formed from various elements;   it included both inhabitants of
the settlements of the Old Line and immigrants from Stavrop,
the Ukraine and the central oblasts of Russia.   In the 1860s,
the lands beyond the Kuban were settled by Black Sea and
Line Cossacks from areas populated earlier, and also by Don,
Tersk and other Cossacks.

In addition to the government resettlement, a constant
stream of independent settlers flowed into the Kuban.   This
increased in particular at the end of the 1860s when ordinary
civilians (from other towns) were allowed to acquire farm

* First published in 'Sovetskaya Etnografiya', 1964, no. 1,
    pp. 22-33.

property there. The settlers included peasants, retired
soldiers and officers, traders, mechanics, and nobility from
Russian (Voronezh, Kursk, Orelsk, Tambov and others) and
Ukranian (Kharkov, Poltava, Ekaterinoslav, and others) provinces. By 1913 these immigrants constituted 57.1 per cent
of the entire population of the region. They settled in the
Black Sea and Line settlements, with a predominance of
Ukranians in the former and Russians in the latter, a trend
which was still evident in the 1920s. Although the wedding
rituals of all the eastern slav peoples have a good deal in
common, the separate elements vary among the different ethnic
groups. The variegated ethnic composition of the population
of the Kuban, the close proximity of the Kuban to the peoples
of the Caucasus, and the particular features of the Cossack
way of life, have all had an influence on the formation of the
wedding ritual of the Kuban population.

In the past the wedding ceremony varied from region to
region of the Kuban (2) as a result of the mixed ethnic origin
of the population. However, by the end of the nineteenth
century and the beginning of the twentieth century, a convergence of the different versions of the wedding ritual was to
be observed. Today the wedding is basically the same in the
whole of the Kuban, although there are slight differences even
now (e.g. in terminology and some details of the ceremonies).

The rural inhabitants of the Kuban usually get married
between the ages of 18 and 25. The most common marriage
age for girls is 18-22, for men, 20-5 (the young men often
get married after completing their national service). The
marriage age, particularly for men, is considerably higher
than before the Revolution.

Previously, the Cossacks usually got married at 18 or 19
and sometimes even earlier, although church weddings were
not permitted before the age of 18 (girls could marry at 16).
If either the girl or young man had not reached the necessary
age, but the parents were determined to marry them, they
would usually approach the priest, with a present (i.e. bribe
him) and he would add the missing months and marry them.
The reasons for early marriages were always economic; on
the one hand, a girl was regarded as merchandise to be mar-
keted as quickly as possible (at 20-2 a girl was already considered too old and could be married only to a widower or a
cripple), and, on the other hand, the Cossacks strove to
acquire an unpaid worker-bride for the household before the
son left to do his military service.

As a rule, before the parents settled on their choice of a
bride or bridegroom, the family discussed the boy or girl and
their financial position, and the objections of the son or

daughter were met with: 'Bear it; you'll love it.' Admitted-
ly, by the end of the nineteenth and the beginning of the
twentieth century a section of the youth, especially the young
men, had already begun to assert their independence in the
question of marriage. Now the motive for marriage is always
mutual attraction.

Marriage usually takes place between people who come from
the same or neighbouring settlements and farms. In the past
Cossacks as a rule chose their brides either from their own
settlements or from a farm attached to the settlement. Now
it is increasingly common for one of the couple to have lived
previously in another region or even oblast. Various circumstances contribute to this, such as national service, courses
cf study at technical colleges and institutions, the meeting of
young people at regional and district rallies of front rank
workers, amateur artistic activities, etc.

Marriages in the Kuban take place at all times of year.
The wedding today, as previously, falls into three cycles,
the prenuptial, the wedding itself, and the postnuptial. The
wedding ritual, however, has been considerably simplified, its
length has been cut, and the significance of many customs
has been forgotten, although the form is preserved. The
matchmaking which begins the wedding cycle is one example of
such a formally preserved custom. Where in the past the
arrival of matchmakers often came as a complete surprise to
the girl and she often didn't know for whom they were
acting, (3) now the bride and bridegroom choose the matchmakers themselves and know when they are coming. The
matchmakers' task is much simpler and easier now. They
know that they will not receive a refusal and as the symbol of
the refusal, a pumpkin (a custom which was widely spread in
the Ukraine and introduced into the Kuban by Ukranian settlers), since the matchmaking is always prefaced by a prep-
aratory agreement between the young man and girl, and discussion of the proposed marriage within the family circle.
The role of the matchmakers is usually taken by relatives or
neighbours of the groom. It is considered a great honour
for the bride and bridegroom if the leaders of the kolkhoz
and the village community consent to act as matchmakers.
The matchmakers, 'elders', 'mediators', are usually talkative,
witty, smart and respected people. When they go to negotiate for a bride, they take with them bread (especially baked
or bought for the occasion) and vodka or wine. The bridegroom himself accompanies the matchmakers. Most often the
matchmakers go to the bride's house in the evening. When
they arrive at the house they knock on the door or window
and ask to be let in. As in the past, the matchmakers gain
entrance to the house by pretending to be lost travellers or
hunters of martens (pretty girls), or merchants who have

heard that there is a calf for sale in the house, or else they
simply say as they enter the house: 'We are not matchmakers
really, but good people, please accept the bread and salt from
Ivan.' The bridegroom stays outside during the first part of
the conversation and only comes into the room later. Following an ancient custom, the matchmakers first of all ask the
consent of the bride's parents who in turn ask that of the
bride and bridegroom. As a sign of her consent the bride
cuts the loaf, which the matchmakers brought, in half, or,
more often, into four pieces, crosswise, after which the bride
and bridegroom leave the room. The matchmakers then place
the vodka on the table and begin talks about the practical
side of the matter; they fix the day of the wedding, discuss
how many guests each side is to invite, etc. At the end of
the ceremony, the bride ties a scarf or handkerchief round
the bridegroom and a towel round the matchmakers and gives
them a loaf in exchange for the one they brought. The contemporary wedding cycle lacks such rituals as 'svody' and
'propoiki' ('zapoi', 'svod' and 'sgovory' among the Line Cossacks, 'magarych' and 'zaruchiniya' among the Black Sea Cossacks). (4) The custom whereby the bridegroom's parents
pay the bride's parents a sum of money ('kladka', 'stolovoe',
'vygovor', 'podmoga') has disappeared entirely. It was
earlier quite widely, though unevenly, spread throughout the
Kuban settlements and was widely known in the Russian provinces. The custom of testing the bridegroom's skills of
husbandry (5) (called 'looking at the yard', 'looking at the
walls', 'looking at the stove', 'looking over the property' by
the Line Cossacks, and 'the inspection' by both the Line and
Black Sea Cossacks), characteristic of pre-Revolutionary
Russian and Ukranian weddings has also died out, or at least
lost its former economic significance. However, in cases
when the bride and bridegroom's relatives are not acquainted
with each other (as occasionally happens if the bride and
bridegroom come from different villages) the bridegroom's
parents gather all their relatives together and invite the
bride's relatives. There are no special ceremonies connected
with such invitations and visits to the bridegroom's house –
the aim is just for the two sides to get to know one another
in a social atmosphere. Typically, this custom continues to
be called 'looking at the yard, the stove', etc. 'Looking at
the stove' at the house of one of the residents of Bolgev farm
(Ust'-Labinsk raion), in 1958, turned out to mean simply that
the bride's relatives – her mother, sister, brothers, aunts and
closest neighbours – from the kolkhoz 'Red October' (Kirpil'sk
village, Ust'-Labinsk raion) came to the bridegroom's house to
meet him and his family. (6)

During the matchmaking or immediately after it, a whole
collection of functionaries are chosen to take on responsibilities
at the wedding – the 'druzhko', his assistant the 'poludruzhke',

the 'starshy druzhko' (the master of ceremonies, 'best man'),
and two female helpers and the 'starshaya druzhka'.   The
most important of these is the druzhko.   He must be a married man, well acquainted with the wedding customs, and
lively, efficient and capable of organising the celebration.
The entire course of the proceedings depends on his manner
and abilities, as it is he who entertains the guests, makes
sure they have everything they want, etc.   His assistant,
the 'poludruzhke' (who does not always figure in the ceremonies) has to carry out all the druzhko's orders.   The
female matchmakers - there are usually two of them - are
chosen by the bride and bridegroom's parents from among
their married female relatives or neighbours.   One matchmaker represents the bride's family, the other the bridegroom's.   They have to be talkative, witty women who know
their job well.   One dresses the bride on the day of the
wedding (sometimes this is done by women famous in the village for their skill in dressing the bride and arranging her
hair and who are specially invited for a small fee).   They
then take the dowry to the bridegroom's house, where the
guests are given a 'karavai' (a round loaf) to eat, and the
presents are distributed.   The 'starshaya druzhka' is one of
the bride's friends from school or work.   She stays with the
bride throughout the wedding ceremonies, going with her
round the village to give out invitations, helping her to dress
on the day of the wedding, etc.   The 'starshy boyarin' plays
a similar role in relation to the bridegroom and is chosen from
among his bachelor friends.   The bride and bridegroom
usually choose their closest friends to be their 'druzhka' and
'boyarin'.   For almost the entire wedding (until the bride
goes to the bridegroom's house), the bride is attended by her
girlfriends and the bridegroom by his unmarried male friends,
the 'boyars'.

As in the past, great importance is attached to the preparation of traditional breads and cake - the 'karavai', 'lezhen',
'dyven', 'giltse', 'shishki'. (7)   The ceremonial baking is
still accompanied by a number of archaic customs which used
to be common among the Ukranians and southern Great Russians.   It is carried out one or three days before the wedding by specially invited married women, relatives or neighbours (earlier the bride's father himself chose happily married
women to be the 'karavainitsy', but this custom has been
dying out since the end of the last century - now the invitations are given out by the bride's mother or the bride herself,
usually to women famous for their culinary art).   The baking
of the ritual breads and cakes, and especially the karavai is
still a ceremonious occasion.   Special songs are sung, e.g.
'Our karavai has gone into the oven, our karavai has found a
place for itself' (Mikhailov village, Udobnaya):   'Our stove is
hot, it wants a karavai' (Staro-Titarov village);   'We've

rolled out our shishki, we've drunk our pepper vodka, we've
finished rolling out our shishki, we've finished drinking our
pepper vodka', 'Our shishki are fluffy and beautiful to see'
(Kirpil village), and others.   They also 'tell fortunes', most
often by baking coins into a 'lezhen' (typically, they mark the
place with the coins in it beforehand and give it to the young
couple to bring them happiness - i.e. there is no longer anything magical about the 'fortune-telling', it has become simply
a game).   Sometimes guests are invited and a meal is cooked
on the day the karavai is baked.

There are special rituals for inviting the guests to a wedding.   The bride herself goes to invite her guests (either on
foot or in a 'lineika', a light carriage), accompanied by her
'starshaya druzhka' and other girlfriends, while the bridegroom's guests are invited by the bridegroom and the 'starshy
boyarin'.   The 'starshaya druzhka' and the 'boyarin' carry
shishki to give to all those invited.   In some villages (e.g.
Udobnaya village, Otradnen region), the shishki are given
only to close relatives (and occasionally neighbours) as a sign
of particular respect.   The custom is for the bride to go to
invite the guests in her wedding clothes - she has to bow to
everyone she meets, (8) and three times to those she wants to
invite.   The bride invites her girlfriends to a party before
the wedding in the same way.   The young people dislike this
custom and cases are increasingly found of her bowing neither
to passers-by or to her guests.

Usually 40-60 people from each side are invited to a wedding.   The circle of guests is considerably wider than it
used to be.   Now not only friends and relatives but also
comrades from work are invited.   It is no accident that the
kolkhozniks use the expression,   'There is a wedding in our
team', for the whole team always goes to the wedding of one
of its members.   Representatives of the kolkhoz management
and of the village community - the president of the kolkhoz,
the secretaries of the Party and komsomol organisations, the
agronomists, livestock specialists, brigade leaders, the president and secretary of the village soviet, the deputies to the
local soviets, etc., are all invited to the wedding.   It is
natural that the presence of comrades from work should be
taken for granted in our society, where family affairs have
shed their former exclusiveness and are closely interwoven
with productive life.

The bride's girlfriends usually gather at the bride's house
on the evening before the wedding, and the bridegroom and
his friends join them later on.   This evening (called 'feast
night', 'girl's night', 'burning evening', 'evening') (9) is
spent in singing and colourful ritual games which give the
wedding the character of a theatrical performance.   The

bride meets her girlfriends at the gate and leads them into
the house.   The men arrive soon after the girls.   They
meet at the bridegroom's house, where they eat, and then
accompany the groom to the bride's house.   The men bring
sweetmeats - sweets, nuts, biscuits - with them for the girls.
The girls sing old traditional songs as well as modern ones
and have to serenade everybody present, i.e. the bride and
bridegroom first, then all the rest.

In the Kuban villages there are many songs used to praise
the guests at the party, and particularly the groom, who is
always presented as a prince with 'chestnut curls and a pink
and white complexion', 'how good you are, how handsome you
are', 'which of us is good, which of us is handsome?', etc.
When the song ends the 'starshaya druzhka' goes over to
those who have been serenaded, while the girls sing a song
praising their 'wealth' and 'generosity', e.g. 'Andryushechka
dangles his purse, Petrovich silver', 'Efimushka, give us,
give us three gold coins, lay them down, lay them down' -
and he puts a few coins on a plate.   The 'starshaya druzhka'
divides the money between the girls.   Sometimes on girl's
night, the bridegroom's friends 'buy' (though it's most often
a symbolic purchase) from the girls the gifts which the bride
has prepared for the bridegroom.   The bride usually gives
the bridegroom a shirt, and he gives her her wedding dress
or material for the dress.   It is this shirt which the girls
'sell' at the girl's evening.   In some villages a few odds and
ends are added to the shirt and the entire bundle is 'sold'.
Thus, for example, in Kirpil village they sell a bundle containing shirts, socks, a handkerchief, a comb and a packet of
cigarettes.   If it seems to the girls that the 'price' is too
low, they sing a song ridiculing the 'stinginess' of the bridegroom and his friends (e.g. 'The men said they'd take the
bundle, they said they'd give a bag of money, then they
tossed us a kopeck as if it was a joke', or 'Our father-in-law
lives in a straw hut' (Kirpil village)).   The girl's night ends
late in the evening with refreshments, and everyone leaves
and meets there again in the morning.

In the past the bride didn't get any sleep at all that night
as at dawn she went out onto the porch to 'wail'.   An orphan
bride would go to the cemetery and wail there.   The old
people still remember how pitifully and dolefully the brides
wailed, particularly the orphans.   These customs were typical
of the southern Great Russian provinces, where often the
bride's wail 'welcomed the dawn', not only on her wedding
day, but also on the morning of each day after the betrothal.
There is no longer any wailing in the modern ceremony,
although in some villages it is still customary for the bride to
visit the cemetery if one of her parents is dead.   Visits to
the cemetery on the day of the wedding are in general very

rare and fewer take place each year.   Early in the morning
on the wedding day, the girlfriends again meet at the bride's
house.   The matchmakers and the 'starshaya druzhka' or a
woman specially invited for the occasion, dress the bride.   A
special long white, or, more rarely, pale pink or pale blue,
dress is worn by the bride.   The wedding dress is usually
rather long with long, or, more rarely, short, sleeves.   The
bride's shoes are made of light or black lacquer with high
heels.   A tulle or nylon veil is worn on the head and decorated with flowers.   Typically, in the Kuban villages and
farms, the bride's hairstyle (little curls framing the forehead)
has not changed in over ten years and is the same everywhere.   However, the bride chooses the cut of her dress in
accordance with her taste and the fashion.   After the dressing ceremony, the bride and the 'starshaya drushka' give the
girls scarves and flowers bought specially beforehand.   The
girls stand round the bride and sing songs until the bridegroom comes.   Such songs include the old traditional songs
(e.g. 'Mar'yushka walked along the new hall, her golden
chain tinkled', 'O let us go, let us all go together through
the green with the pretty young girl', and many others), the
so-called 'cruel' romances ('My mother loved me, I respected
her', 'Where have the flowers gone, which graced the vales?',
and others), folk songs ('Frost, frost, don't freeze me', 'Oh,
the wind from the field, the foam from the sea', 'A steep hill
stands' and others), everyday songs of family life, and the
songs of Soviet composers ('Rowanberry', 'Where do you run,
little path?', 'Moscow evenings', 'Virgin soil', 'Kuban Field',
and others).

Meanwhile, the final preparations for the trip to the bride's
take place in the bridegroom's house.   All the bridegroom's
friends, the boyars, come to his house, and they, the druzhko
and the matchmakers form the wedding procession.   Usually
they fetch the bride in cars decorated with branches, flowers
and streamers;   they often tie a banner bearing the names of
the bride and bridegroom to the side of the car.   The members of the wedding procession sing and dance as they go.
Before the Revolution, the bridegroom, the druzhko and the
matchmakers used to go to get the bride in a light carriage
while the boyars, dressed in Cossack style, galloped there on
horseback.   The boyars accompanying the groom would shoot
in the air, cut capers on their horses and show off their mas-
tery of riding.

Fancy riding is now very rare at weddings, though it can
still be met with in some villages.   Thus, for example, in the
village of Ubornaya the boyars wear Cossack costume (the
kolkhoz has a selection of outfits), and they display their
equestrian skill as they accompany the groom.   In the court-
yard of the bride's house 10-15 young men (the bride's

relatives and neighbours) wait for the wedding procession's
arrival, armed with brooms, staves, buckets and even guns,
to keep the gates closed so that the bridegroom cannot get
through to the bride without paying a ransom.   As the bridegroom approaches, they and the members of the wedding procession shoot at each other (with blanks).   They only open
the gate after the druzhko has paid the ransom.   Sometimes
the boyars try to force their way into the house.   As a rule,
the ransom at the gates is a lively ceremony and the occasion
of much laughter and joking.   After receiving the ransom,
the guards open the gates and let the bridegroom's procession
into the yard.   The druzhko goes to the house to 'buy' the
bride's table and plait of hair. (10)   In the past the custom
of selling the table and plait was common among all the eastern
slav peoples.   The survival of these customs today when they
have lost their original meaning (for example, the plait is still
sold now although there is no longer any distinction between
the hairstyles of married and unmarried women, and the brides
often have short hair) is explained by the fact that they have
been turned into games.   The girls sing songs in which they
make cruel fun of the sluggishness or the stinginess of the
matchmakers, and the bridegroom's friends.   One song starts
'You, druzhko, don't mess about, you, druzhko, go and feed
the pigs, you old clown, you black dog.'   Other words go
'Stingy boyars, stingy boyars, won't you give us something?',
and so on.   They hold contests of wit with the druzhko.
The table is 'sold' by the 'starshaya druzhka', who haggles
for a long time, although the price has usually been decided
beforehand.   The plait is 'sold' by a small boy, one of the
bride's relatives, and he gets sweets and gingerbread for
this.   After the 'sale' of the table and plait the best man
leads the bridegroom into the house and shows him to a seat
next to the bride.   The people accompanying the bridegroom
sit down at the table by him together with the guests from
the bride's side and the merrymaking continues.   The girls
leave the room singing, or remain at the table.   A playful
scene ensues between the 'starshaya druzhka' and the 'starshy
boyarin'.   Two identical bottles, tied up with red ribbon, and
decorated with wheat stalks ('kolosovye' 'krasnaya' 'bugai') are
placed on the tables.   One is filled with wine, the other with
coloured water.   The one who chooses the water is subjected
to severe teasing.

One of the most important moments of the wedding is the
presentation of gifts to the young couple. (11)   This is an
old custom and probably originated as a form of collective
mutual aid.   According to an old tradition, the young couple
stand on a sheepskin coat spread out on the floor.   The
parents present their gifts first, followed by the close relatives, and then all the rest.   Before the Revolution the
young boys and girls did not give presents to the couple.

Now they do, though not always.   The girls most frequently give toilet articles - soap, powder, scent;   the boys, money (1-5 roubles).   There are all sorts of possible wedding presents - crockery, tablecloths, clocks, gramophones, material for dresses and shirts, linen and money.   Gifts of money are usually accompanied by some message, e.g. 'for an awl, for soap, for red dye', or 'for petrol so that you get the bride home without getting lost'. (12)   During the presentation numerous toasts are drunk to the health and happiness of the young couple.   The ceremony often ends with the couple having to buy the gifts from their relatives and neighbours. Then the merrymaking continues and the young couple and those who go with them prepare for their journey.   Before they go, the couple and the guests are photographed.   No kolkhoz wedding in the Kuban ever takes place without photography.   As a rule, the photographer is invited to both the bride's and bridegroom's houses.   Sometimes the couple themselves go to the photographer on their way to the village soviet or the bridegroom's house.

If the registration of marriage is performed on the day of the wedding, (13) the couple and their party go through the main streets of the village to the village soviet.   The registration of marriage is usually performed in a solemn atmosphere.   The chairman and deputy of the village soviet congratulate the couple and wish them luck.   At the end of the ceremony they drink to the happiness of the newlyweds with wine (often champagne).

An integral part of the wedding ceremony is the transfer of the bride's dowry to the bridegroom.   The dowry must include a bed, bedding, and a wardrobe and very often a hand or treadle sewing machine, a bicycle, etc.   The druzhko and the matchmakers 'buy' the dowry (this ceremony is basically a repetition of the buying of the table and plait) and, accompanied by some of the bride's female guests, they take it to the bridegroom's house singing joyfully and trying to include almost the whole village in their route.   The young people on the whole dislike this method of transporting the dowry, but it is still done like this everywhere.   The dowry is transferred either on the day before the wedding (e.g. in the village of Staro-Myshastov and the town of Korenov, and others) or on the day of the wedding (in Berezan, Tikhorets region, and the village of Gostagaev, Anap region) or when the gifts are presented in the bridegroom's house (in the village of Lineinaya, Belorechen region, and others).   If the bride and bridegroom come from different villages, the dowry is usually transported in the car in which the young couple go away.

When they arrive at the bridegroom's house, the wedding feast recommences.   As at the bride's house, refreshments

are served and the guests sing, dance and give presents to
the newlyweds.   The bride's guests either come with her or
stay behind and go on celebrating in her parents' house.
The wedding feast in the bridegroom's house concludes the
first day of the wedding, but this is not the end of the celebration.   On the morning of the following day the guests
gather again in the bride's and bridegroom's houses.   After
breakfast the couple goes to the home of the bride's parents.
They are accompanied by their relatives and neighbours and
many members of the procession wear gipsy costumes.   One
man always dresses up as a doctor, always ready to adminis-
ter 'first aid', i.e. to pour out more wine.

Today weddings usually begin on Saturday and last for two,
sometimes three days.   On the last day of the wedding, the
guests again meet at the young couple's.   It is customary for
them to bring chickens with them and cook them there.   The
wedding customs described above are still widespread today
among the rural population of the Kuban.   It is very rare for
a couple to get married without observing all or part of the
ceremony, although it does happen.   In such cases the weddings are like ordinary parties, but longer.   Thus, for
example, two of the sons in the family of the Hero of Socialist
Labour P. Shatsky (of the Lenin kolkhoz, Labin region) were
married without the traditional wedding.   However, guests
were invited to celebrate the marriage and the merrymaking
went on for days. (14)

The kolkhozniks of the Kuban are prosperous and don't stint
money on their weddings.   A large number of guests are invited and they buy and cook all sorts of dishes, zakuski and
wines.   The most widespread traditional dishes are borshch,
chicken and noodle soup,'sauce' (stewed meat and potatoes),
roast duck or goose, 'cold dish' (boiled chicken with green
onions, lettuce and sour cream), jellied meat, omelettes, roasted and boiled meat, marinated fish, herring, fresh cucumber,
radish or tomato salad, stuffed peppers, pies and tarts filled
with curd cheese and fruit, yoghurt, compote, fruit jelly and
nuts.   The wedding feast nowadays always includes ready-
prepared groceries and confectionary - sausages, ham, cheese,
various canned goods, biscuits, sweets, etc.   The kholkhoz
usually helps in the organisation of the wedding, by providing
cars for the wedding procession and for transporting the
dowry, by supplying products (usually meat and wine) at a
wholesale price from the kolkhoz store-room, and by giving
financial help to the newlyweds.   For example, in 1960 the
management of the Lenin kolkhoz (Din region) agreed to grant
a house on credit and an interest-free loan of 200 roubles to
V. Bezinskaya and her husband V. Zanozdrev, both tractor
drivers. (15)   The kolkhozes usually take an especially great
interest in the organisation of komsomol weddings, where the

kolkhoz community as a whole or in part takes the responsibility for the wedding arrangements upon itself. Komsomol weddings were introduced comparatively recently (two or three years ago) but they have already won the recognition of the youth. These weddings are most often celebrated in the clubs or Red Corners of the farms and brigades. Komsomol weddings are performed either without the observance of the popular traditions, or the form of the ritual is kept, but some of the obsolete customs are discarded, and the element of entertainment is brought to the fore. Thus, for example, in the Lenin kolkhoz of Din region the first komsomol wedding was held on 1 May 1966. The wedding was based on the popular traditions, but differed in some ways from the customary ceremony. Thus, the bride and bridegroom did not bow to those they invited to their wedding, the bride did not do the inviting in her wedding dress, the bridegroom did not hand out shishki, etc. They sang only Soviet songs - 'Virgin land', 'Kuban fields', etc. The role of 'matchmaker' was played by the secretary of the kolkhoz komsomol organisation. (16)

As has already been said, the contemporary wedding still preserves the old traditional forms and retains the poetry of the rituals - even now one can hear the traditional songs associated with particular stages of the weddings as well as those sung throughout the wedding. However, all traces of social and economic inequality have disappeared from the modern wedding ceremony (e.g. the custom of inspecting the bridegroom's husbandry), as well as the unequal position of women in the family. All the same, even now there are cases when young people, on the instructions of their elders, blindly observe all the ceremonies without considering what they mean. Thus, for example, in one of the weddings which took place in 1958 in the kolkhoz 'Red October', Ust'-Labin region, the bride wailed periodically simply because this was required by the old custom. (17) Rural society must activate mass-enlightenment work among the youth, lead the struggle against the obsolete customs and aid the formation and spreading of the new traditions, which correspond to our new reality.

NOTES

1 This article is based on personal observations, field materials and questionnaires. The information was collected by the author and the members of the Kuban section of the Combined Expedition of the Institute of Ethnography of the Academy of Sciences of the USSR, during expeditions to Krasnodar Territory in 1954 and 1958-61. In addition, the author has used descriptions of weddings of the nineteenth and early twentieth centuries in individual

settlements of the area, included in 'A Collection of Descriptive Materials on the Regions and Tribes of the
Caucasus', vol. 1, 1883, vol. 29, 1901, vol. 36, 1906 and
others; 'Collected Papers on the Kuban', vol. 1, 1883,
vol, 2, 1891; the local newspaper, 'The Kuban Region
Gazette', 1863-1909; and also general works on the history of the area and the wedding rituals of the eastern
Slavs.   Materials on the wedding songs were kindly made
available to the author by a teacher in the Krasnodar
Pedagogical Institute, Candidate of Philological Sciences,
E.F. Tarasenkova.

2   The most essential differences were observed in the wedding ritual of the Nekrasov Cossacks (a wedding of the
Nekrasovtsi, who migrated here from Turkey, is described
in detail in the work of V.F. Tumilevich, The Wedding
Ritual of the Nekrasov Cossacks and Proceedings, vol.
45, 'Works of the Historical Philological Faculty', no. 6,
Rostov, 1958, pp. 129-68).   However, in the last ten
years, the wedding customs typical of the whole of the
rural population of the Kuban have even spread to the
former Nekrasov Cossacks (the inhabitants of the farms of
Novo-Nekrasov and Novo-Pokrov in Timashev District).
The differences chiefly concern the wedding customs of
the Line and the Black Sea Cossacks.   Thus, in Black
Sea settlements, as in many Ukranian and Belorussian
villages, after the wedding ceremony, the wedding procession and the young couple go to the bridegroom's house,
then to the bride's house and from there the young
couple leave for the husband's house.   Among the Line
Cossacks, the bride goes to her husband's house immediately after the wedding ceremony.   The functionaries
at the Black Sea wedding include the 'svetilka' (a girl,
the sister or another female relative of the bridegroom,
who sits beside him at the wedding table, holding lighted
candles).   The wedding songs of the Line Cossacks are
usually sung with a distinctive refrain ('oi leli', 'oi, lada',
etc.), which does not exist among the Black Sea Cossacks.
The wedding customs of the Cossacks and the immigrants
were basically the same, but the immigrants never went in
for horse-riding and when the bride's brother 'sold' her
plait, he sat with an axe or a stick in his hand, not with
a sabre, as the Cossacks did.

3   In the late nineteenth and early twentieth centuries, be-
trothals in the Kuban were sometimes made 'with hats on'
i.e. without the couple seeing each other.   It was usually
the daughters of poor people who were betrothed to the
unsuccessful sons (cripples, hooligans, drunkards) of
Cossack officers in this way.   In 1914, the immigrant,
T.I. Kovalenko who worked as a farmhand for a rich Cossack of Tengin village was betrothed in this way.   The
matchmaker, the bridegroom's father, boasted extravagant-

ly about his son's virtues, and above all, about his
wealth. Only afterwards did Kovalenko discover that her
husband was notorious in the village for his evil ways
(field notes of the author, 1954, kept in the Department
of Ethnography, Moscow State University).

4 These rituals, which have much in common with the
rituals of 'rukobitya' and 'zaruchin', widespread among
the Russians and the Ukranians in the past, were in many
ways a repetition and reinforcement of betrothal. A
large number of the bride and bridegroom's relatives were
invited to the 'svody' and 'propoiki' to discuss the time
and condition of the impending marriage. It was extremely difficult to cancel the wedding after the 'svody' and
'propoiki' - the injured party had the right to demand re-
imbursement of all the expenses they had incurred and an
additional sum of money for the insult to their honour.
Cases of calling off the wedding after these rituals had
been performed were very rare and were even taken to
the village court.

5 The Kuban Cossacks always used to observe the custom of
inspecting the bridegroom's husbandry, but it was only in
wealthy families that much importance was attached to it
and they tried to inspect his property before the 'svody'.

6 The author's field notes, Archive of the Institute of
Ethnography (AIE), Collection of the Russian Ethnographical Expedition, Kuban Section, 1958, document no. 7, line
183.

7 The 'karavai', formerly an essential ingredient of Ukranian
and southern Great Russian weddings, are baked both at
the bridegroom's and at the bride's houses, or, more
often, only at the bride's. Today the karavai is placed
on the wedding table and cut during the present giving.
The matchmaker gives everyone who gives the young
couple a present a glass of vodka and a piece of karavai.
'Lezhen' is a large, richly decorated pie with a filling.
The lezhen is given out at the end of the wedding feast.
They are baked more in villages settled by migrants from
the central provinces of Russia. The 'dyven' is a sort
of ring-shaped biscuit. On it are placed three sticks,
made out of baked dough and decorated with two dough
doves, to symbolise the bride and bridegroom's mutual
love and fidelity. The young bride takes a dyven with
her when she goes into the bridegroom's house; the next
morning, she gives half of it to her mother, the other
half to the bridegroom's guests. The 'giltse', formerly
very common in the Ukraine, is the bough of a cherry
tree, or other, usually fruit, tree, made of sweet baked
dough and decorated with dough figures, biscuits,
sweets, apples, paper or cloth flowers, ribbons and roses;
it is placed on the table in a bucket of grain or earth or
stuck into a pumpkin or loaf. The giltse are given out

when the bride takes leave of her girlfriends.   'Shishki'
are little round loaves;   they bake an enormous amount of
them, between 300-500.   The shishki have various functions: they play the part of an unusual sort of invitation
card and are handed out as wedding invitations;   the
girls receive shishki when they take leave of the bride;
everyone who gives the couple a present receives shishki
as well as karavai.   Like the karavai, the shishki were
characteristic of the traditional Ukranian and southern
Great Russian weddings.

8   As is known, the Kuban settlements have a large population, often of 10,000 or more, so one can easily imagine
how many times the bride has to bow, sometimes to complete strangers.

9   Before the Revolution, parties were held throughout the
period between the official betrothal or 'propoiki' and the
wedding.   However, these were never called 'girl's evenings'.   At these parties, the girls busied themselves
with needlework to help the bride prepare for the wedding, and the young men gave them sweetmeats and generally tried to amuse them.   These parties were of great
importance in the past, as they were almost the only official place (except for sit-down gatherings and the
streets), where young men and girls could meet.   Also,
the people at the party gave the bride practical help in
preparing her dowry and the presents for the future
relatives.   These parties are hardly ever held now and
have lost their point.   Now the House of Culture, the
cinemas, the reading room, etc. have become the main
places for young men and girls to meet and the bride
buys everything she needs for the wedding in the shops.
However, the term 'parties' is in some places preserved
to denote the feast night.

10   The selling of the plait is conducted in rather an unusual
way in the Kuban.   Thus, while in the Ukraine and
other regions of Russia, the boy who sells the plait was
armed with a stick or axe, in the Kuban, he holds a
sabre in his hand.

11   If the bride and bridegroom come from different villages,
the bride's guests give her her presents in the house.
If they come from the same village, either the bride's
guests give her their presents in her house and the
bridegroom's guests in his house, or all the guests give
out their presents in the bridegroom's house.

12   The author's field notes, AIE, Collection of the Russian
Ethnographical Expedition, Kuban Section, 1958, document
no. 7, line 148.

13   It should be noted that in the Kuban, the majority of marriages are registered before the wedding, although cases
of registration after the wedding are still encountered.
Church weddings are extremely rare in the Kuban and
only take place under pressure from old people.

14 The author's field notes, AIE, Collection of the Combined
    Expedition, Kuban Section, 1960, document no. 7a, line
    344.
15 Ibid., line 155.
16 Ibid., line 8.
17 Ibid., document no. 7, line 9.

7 The connections between the contemporary town and village family
D.M. Kogan*

A study of the connections between the town and village population enables us to explain some aspects of the life and culture of the inhabitants of the town. (1)

The present work is limited to a study of the connections
between the inhabitants of the town of Kaluga and their relatives in rural districts.   It is based on a selective survey,
conducted by questionnaire, of 3,041 people, working in ten
different enterprises and institutions. (2)   An analysis of
the results of the questionnaire shows that a section of the
different groups of townsmen maintain relations with people
living in the country.   It also reveals the conditions and the
concrete forms of these connections.

More than two-thirds of our respondents were not original
inhabitants of Kaluga. (3)   A significant majority of them
(67.3 per cent) had come from rural districts.   The time of
arrival in the town of the former rural inhabitants who today
work at the various enterprises can be seen from Table 7.1.

Table 7.1

	Before the Revolution [†]	1917–20	1921–9	1930–40	1941–5	1946–55	1956–9	1960–6
Percentage of the total number arriving from rural districts		0.2	4.7	18.2	8.7	34.8	12.0	21.4

[†] No statistics given (T.D.).

The table shows that a large number of the former rural
inhabitants migrated to the town in the post-war years.   In
this both the natural decrease in the population and the ter-
mination of the working life (due to retirement) of people who

* Based on a questionnaire conducted in the town of Kaluga.
  First published in 'Sovetskaya Etnografiya', 1970, no. 6,
  pp. 105-10.

migrated from the village from 1917 to 1940 should be taken
into account.   The influx of the rural population in the post-
war years was a result of the rapid economic development of
the regional centre: in this period new industrial enterprises
were constructed and the old ones reconstructed, there was
large-scale housing construction and public services and amen-
ities were organised.   The town of Kaluga also gained stature
as a cultural centre.   The special secondary schools and
higher educational institutions trained engineers, technicians,
teachers, medical workers, etc.

Over one-third of the townsmen (38.4 per cent) who completed the questionnaire have relatives in the country.   Of
the townsmen, 61.7 per cent in this category come from the
country;   19.2 per cent have migrated to Kaluga from other
towns;   17.2 per cent (4) natives of Kaluga or inhabitants of
the nearby villages, working in the town (the so-called 'suburban' population);   2.6 per cent (5) have other antecedents.

Table 7.2

Groups of townsmen	Have both parents or parents' family	Have only the father	Have only the mother	Have brothers/ sisters living independently with their families in rural districts	Have other relatives in the collateral mother and father-in-law, cousins, etc.
			In percentages		
Local, inc. (a) natives	39.6	1.3	6.6	8.9	43.6
of Kaluga (b) suburban	26.0	1.6	5.8	4.0	62.6
population	55.9	0.9	7.9	14.7	20.6
Arrivals from the village	44.5	1.8	22.8	16.3	14.6
Arrivals from other towns	44.3	2.4	18.4	11.7	23.2
Others	42.8	0.6	20.0	22.2	14.4

Table 7.2 lists the data on the relatives of various degrees
of kinship of the groups of townsmen in the rural districts.
It can be seen that a substantial proportion of the members of
almost all the groups have parents (6) or parents' relatives (7)
in the country.   This proportion is particularly high among
the 'suburban' population (55.9 per cent).   Table 7.2 shows

that the number of townsmen whose fathers alone remain in
the rural districts is small (in various groups from 0.6 to 2.4
per cent).   This can be explained by the fact that many of
them lost their fathers in the Second World War.   Moreover,
single men tend to marry more often than single women.   The
percentage of townsmen whose widowed mothers live in rural
districts is naturally considerably higher than the percentage
of townsmen who have widowed fathers in the village.

In all groups the percentage of people who have brothers
and sisters in the village is comparatively small.   This may
be connected with the fact that the townsmen's brothers and
sisters, when they reach their teens, also tend to go to the
town to continue their education or work in industry.   In
this they are helped by their relatives in the town.

An analysis of Table 7.2 shows that all the groups also include people who have 'other relatives in the collateral line'
in the country.   The proportion of people who have relatives
in the collateral line in rural districts is especially high among
the natives of Kaluga.   This is because the parents of many
Kalugans migrated from the country, leaving their brothers
and sisters behind.   In addition the inhabitants of Kaluga
who marry immigrants from the village form kinship relations
with their husband's or wife's relatives living in rural districts.

Only 6 per cent of our respondents did not keep in touch
with their relatives in rural districts.   The highest proportion of people maintaining relations with the village is found
among the former rural inhabitants (47.1 per cent).   Among
those who have migrated permanently to Kaluga from other
towns, 31 per cent have connections with the village, among
the inhabitants of Kaluga and its suburbs, 34.5 per cent.

Of the single townsmen who answered our questions, 56 per
cent maintained ties with the village.   The largest group of
these consists of people of 20-9 years of age and boys and
girls of 16-19.   Men make up 48 per cent and women 52 per
cent of the townsmen with families who have not lost touch
with their country relatives.   Table 7.3 gives data on the
sex and age groups of people in this category.   As it shows,
the majority of people in this category of townsmen are

Table 7.3

	16-19	20-9	30-9	40-9	50 and over
Men	6.2	33.4	37.7	16.5	6.2
Women	14.2	27.1	30.4	23.5	4.8

between 20 and 29 and 30 and 39 years of age. There are comparatively few people over 50 - evidently the relatives of people in this age group have died.

We also grouped the families according to the number of members. Each group naturally includes families of varying types. We will devote our attention to families with the most typical composition.

Two-person families make up 15.3 per cent of all those questioned (including single people). These were mostly married couples (53 per cent). A little over one-third of these families maintained ties with rural relatives, usually their parents or their parents' families.

Three-person families account for 31.4 per cent. The majority of these (68 per cent) consist of a couple and their son or daughter. Of these families, 38 per cent have contacts with the village.

Four-person families account for 28.5 per cent. About two-thirds of these included two generations (i.e. a couple and their children). Of these families, 37.4 per cent preserve relations with relatives in the country. A little over one-fifth of the four-person families included three generations. Of families in this group, 56.4 per cent maintain ties with the village (mainly with relatives in the collateral line).

Five-person families account for 10.7 per cent. Of these, 46.3 per cent include three generations. Those who maintain kinship relations with members of the rural population number 44.2 per cent. There are comparatively few families of six, seven or more people. They were too unrepresentative to be worth an independent examination.

Our field materials show that it is usually young families, consisting of a married couple and their children, who preserve ties with the village. The preservation of contacts with the village is also typical of families which include members of the older generaton.

It is interesting to examine the question of the townsmen's connections with their country relatives in relation to their social-professional groups. The townsmen were divided into the following groups: (a) workers; (b) engineers and technical workers; (c) education and health workers; and (d) white-collar workers (office workers and others). The workers in each of the above social groups were then divided into sub-groups according to their degree of qualification or level of education. Table 7.4 shows the percentage of people in each social group or sub-group who have relatives in the country and keep in touch with them.

Table 7.4

Social group	Have relatives in rural districts	Maintain connections with the village
Workers	40.4%	37.6%
Qualified	44.3	41.4
Semi-qualified	41.0	38.2
Unqualified	34.8	30.4
Engineers and technical workers	35.6	35.4
Specialists with higher or secondary education	33.1	31.9
Practical workers	39.0	38.7
Educational and health workers	16.4	15.7
With higher education	11.6	10.0
With secondary special education	20.3	20.2
White-collar (office) workers	29.4	28.3
Semi-qualified	29.8	29.0
Unqualified	29.2	27.8

We find that quite a high percentage of people in the group of workers have relatives in rural districts. This proportion is higher among workers with higher and secondary education than among unqualified workers. This is connected with the fact that a large proportion of workers (72.3 per cent) - migrants from the country - qualify at a comparatively early age. Courses in professional and technical schools, national service, etc., contribute to this. A rather smaller percentage of the unqualified workers have relatives in the country (34.8 per cent). This can be explained by the fact that this sub-group contains a large number of people over 45, who have lived in the town for 25 years and more. A considerable proportion of these moved to Kaluga with their parents. The relatives they still have in the country are mostly in the collateral line.

A little over one-third (35.6 per cent) of the engineers and technical workers have relatives in rural districts. This proportion is slightly higher (39 per cent) among workers without higher and secondary special education. As for white-collar workers, not more than 30 per cent of them have relations in the country. White-collar workers help their relatives to move to the town and take up a profession more often than manual workers do. It should also be borne in mind that 95.5 per cent of white-collar workers are women.

An even smaller proportion of the educational and health workers (16.4 per cent) have relatives in the country. They make up a little over one-tenth of those with higher education and 20.3 per cent of those with secondary education. This is explained by the fact that 70 per cent of this social-professional group consists of either hereditary townsmen or natives of Kaluga whose parents migrated from rural districts. Also, a large number of the doctors and teachers (migrants from the village) are now elderly (49 and over). Naturally, few of them have relatives left in the country.

It is clear from the above that the proportion of people who have relatives in the country varies considerably among the different social-professional groups. This in turn affects the proportion of people in each group who maintain ties with the village.

Our data reveals that the highest proportion of people maintaining ties with the village is to be found among the manual workers and engineers and technical workers. This is evidently because these groups include a particularly large number of migrants from the rural districts. The proportion of people maintaining ties with the country among the white-collar workers is considerably smaller than in the first two groups. Almost all the educational and health workers who still have relations in the village still keep in touch with them.

The number of people who are in contact with relations in the country in the individual enterprises and institutions involved in the questionnaire varied greatly from average for the collective as a whole (58 per cent of workers in the building trade maintain ties with the village; 45.4 per cent in the bus depot; 44.8 per cent in the department store; 29–39 per cent in the engineering works, light industries, on the railway and in the communications industry). A much smaller proportion of people have connections with the village in the town 'combine' of social services (15.5 per cent), the polyclinic (17.9 per cent), and the secondary school (20 per cent). The small number of workers in the combine of social services who preserve relations with relatives in the country, in our view, is explained by the following circumstances: 53 per cent of the formal rural inhabitants who work in the combine have lived in Kaluga 20 and more years, 29.3 per cent for 10-18 years. If the composition of this group by age is analysed, it turns out that 34.6 per cent of them are aged 40-9, and 29.3 per cent are 50 and over. It is highly likely that many of the people in this group have worked in Kaluga over a prolonged period and have either helped their relatives to move to the town or their elderly parents who stayed behind in the country have died.

The analysis of the results of the questionnaire shows that among the workers in the industrial enterprises, construction industry, town transport services, railways, communications and trade, a significant number of those who preserve contact with their relatives in rural districts maintain ties with their parents or parents' families. Thus, on the railway and in the bus depot, it is over half, in the building works, in the engineering factory, in the communications industry and in the department store it is just under half.

As we have already remarked, (8) the ties between the town and village population are reflected in many aspects of their life - economic, social, cultural and other.   The townsmen's social group, their lifestyle, culture, psychology, etc. (9) all play a part in determining the nature of their relations with the village.

Most townsmen who have relatives (parents, brothers, sisters) in the country as a rule maintain some sort of connection with the village.   This can take the form of financial aid, visits or holidays, correspondence and joint celebration of family occasions (the birth of a child, a wedding, etc.).   If the village in which the relatives live is not far from the town (a distance of 25-75 km), the townsmen (especially single people) usually go there comparatively often (once or twice a month).   In this case they hardly ever write to each other. If the relatives live a long way from the town, correspondence takes on an important meaning.   In this case the townsmen visit the country comparatively rarely (once a year to mark some important event in the family life of the relatives).   The connections of the single townsmen with the country mainly take the form of visits or holidays (42.4 per cent), or financial aid (41.5 per cent).   Young men and women who move to the town usually receive material aid in the form of small sums of money or food from their parents.

The type of connection varies among the different social groups.   For example, among people with higher education (we took medical workers as an example) they are usually limited to visits of 1-2 days, the giving of presents and financial aid to their relatives in the country.   The connections of the working-class townsmen with their relatives in the country are usually of a more varied and mutual nature.   They go to visit their country relatives and spend their holidays with them, help them with the farming, give them financial aid. The country relatives, in turn, provide the townsmen with agricultural produce.

According to the questionnaire, 52.8 per cent of the workers who have relatives in the country go to visit them and spend their holidays with them;   14.4 per cent preserve some sort of ties with their country relatives. The situation is approximately the same among the engineers and technical workers. For workers in education, the health service and cultural institutions the typical forms of contact with relatives in the country are visits and holidays, and also financial aid.

To conclude, we will remark that our work has far from exhausted the question of ties between the town and country population. The materials presented above can, in our view, be of use in solving many of the problems connected with the ethnographical study both of the town and of the country.

NOTES

1 The question was formulated in another of our articles. See D.M. Kogan, Ties between the Urban and Rural Population as one of the Problems of the Ethnography of the Town, 'Soviet Ethnography', 1967, no. 4, pp. 40-7.
2 For more detail on this, see L.A. Anokhina, M.N. Shmeleva, The Utilisation of Statistical Information from Questionnaires in the Ethnographic Study of the Town, 'Soviet Ethnography', 1968, no. 3, pp. 17-18.
3 Ibid., pp. 19-20.
4 We treated the natives of Kaluga and the inhabitants of the nearby villages, who worked in the town, as locals. The first made up 9.4 per cent, the second 7.8 per cent of the people questioned.
5 The rest included new arrivals, demobilised soldiers and others.
6 In this category we include fathers- and mothers-in-law, on both sides.
7 The parents' family includes the parents, or one of them and the brothers, sisters, grandfather and grandmother, etc. who live with them.
8 See D.M. Kogan, op. cit., p. 46.
9 These questions, which are of great importance for the ethnographical study of the urban population, need further research. It is not possible for us to discuss them in detail in the present study.

Part III
BALTIC STATES

INTRODUCTION

The Baltic States comprise Latvia, Estonia and Lithuania, nations whose past history has swayed between independence and domination by powerful neighbours, notably Germany and Russia, finally, in 1941, being taken over by Stalin's Soviet forces, and, since then, forming three Union republics of the USSR. They have retained their alphabet (Latin script) and have a thriving literature in their own languages, but a government policy of settling Russians in those areas has resulted in many people being bilingual. The universities of Tartu, and at Riga, Vilnius and Tallin have an older generation of scholars well versed in the German tradition in ethnography and a younger generation more familiar with Soviet Russian approaches.

Marxist cadres were sent from Russia in the post-war period to train the local scholars. Terent'eva was among them. From then on she had continually returned to do her own field work there and, thanks to her energy and loyalty, on the one hand, and her academic reputation through her sound knowledge of Baltic languages and ethnography and long list of publications, on the other, she rose to be Deputy Director of the Institute of Ethnography of the USSR Academy of Sciences in Moscow. Both her erudition and her position are reflected in the first and second parts of her paper respectively. The text on Soviet times, in sharp contrast to the painstaking precision of archive research of the previous period safely in the past, is elusive on detail and abundant in official commentary which is used uncritically by some Western scholars as evidence of the Sovietisation of ritual with no reference to the punitive conditions imposed on the national minorities to refrain from 'unprogressive' practices, or the conditions in which Soviet scholars write. In the Baltic States, nevertheless, a strong school in the study of material culture thrives, as do folklore studies, and they certainly provide one of the most fascinating areas of European anthropology for comparative analysis.

Some time before her death, Professor Terent'eva and I went through the original text and together slightly condensed it for publication in the present volume.

129

8 The Latvian peasant family
L.N. Terent'eva *

The author of the present work has devoted herself for
several years to the study of the family life of the kolkhozniks
(collective farmers. T.D.) of the Latvian Soviet Socialist
Republic. This article is based both on field work and materials from the Central State Archives of Latvia SSR and on the
personal records of members of the rural population of Latvia.

Our research covers a period of about half a century: from
the beginning of the twentieth century to the present day,
i.e. the last years of Tsarism, the period of the Great October
Socialist Revolution and the establishment of Soviet power in
the Baltic States (1917-19), the years of the bourgeois dictatorship in Latvia (1920-40) and the twenty years which
elapsed between the establishment of Soviet power in Latvia
and its inclusion in the Soviet Union (1940-60). (1)

Under the Tsars in the nineteenth century, Latvia was divided into three parts for administrative purposes: the 'uezds'
bordering the northern river Daugav made up Liflyands
'gubernia', to the south of Daugav was Kurlands gubernia;
and the eastern uezds of Latvia (approximately a quarter of
the territory of the republic) were joined with Vitebsk and
Pskov gubernias respectively. (Uezd = an administrative
region; in Tsarist times the regions were divided into
'gubernia', 'uezd' and 'volost'. T.D.) These administrative
divisions reflected the stage of historical development reached
by the country before its annexation to Russia. (2) The
unification of Latvia took place only after the Great October
Socialist Revolution.

Differences in the political and social-economic development
of the three parts of Latvia continued to exist in varying
degrees even after it became part of the Russian empire.
The gubernias of Liflyand and Kurland, which were amalgama-
ted with neighbouring Estlyand under the general name of the
Prebaltic gubernia, occupied a special position in Tsarist
Russia. The German baron-landowners were the virtual
rulers of the area, preserving political rights (in the form of
nobles' self-government) and other privileges. The agrarian

* First published in 'Trudy Instituta Etnografii Akademiya
  Nauk SSR', vol. 77, Moscow 1962, pp. 62-93.

laws operating in these gubernias were different from those of
Russia. (3)   However, in the Latvian uezds of Vitebsk and
Pskov gubernias the agrarian laws and the administration were
the same as those in the rest of Russia.

There were essential differences between the forms of agriculture and types of settlement existing among the Latvian
peasants.   In the Prebaltic republics private farming and
settlement in individual homesteads was established long
before their unification with Russia. (4)   In the Latvian
uezds of Vitebsk and Pskov gubernias, as in other parts of
these and the majority of the other gubernias of Tsarist
Russia, farming by the commune ('obshchina') and settlement
in villages predominated up to the beginning of the twentieth
century. (5)

The process of development of capitalism in agriculture proceeded with varying degrees of intensity in the different
gubernias.   At the end of the nineteenth century. V.I. Lenin
saw the Prebaltic gubernia as the area where capitalism was
most highly developed in agriculture. (6)

The main commodity-producing branch of agriculture in
these gubernias was dairy farming.   By the beginning of the
twentieth century it was the leading producer in European
Russia.   The agriculture of the Prebaltic gubernia was also
of an intensive character.   The many-field system was adopted not only on the landowners' but also on kulak, and to
some degree on the middle peasants', farms.   The practice of
sowing grass and fodder crops was also common.   The widespread adoption of agricultural machinery provided further
evidence of the high degree of capitalism in agriculture. (7)

The eastern 'uezds' of Latvia (Latgaliya) embarked on the
road of capitalist development in agriculture much later.
The distance of these 'uezds' from convenient sea routes
slowed down the rate of their economic development.   The
poor development of industry had a negative influence on
agriculture, which remained extremely backward. (8)

Capitalism developed in the Latvian republic along Prussian
lines.   Right up to 1917 the land was owned by a privileged
feudal class - German barons in Liflyand and Kurland gubernias and Polish landowners in Latgaliya.   At the beginning of
the twentieth century, about half of all the land - 48.3 per
cent - was concentrated in the hands of the landowners, while
38.5 per cent belonged to the peasants, the remaining 13.2
per cent of the land being the property of the state, the
towns and the church. (9)   The Latvian peasantry suffered
from an extreme shortage of land.   In 1905 the number of
landless peasants amounted to over 60 per cent and, in Kurland, to almost 75 per cent of the agricultural population. (10)

About 22 per cent of the peasant proprietors owned small plots (from 1 to 2 hectares), and approximately the same number possessed from 10 to 22.   Only about 20 per cent of the peasant land belonged to these small and middle proprietors, while over 80 per cent of the land was concentrated in the hands of the bigger peasant owners (they made up 56 per cent of the total number).   These owners (with 22-100 hectares, and more) were mainly kulaks who had developed the system of hired labour.

Class differentiation was thus highly developed among the Latvian peasantry.   In spite of the obstacles to the development of peasant proprietorship created by the nobility, there was a stratum of rural bourgeoisie exploiting hired labour;   a rural proletariat and a large semi-proletarian stratum (the so-called 'batraks' - hired labourers who owned tiny strips of land) was formed;   there was a large group of very poor peasantry (especially in Latgaliya);   and also a layer of middle peasants.

The agrarian problem was one of the central political questions in Latvia, as the events of 1905 very clearly show.   In 1917 and 1919 Soviet power was established in the unoccupied territory of Latvia;   its most important act was the confiscation of the landowners' estates and the nationalisation of the land.   When the Latvian counter-revolutionary bourgeoisie came to power in 1919, they immediately undid the nationalisation of the land and restored the estates confiscated in 1918 to the landowners.

However, the pressure of the growing revolutionary movement of the peasants forced the government to undertake agrarian reform.   The results of the bourgeois reform can be briefly indicated by the following figures. (11)   In 1929, after the completion of the reform, there were 50,000 nearly landless peasants in Latvia;   with the peasant holders of small plots they added up to 130,000 families (i.e. about half of the agricultural population).   They owned less than one-seventeenth of the total stock of land.

At the other extreme, were the owners (about 68,000 of them) of plots of over 70 hectares of land.   These included most of the kulak-capitalists, and over two-thirds of the agricultural land was in their hands. (12)

The bourgeois government, in its policy of agrarianisation, showed an exclusive concern for the development of kulak production.   They were given contracts for the supply of produce, state grants, subsidiaries, etc.   All this resulted in the concentration of the main means of production (land, productive and working livestock, and agricultural implements and machines) in the hands of the kulak-capitalist minority, and hastened the process of class differentiation in the countryside - inevitable under capitalism.

Thus, according to the 1935 figures, the Latvian village proletariat numbered over 280,000 - more than 20 per cent of the rural population.

Of the total number of peasant proprietors (270,000), 20.2 per cent had less than 2 hectares of land, and 24.3 per cent belonged to the group of 'poor peasants'. These peasants had to work to the point of exhaustion to secure a meagre subsistence for themselves and their families. Some of them had to resort to selling their labour power. In 1933, 28.3 per cent of the proprietors were 'middle peasants'. The remaining 27.3 per cent were kulaks and big capitalists. (13)

The ratio of the above groups of peasant proprietors varied from oblast to oblast of Latvia. Latgaliya had the greatest number of small proprietors in 1935 - over 60 per cent of all the small, and almost 50 per cent of the middle, peasants of Latvia were concentrated there. (14) (15)

The degree of intensity of peasant agriculture also varied greatly from oblast to oblast. The 'uezds' which had earlier formed part of the Prebaltic 'gubernia' were the most economically developed. The agriculture of Latgaliya remained backward. The main reason for this was the economic policy of the bourgeois government, which hindered the development of industry and the more profitable branches of agriculture (above all, the breeding of dairy cattle). The bourgeois government of Latvia saw Latgaliya as a reservoir of cheap labour (farm labourers, unskilled workers, navvies, shepherds, etc.) for the economically developed 'uezds'. (16)

The nature of the social-economic development of the Prebaltic 'gubernias' - and earlier transition to commodity-money relations, a much more intensive development of capitalism in agriculture than in the interior 'gubernias', and also the predominance of an individual homestead-type of farming - had a direct influence on the internal structure of the Latvian peasant family and the whole family system. Unlike the Russian peasants, whose family relations remained mainly on a patriarchal basis right up to 1917, money relations had long dominated the life of the Latvian peasantry. This was true above all of the groups of propertied peasants.

The fierce, stubborn struggle for land, for property, and for economic independence which the peasants were forced to wage under Tsarism, inevitably had its effect on family relations. Under these circumstances, the search for an advantageous marriage for a large inheritance appeared in its most undisguised forms. The relations between the members of a family depended on the rights of each member of the family to its property. It was this that determined the relations between parents and adult children, between brothers and sisters, husband and wife, and also the family's attitudes to sons- and daughters-in-law.

The further development of capitalist relations under the bourgeois dictatorship led to a worsening of peasant family relations, and was often the direct cause of the disintegration of the family.

The author began her study of the Latvian peasant family by examining its form; for this she studied the genealogy of the family and its forms of property, and also drew on materials on the nature of the settlement of the peasantry. An analysis of this data showed that the small family has long been established in most parts of Latvia. It is extremely difficult to determine the date of the transition from the large to the small family because of the particular historical circumstances whereby the natural course of this process was forcibly interrupted by the German feudal nobility. Literary sources provide almost no information on this question.

Our research provides grounds for asserting that the process of the disintegration of the large family proceeded with varying degrees of intensity in Latvia. In the western and central raions it was completed earlier, in the eastern, considerably later. Thus, for example, in villages studied in Ekalpils raion, bordering Latgaliya, the process of the disintegration of large families seems to have been completed by the middle of the eighteenth century. In some of the eastern Latgaliyan raions the peasants were still living in large families at the beginning of the nineteenth century. (17)

The small family usually consisted of two to three generations of relatives in the direct line, i.e. couples and their children, or couples, their children and their parents. There were sometimes cases of the cohabitation of near relatives in the collateral line - unmarried brothers or sisters of the couples (for more on this see below). The head of this family was the father, if he had not yet bequeathed his property to his heir, or an adult married son, if he had already entered into his inheritance.

In large families in addition to the owner's parents some of his married sons and sometimes also his married daughters and their children shared the house and farming with him. The head of the family was the father, and after his death the eldest son. The disintegration of large families and their replacement by small ones was a drawn-out process. The various degrees of communal living practised in the family showed that it was still taking place in Latvia, at the beginning of the twentieth century. In many families, the married brothers (especially in families where they had additional earnings) farmed together, but already lived apart and rarely shared a common table.

As the large families disappeared, two forms of inheritance became common among the Latvian peasants: the division of the father's property among the members of the family (in Latgaliya), and single inheritance (in the rest of Latvia). In large families, all the property was held in common and was not subject to inheritance.

One of the main features of single inheritance was that the property remained intact, since it passed in its entirety into the hands of one man. However, the predominance of this form of inheritance hastened the process of the dispossession of the peasants. Of the peasant sons who did not inherit very few ever came to be in a position to start homes of their own. In most cases the migration of landless peasants to the town was accompanied by a complete break with the land.

The situation was different in 'uezds' where the system of dividing the inheritance prevailed. On each successive transfer of inheritance the land was split up into yet more plots, with disastrous economic results. However, by the end of the nineteenth century, single inheritance was beginning to spread among the more prosperous peasants of Latgaliya. In the bourgeois period the government placed some restrictions on the division of property on inheritance.

The division of the land, as opposed to single inheritance, considerably retarded the process of dispossession of the peasantry. It tended to tie the peasants to their farms, forcing them to cling to a tiny scrap of land. Even so, the grave shortage of land in Latgaliya forced many peasants to look for additional sources of income. In Latgaliya migration to the towns was usually seasonal, and the workers left their families on the land.

Under both forms of inheritance, the heirs were relatives in the male line. In the direct line these were the owner's sons, and, in the case of their death, his grandchildren. In the collateral line the owner's closest relatives included his brothers and consequently also their sons. Daughters, as a rule, only inherited their father's property in families where there were no sons. In such cases, the heir would be a daughter who already lived with her husband in her father's house.

The mode of inheritance was determined by local customary law as well as by the ordinary civil code.   Under single inheritance one son, usually the eldest, inherited all his father's property (however, this was not strictly adhered to and any of the sons could inherit depending on family circumstances).   The father (or the brother who inherited) had to pay the other sons for the labour they put into the property - in the form of daily wages, or in kind (the latter more rarely).   The daughters had to be provided with a dowry. The property rights of the widow were extremely limited.   If she was left with young children, they would be looked after until they came of age.   If the widow had no children, she had to leave her dead husband's land, taking only her dowry with her.

The task of supporting his elderly mother (and, if the property was transferred to the son in his father's lifetime, of both parents) devolved on the heir.   The terms of the inheritance were usually specified in a will.   At first oral wills sufficed, later (in the second half of the nineteenth century) they were replaced by written ones, drawn up by a lawyer in the presence of witnesses.

In the wills (testaments) the conditions of the transfer of the inheritance and the obligations of the heir in regard to other members of the family were stipulated down to the smallest detail.   Our examination of the wills revealed no consistent norms for determining the amount paid to the sons who did not inherit - it was arbitrarily decided by the legatee. The amount of the daughters' dowries and the elderly mother's allowance was decided in an equally arbitrary way.   This depended to a great degree on the financial situation of the owner of the property.   We will give examples of some of these documents.   The will of the peasant P. Lezdins (formerly of Smiltan 'volost', Rizhsk 'uezd'), drawn up in 1882, lays down that the two sons inheriting are obliged to pay their brothers 100 roubles each, and to provide their sisters with a dowry of a wardrobe worth 15 roubles and two cows worth 20 roubles.   The will ends with the stipulation that if one of the eldest sons dies, his property will go to the son next to him in age. (18)

The wills of the peasants P. Liepins (formerly of Yaunpiebalg volost, Tsesis uezd 1939) and R. Lieitis (formerly of Siguld volost, Rizhsk uezd, 1930) set out the allowances to be paid to their elderly mothers.   The first will prescribes that the mother should have a flat on the farm, with heating and lighting, good food at the common table, good care and clothing.   It goes on to say that each year she should be provided with wool of her choice, 10m of bleached linen, a pair of boots of her choice, 3 pairs of mittens, 3 pairs of stockings,

3 pairs of shoes, 2 sheets, 60 Latvian roubles a year, a horse
with harness and a driver for outings, medical care and medi-
cines.   If she wished to leave the farm, in addition to the
above she would get a yearly 240 kg of rye flour, 60 kg of
wheat flour, 90 kg of bacon, 10 kg of fresh mutton, 30 kg of
butter, 40 kg of sugar, 164 kg of barley and barley flour,
25 kg of curds, 6 kg of salt, 6 kg of rice, 3 kg of coffee,
10 kg of tea, 6 litres of hempseed oil, 26 kg of peas, 6 kg of
soap, 3 litres of fresh milk (daily) and as much potatoes,
vegetables, cabbages, apples, plums and berries as she liked.
It also laid down the nature and cost of her funeral arrangements. (19)   The extent of the mother's allowance indicates
that the owner of the farm was wealthy.

The peasant R. Lieitis allows his aged mother much less in
his will.   His heir is obliged to supply her with a room to
herself in the farmhouse, to give her food, and, if she falls
ill, medical treatment.   Further on the will stipulates that if
she cannot live with her son, he must give her 'one milk cow
and supply food for the cow'.   In addition, he must give his
mother yearly 10 puds of rye flour (1 pud = 16 kg. T.D.),
4 puds of barley, 2 puds of oats, one suckling pig not less
than 25 kilos in weight, a desyatyn of land for vegetables
(desyatyn = pre-Revolutionary land measurement, = 1.09254
hectares.   The area covers a tithe of land.   T.D.) (this
plot he is obliged to cultivate himself, and plant with potatoes
and vegetables), and also 50 Latvian roubles pocket
money. (20)   The more meagre provisions for the mother
here are obviously due to the straitened circumstances of the
family.   R. Lieitis's land was burdened with debts.   The
will says that he bequeaths to his son 'all my land with all
outstanding debts'.

In the Latvian uezds where it was the custom to divide the
property between several heirs, these were again the sons.
If the property was divided up after their parents' death, all
the sons received an equal share of the inheritance.   If their
parents (or one of them) were still alive, one son would
undertake to support them and would receive a larger portion.
Sometimes the parents lived on their own after transferring
their property.   In this case all the sons by arrangement
contributed to their upkeep.

As in the uezds where single inheritance prevailed,
daughters only got dowries.   In some volosts of Latgaliya it
was the custom to give the daughters and widowed mothers a
share of the inheritance, but much less than the sons.
Judging from the wills, this share equalled one-fifth of the
immovable and one-seventh of the movable property.   The
mother's share was for her upkeep during her lifetime, and
on her death reverted to her sons.   When a daughter died,
her share was inherited by her children.

When an inheritance was transferred, the land, buildings
(which were often split up into parts), working and productive cattle, stores of grain, fertiliser (manure) and household
goods were all divided up.   The division of the property of
the peasant Leisavnieks, a former inhabitant of the village of
Kurn, Balvsk 'volost', among his sons, is an example of this.
The division took place in 1905, in the father's lifetime, and
marked the break-up of a large family, which had until then
consisted of the parents and three sons, two of whom were
already married and one of whom had five, the other two,
children.   They had all owned the property in common and
farmed communally.

At the time of the division, the father was 80.   The property was divided up on the initiative of the eldest son.
There were 13 desyatyn of land which was divided into three
equal parts (between the three sons).   The buildings were
divided as follows: one son obtained his father's hut and
entrance hut, the second the shed and the old cattle stall,
the third son, the new cattle stall.   Two of the brothers
also received storerooms, and the third, the three-walled
annex to the storeroom.   At the time of the division, the
family had 2 horses, 3 cows, 4 sheep and 2 pigs.   Of the 3
cows, 2 were the dowries of the brothers' wives and were not
included in the division;   the father took the third cow himself.   This left 2 horses and the heifer to be divided among
the three brothers.   They estimated their market price and
paid the others the difference to make their shares equal.
The division occurred in spring.   They kept the winter crop
of rye in common and divided the previous year's harvest up
equally.   They shared out the stubble from the fields, dividing it up into equal cartloads.   Each brother had already
sown and harvested his spring crop separately that year.
Their father agreed not to take a share of the immovable
property on condition that each of the brothers paid him a
yearly allowance of 4 measures of rye, 4 measures of barley
and 2 measures of oats.   The father was to live with each of
his sons in turn, bringing only himself and his cow with him.
During his stay the son in question was bound to provide him
with a potato plot and manure to fertilise it with.   Each son
had to mow hay for feeding his father's cow and give him 2
berkovtsi of straw and 3 puds of chaff.   (Berkov = pre-
Revolutionary measure, = 400 Russian pounds, i.e. equivalent
to 361.12 lb.   T.D.)   In addition, the sons had to give their
father 13 pounds of trepanned linen a year to make cloth out
of.   The father agreed to give the spinning and weaving of
the linen out to some other woman so as not to burden his
daughters-in-law. (21)

Numerous documents, kept in the Central State Archive of
the Latvian SSR (inventories of property drawn up when farms

were divided, legal judgments on questions of inheritance),
reveal the peasants' characteristic attitude to property and
the tenacity with which they clung to every bit of their farm,
however small its value.   This can be seen by looking at the
inventory of the property of a deceased peasant, formerly of
Livan volost, Daugavpils uezd, Liepniec (1923).   Besides
the land (an area of 15 hectares), buildings and livestock
(cows, calves, horses, sheep, lambs), the following items
were included in the inventory for division between his
heirs: 1 unpainted table, 1 brown stool, 2 unpainted beds,
1 small table, 1 box, 1 small cupboard, 6 pots, 2 wooden
pails, 1 axe, 2 saws, 1 hand saw, 1 chisel, 2 benches, 1 old
fur jacket, 1 blanket, 1 horse-cloth, 1 broken sledge, 1 old
harness, 1 bow with rings, 2 pieces of iron, 1 two-litre bottle,
1 winter hat, 1 lamp, 1 zinc cup, 3 pottery plates, 2 beer
barrels, etc. (22)   In the same kind of document, the peasant Francis Liepniec in 1922 divided between his inheritors,
among other things: 'One large pot, a blanket, an old
jacket, 2 large bottles, a zinc mug, 4 icons, 3 viushky
(viushky = trinkets.   T.D.), a frying pan' and so on. (23)

If problems arose during the division of the property (for
example if it proved impossible to divide it up equally), each
item was valued separately.

Interestingly, the land was also included in the valuation,
for example, a document of 1923 seen by the author, valued
land at 720,000 roubles when the whole estate was valued at
798,000. (24)

To conclude this section of the article, one must mention
the mode of inheritance when the heir was a daughter.   The
will of the peasant Jekabs Liepa, a former President of Ozols
'volost', in the Cesus uezd, is an interesting example of this:

I, Jekabs Jana Liepa, after my death bequeath my property
to my three daughters.   Minna Anderson, Matilda Enzele
and Madala Paula.   The far room is to go to Madala Paula,
the middle room where I myself live, with the kitchen and
larder (ankambar) to Minna Anderson. (25)   The big room
with the kitchen and larder (ankambar) is to go to Matilda
Enzele.   Minna and Madala must manage with one kitchen
and larder (ankambar).   The stables are to go to Minna
Anderson, the small storeroom, the small goatshed, the pig-
sty and the main cattle shed are to be divided into three
parts.   The big storeroom is to be divided between Matilda
and Madala.   One hay shed is to go to Matilda Enzele, the
second to Madala, Minna will have to keep her hay in the
space under the storeroom.   The threshing barn with the
threshing floor are to be shared by all three.   Everyone
should contribute to the repair of the stove in the threshing

barn.   The stove in the house and the kitchen range are
also to be shared by all three.   Matilda is not to forbid the
others to use the range and when it breaks down everyone
must contribute to its repair.

The land and fields are to be divided into three equal
parts.   If one of my daughters does not want to live here,
she must sell her part of the land to her sisters for a
reasonable sum.

After the death of these three heirs, the farm of Lejas
passes to Janis, son of Matilda and Aleksandr Enzelis, i.e.
he is to receive half of all the property and the other half
is to go to Marta, daughter of Madala and Karlis Paulis.
Minna's adopted child will not inherit anything after her
death.   When Matilda dies, Janis Enzelis is to receive half
of his mother's property immediately after her funeral.   If
Janis does not live to this time, Matilda's second son,
Valdemars Enzelis is to receive her property.   Also, when
Madala dies Marta or her sister are to inherit her portion
immediately after her funeral.

None of the heirs mentioned above can move a third party
into their room without the consent of all the co-heirs.

If one of the appointed heirs does not want to live on the
farm Lejas, their part of the land will be worked by those
who live on the farm for a corresponding payment.

The roofs are to be kept in good repair.   The wood is
not to be sold for timber and the fences around the fields
must be kept in good condition.   The apple trees belong
to everyone and everyone must look after them.   The hops
also belong to everyone.   No one is to dispose of any part
of the property before Janis and Marta inherit.   Whoever
plants fruit trees after my death is to have the fruit from
them.   The berries also belong to everyone.   Janis and
Marta should choose guardians for themselves, to ensure that
the timber is not sold.   Aleksandr Enzelis is not to rent
out the land.   If Matilda cannot manage, Janis as the heir
may rent it.

If any of the above-mentioned heirs or anyone else contests this will or doubts its authenticity, let it be known
that I have hitherto put my signature to no document.
Any later additions must however be accepted as genuine.

This will is written in two copies and cannot be altered.
This will is written by Jekabs Jana Liepa 30 April 1923.

Note.   The room given to Madala above is to remain at

her disposal. I have put in Madala's room: 1 bed, 2
chairs, 1 little table, 1 box containing my clothes, a big
mirror, 2 framed portraits and 2 small picture frames, one
moulded, one joined; the cupboard I bequeath to Janis
Enzelis. Signed Jekabs Jana Liepa. 30 April 1923. (26)

There are several points to note in this document: since
there were no sons in the family, the married daughters inherited and their father divided his property equally between
them, which was unusual in that area. Typically, Liepa also
stipulates who shall inherit after his daughters - his grandchildren Janis and Marta - and tells them to choose guardians
for themselves immediately after they come into their inheritance. This is presumably done to prevent any possibility
of his sons-in-law - Aleksandr Enzelis and Karlis Paulis -
seizing the property from the owner's daughters. The pro-
vision that the adopted child of one of his daughters (who has
no children of her own) may not be regarded as the heir to
her mother's portion and that all the property inherited by
her mother must pass to her father's grandchildren (the children of her sisters) (27) is also typical.

Daughters had thus very limited rights to the property they
inherited. The son-in-law, 'primak' (living with his wife's
family), had still less right to the inheritance. Peasants
entering into primak sometimes obtained various rights to their
wives' inheritance through written agreements concluded with
their future fathers-in-law at the time of their marriage.

The agreement stipulated what the son-in-law living with his
wife's family should bring with him to his father-in-law's farm,
what property rights he would have, and what was demanded
from him in return. Two documents provide an important
example of this: the first begins:

I, Anton Andrejs Soms, came in 1899 in primak to the house
of Donats Kaire's in the village of Samogol bringing with me
movable property worth to the value of 200 roubles, a horse
valued at 25 roubles, and 50 roubles in cash. I give 50
roubles of my own money to my father-in-law Donats
Keiris. (28)

In the other document, dated 21 March 1902, the agreement
becomes two-sided:

I, a peasant of Likknenesvolost, Nicgales village, Samogol,
Donats Keiris, lay down that my children shall until my
death accept my son-in-law Anton Andrejs Soms as part of
the family.

In return, I, Anton Andrejs Soms, according to the wish

of the father (of my wife) Donats Keiris, am obliged to pay
a hundred roubles (100) on the marriage of my wife's sister,
Anna Keiris Donats.   And to arrange the wedding.   Witnesses present: 1) Francis Slogars, 2) Andreja Pudans,
3) Janis Rasnacs, 4) Andrjs Kunickis, 5) Yazafs (surname
indecipherable). (29)

Under such an agreement the primak becomes a co-owner of
the property left by his wife's father.

Other documents show that it was usual in such cases for
the property to be divided equally between the daughter-heir
and her husband entering as a primak (primak = Russian word
for husband living on his wife's property. T.D.).   The
peasant woman Jekla Visvnavska, born in 1888 (today a
kolkhoznik of Daugvils raion of the LSSR) corroborates this.
She informed us:

My daughter Emilya married in 1931 at the age of 22.   She
brought Eduards Baltacis from Keisi into the house as
'primak'.   When he entered as primak, we wrote a will by
which half of all the immovable and movable property would
pass into his possession and the other half remain my
daughter's. (30)

The practice of concluding agreements with the primak was
quite widespread in Latgaliya, but not universal.   The lack
of an agreement greatly reduced the primak's status in the
family.

Before we pass to a description of relations within the
family, we should note how well the words of K. Marx and
F. Engels in the 'Communist Manifesto' apply to the Latvian
peasant family: 'the bourgeoisie tore the touching sentimental
cover from family relations and reduced them to purely mone-
tary relations.' (31)

First, let us look at the relationship between parents and
their adult children.   The head of the family, the owner of
the property, was, as has been said, the father.   However,
the father's power over his children, their subordination to
him and their respect for both parents usually only lasted
until the father transferred the inheritance to his son.   Then
the adult children, and in particular the heirs, changed their
attitude to their parents abruptly, and, when the latter grew
too old for work, often became unspeakable.   This gave rise
to the custom of written contracts between the father be-
queathing and the son inheriting the property.

After this the pattern of relationships between the heir and
his father differed from family to family.   In some families,

the parents lived peacefully with their son's family, while in
others (usually the more well-to-do) the children limited their
relations with their parents to fulfilling the terms of the con-
tract, which they regarded as a heavy burden from which
they impatiently awaited their release.   It sometimes happened that the son did not fulfil the conditions of the con-
tract.   To prevent this, some parents, in addition to a con-
tract, got a lawyer to mortgage the property they were be-
queathing to their sons for a sum equal to the cost
of their upkeep.   The mortgage agreement in the parents'
favour could only be liquidated when the son produced satis-
factory evidence that his parents had died. (32)

Among the documents of the volost courts there are many
complaints about the heirs' nonfulfilment of the obligations
towards their parents placed on them by the laws of the day
or the terms of wills.   For example, the complaint of the
peasant woman Franciska Lipeniec, formerly of Livan volost
of Daugavpils uezd, shows that after the death of their father
(her husband) her sons seized all the property and excluded
her from the use of the land.   Franciska Lipeniec asks the
court to divide all the immovable and movable property
between the heirs according to the custom of the
'volost'.... (33)   (Two more examples were originally given
by the author of similar complaints.   For sources see notes
34 and 35. T.D.)

The relationship between adult brothers, or between adult
brothers and their sisters was also governed by financial considerations.   In uezds where the father's property passed
intact to one of his children, relations between brothers and
sisters were governed by the possible rights of one or the
other to the inheritance while they were still in their father's
house.   Everyone in the family was afraid of the future heir
(and fawned on him).   This was true of the neighbours too.
The future owner was an object of respect for the whole district.   If the father chose a daughter as his heir, she too
became the centre of attention of the family and local society.
The other children knew their fate in advance - they had to
look for other sources of income or stay on their brother's
farm in the position of dependent labourers.

In Latgaliya, where the custom was to divide the property
equally between the sons, they occupied more or less equal
positions in the family.   However, here, too, relations
between the brothers worsened and friction arose as the time
of the impending division of the property approached.   On
questioning peasants and examining the archives of the volost
courts we discovered that complaints about the division of
property arose not only when the father died intestate but
also when a will existed.... (The author originally cited a

case of a brother taking his younger brother's inheritance
from him. For source see note 36. T.D.) Cases of
widowed mothers and sisters being denied their rights of
inheritance were especially frequent in Latgaliya. In 1920
the peasant Tekla Malnats went to court because her brother
took all her father's inheritance and wanted to throw her
out. (37) The same complaint was made by the peasant
Victoria Pug. (38) An interesting case is that of Maria
Hadson in 1925 who complained that she and her two
daughters were being deprived of the use of their inheritance
by her sons (their brothers). The court agreed with her
that they were each entitled to one-seventh of movable and
one-fifth immovable property. (39)

That financial considerations governed relationships between
the very closest members of the family - between brothers or
between children and their parents - is confirmed by the one-
sided transactions and the buying and selling that went on
between the different members of the same family with interests in the inheritance. The peasant Sliksans (of Ekabpils
raion) told us of a highly characteristic case which occurred
in 1957. His father owned a farm of an area of about 20
hectares which was encumbered with debts and was about to
be put up for auction. The eldest son agreed to rescue his
father; he paid off the debt and thus prevented the sale.
But after this the eldest son became the owner, and exercised
his right to force his father and mother and their younger
children to leave the farm.

Relations between husband and wife, their status on the
farm and in the family, were also largely determined by their
relationship to the ownership of the land and immovable property. The real head of the family was always the one regarded as the owner of the farm, i.e. in whose name the inheritance was registered.

The position of a bride in her husband's family was determined by who ran the farm. If it was her father-in-law,
both she and her husband had to obey her husband's parents
in all matters. If her husband inherited the property, her
position in the family changed: she became the mistress and
her husband's parents fell into a dependent position which
increased the less capable they became of working.

The husband's parents usually disapproved strongly of a
widow remarrying outside the family. To stop this, they married her off to one of her late husband's closest relatives,
usually his brother, as quickly as possible. If the bride did
marry a man from another family, and then had children by
him, the new family had only a temporary right to the land
and property of her deceased first husband. This right

lasted until the eldest son of her first marriage came of age.
Then everything was up to him.   Cases are known when the
mother, the stepfather and their children were forced to leave
the farm when the young master entered into his rights;
there are also cases where the eldest son gave his mother and
her new family a small patch of land somewhere on the farm
on which to build themselves a hut.   The children of the
second marriage had no right to their stepbrother's property.
This is confirmed by a court case between two stepbrothers
Osips Yuksa Mukans (the son of the mother's first husband)
and Janis Mukans (the son of her second marriage) over an
area of 5.1 hectares of land.   The court recognised Yuksa's
right of inheritance and excluded his stepbrother from the
property left by the first husband to his widow after his
death. (40)

The relations between heirs who were the children of the
first and second marriages of their father were no less complicated.   The main right of inheritance again belonged to the
children of the first marriage.   This can be seen from a
court case started by the peasant woman Monika Miglane
(1927), the second wife of the deceased peasant Benedicts
Miglans.   A widow, left with four small children, she complained that the guardian of the children of her husband's
first marriage had taken the land (11 hectares) and the rest
of her husband's property into his hands and would not allow
her and her children to use it.   In her plea she insisted that
the appointed part of the movable and immovable property
should be given to her and her children. (41)

The position of the son-in-law-'primak' was even worse than
the position of the bride.   In Latvia there are two words for
son-in-law: the more respectful 'znots' if the daughter leaves
her parents' house, and 'iegnatis' which has a shade of con-
tempt and is used for a son-in-law who settled in his father-
in-law's house, when his wife was the heir to the farm.
The 'iegnatis' not only had no rights to the land (unless they
had been granted by a special agreement), but had to suffer
the continual reproaches of his wife's parents and his wife,
too, for his intrusion into the family.   All the other members
of the family would order him about shamelessly.   'If he
didn't like it,' our informants told us, 'the "primak" could go
back where he came from.'   There were various popular
jokes about the 'primak''s position in the family.   They used
to say of him: 'At Easter everyone goes to church, but the
"primak" stays at home to bewail his lot,' or 'Before you
decide to become a "primak", you should sit for 24 hours on
an ant hill, if you can bear it - you should risk it.'

The young had far greater freedom in the choice of a husband or wife in predominantly Lutheran raions than in

Catholic areas.   But, in both cases, marriages were dependent on the respective wealth of the parties and were therefore usually concluded for financial reasons.   The benefit or
detriment it would bring to the farm always weighed heavily
with parents in deciding the question of their children's
marriages.

The view of marriage as a financial transaction became even
more widespread in the years of the bourgeois dictatorship.
The rural bourgeoisie tried to use the marriage of their children as a means of strengthening their connections with the
commercial and financial bourgeoisie of the towns.   These
marriages were considered the most advantageous.   In the
countryside marriages between representatives of different
classes or different social groups were the exception;   they
led to rifts between children and their parents, who sometimes
took the extreme step of disinheriting them.

Whatever their social group, people did not get married
young: 25 was normal for girls, 30-35 for men.   At the ex-
tremes of the social scale, i.e. among the wealthiest peasants,
and the hired labourers, the marriage age was still higher.
Among wealthy peasants this was evidently because the eldest
son waited to get married until his father transferred the
property to him, and his father was in no hurry to do this,
since he would fall into the background, and then gradually
into a subordinate position.

Among the poor peasants and especially the landless labourers, the postponement of marriage to a later age reflected
their desire to improve their lot and reach a position where
they would be able to support a family.   This usually turned
out to be an unrealisable dream, and after they got married
labourers would continue to live in the house of their master,
crammed together with several other families in the same room,
and all working for him, large and small.

Marriages between people of different ages became increasingly common in these years.   The difference in the ages of
the couple was sometimes as much as 26-7 years.   The
reasons for such marriages were always economic.   Great
importance was attached to the dowry.   There was a custom
of bringing the dowry to the bridegroom's house before the
wedding, to be examined by the bridegroom's relatives.   A
girl with no dowry or a small dowry had no chance of an early
marriage.   A man who brought a penniless wife into the
family would have to endure his parents' bitter reproaches.
In rich families, the dowry, usually made up of household
goods and livestock, often amounted to a considerable sum.

In summing up what has been said about relations with the

family, it must be emphasised that it chiefly refers to the groups of propertied peasants. Among the poor landless peasants and the hired labourers, personal attraction played a decisive role in marriage, as in other relationships. In this sphere, marriage for financial considerations was the exception and happened when the couple were usually of 'unequal ages'.

One unfortunate result of the capitalist system was the high proportion of unmarried people of both sexes among the hired labourers. Their number grew year by year as married labourers were more and more often refused work and unmarried people preferred.

A no less typical phenomenon was the family with few or no children and the simultaneous existence of illegitimate children. In wealthy peasant families parents often consciously limited the number of their children to those they could afford to maintain in their social group and provide with land. Poor peasants had to keep in mind not only the question of their children's future, but also whether they could feed and shelter them. The rate of child mortality was high.

The birth-rate among the groups of poor peasants, and especially among the landless labourers, was so low that it even caused alarm in leading bourgeois circles, and found reflection in print. A series of articles on this subject was published in the Ekabpils uezd newspaper. The agronomist J. Kengis in the article 'Our aim is for workers to have families' wrote:

> The question of a labour force for agriculture will only be satisfactorily settled when we devote ourselves to guranteeing the natural growth of the population as well as improving conditions of life and work in the countryside. This applies equally to the families of peasants and of hired labourers.

The author of the article also remarks 'The number of workers with families has decreased still further since the owners began to give preference to unmarried labourers.' He tries to convince farmowners of the advantages of hiring workers with families, showing that this would not only benefit agriculture but would also ensure the 'production' of new ploughmen. He also lists various privileges the government was thinking of granting to workers with families to encourage people to have children. (42)

Another apparently contradictory phenomenon accompanied the tendency to have less children, that of adopting other people's children. They were mostly adopted (audžu bērni) by families of peasants who based their agriculture on the

exploitation of hired labour.   The practice of adopting and
'educating' orphans, for which they got a state grant, was
nothing other than a hidden form of exploitation of child
labour.   The foster parents preferred to take on the education of girls.   A former orphan explained to us: 'It was
more profitable.   We had to do all the work of looking after
the livestock and the house and they didn't have to worry
about giving us a share in the inheritance.   Even their own
daughters only got a dowry.' (43)

Most of the illegitimate children were the sons and daughters
of hired labourers.   Some hired labourers, seeing no possibility of ever enjoying a normal family life, consciously decided
to have children and then abandon them;   others were forced
to live together by their masters.   It was easy to tell who
was illegitimate in peasant society because they were custom-
arily given their mother's instead of their father's name as
their second name, e.g. Ivan son of Anna, etc.

The consolidation of private property and the intensification
of competition led to a weakening of family ties, a narrowing
of the circle of relatives and the disappearance of family feel-
ing.   This, in turn, had a negative effect on neighbourly relations.   The mutual coldness and aloofness of the time can
be seen through the custom of visiting relations and neighbours only by invitation.   It was not even done to go to a
funeral without an invitation.   Good neighbourly relations
were usually only formed between people of the same social
group, especially among the wealthy peasants.   They tried to
meet other people only outside the farm.

The disunity, the terror of losing advantages gained in conditions of fierce competition that governed relations between
peasants in the Latvian countryside under the bourgeois government, also determined relationships in daily life.   A neighbour who visited the farm without invitation would be greeted
with unconcealed surprise and considerable suspicion.   Why
had he come?   What did he want to see?   What favours did
he want to ask?   Conversation would be held on the porch,
and he would not be invited into the house.   As one peasant
woman E. (Ekabpils raion) remarked to us:

At the end of the 1914 war, almost everybody had been reduced to a condition of poverty and we lived in an abnormal
way.   We often went to see people on neighbouring farms
and spent our spare time with them.   But once our affairs
had been straightened out and we again lived like farmowners our relations noticeably changed.   Everyone began
to look at each other through wolfish eyes.

This happened less among the poor peasants who were united

to a certain degree by the hopelessness of their position,
which was one of continual bondage.   Competition within
these groups of peasants also prevented them from behaving
naturally and openly with each other.   However, the daily
relations between agricultural workers were largely free from
financial calculations.

The conditions in which the oppressed majority of labourers
lived under the bourgeois regime - with no family and in total
isolation from their masters - gave them a desire to meet
people of a similar situation.   However, the possibilities of
such meetings were extremely limited.   Many owners not only
forced their labourers to work all week from early morning to
late evening, but also encroached on their spare time or found
various ways of preventing them from meeting other people.

The differences in social and family positions, resulting from
property and social inequality, were reflected in the way the
peasants addressed one another.   Peasants who owned large
farms were earlier (the end of the nineteenth to the beginning
of the twentieth century) given the name of their piece of
land with the addition of the title 'master' ('saimnieks') or
'mistress' ('saimniece'), for example, master of Birinei, mistress of Rishchkan.

In the bourgeois period when the government's policy of
agrarianisation of the country gave the rural bourgeoisie an
especially privileged position in Latvia, they began to borrow
forms of address from the town - Mr ('kungs'), Mrs ('kundze).
Poor peasants were never addressed in this way.   They were
usually called simply by their surname or by the name of the
farm, but without the addition of master, still less Mr.
Hired labourers, landless peasants and share croppers were
called by their first names, not their surnames.   If there
was more than one person of the same name in the neighbour-
hood, the father's name was added on, e.g. Peter son of Ivan,
Anna daughter of Ivan, etc.

I began my study of the contemporary kolkhoz family and of
the changes in the structure of the family, produced by the
establishment of Soviet power, and the introduction of the
kolkhoz system in Latvia, by examining the size and composition of the family.   With this aim I conducted a questionnaire
on the family in the kolkhozes of Ekabpils, Davgavpils, Abrens
and Kraslavs raions of LSSR.   In all, about 1,200 families
were studied.   The completed questionnaires helped to give
an idea of the size, the sexes and the ages of the family, of
the number of generations and of children, their nationality,
their level of education and their occupation.   The first thing
an analysis of this material reveals is the small size of the
families.   Only two or three people lived in many of the

kolkhoz household units studied.   There was a considerable
number of solitary kolkhozniks.

Another noticeable feature was the extremely small number
of families of three generations, and, on the other hand, the
existence of quite a large group of families of one generation.

A further analysis of the results of the family questionnaire
established the composition of each group.   It turned out
that the vast majority of the group of solitary kolkhozniks
were old people.   An additional questionnaire revealed that
some of the solitary kolkhozniks had adult children who lived
apart from their parents, some in the same kolkhoz.

Most of the one-generation families were couples.   However,
some kolkhoz household units were occupied not by families but
by close relatives, usually elderly unmarried brothers and sisters, who lived and kept house together.   A large number of
the one-generation families had children, who lived apart from
their parents, mostly in the same kolkhoz.   Some of the
couples were childless.

The two-generation families usually included parents and
young or adolescent children, or parents and their adult married and unmarried children.   In all these cases, besides
complete families (with both parents) there are many families
where only the mother is alive, and a small number of families
where only the father is alive.   Three-generation families
usually include the married couple (or one of them), their
young children, and their parents (or one of their parents,
most often the mother).   It should be noted that in more than
half of these cases the couples live with the wife's parents
(this is partly connected with the practice of 'primachestvo'
(primak: T.D.) in the past).

The vast majority of the families studied had few children,
usually 1-2, and more rarely 3, and only a very small number
of families had 4, 5 or more children.

The information provided by this kolkhoz family questionnaire shows that in Latvian SSR, a place where the kolkhoz
system was comparatively recently established, the peasant
family is in a transitional stage of development.   The family
has many features inherited from the past - in particular,
with regard to its structure and size.   The main legacy of
the past is the high percentage of single people, without
families, in the kolkhoz.   A comparison of the data on the
structure of the family with the data on social groupings of
peasants in the past shows that the vast majority of the
solitary old people come from the group of former landless
peasants and hired labourers, the hopelessness of whose

position as regards marriage was discussed above.   The large
number of families with few or no children (44) and also those
with only one parent - the mother - is another sad legacy of
the past.

These are either widows whose husbands died young (usually
from over-work) or mothers of illegitimate children. (45)
Another transitional problem is disintegration of the family
especially during the first stages of collectivisation.   A more
detailed acquaintance with the composition of kolkhoz families
established that this process, a natural consequence of the
kolkhoz system, was less widespread than it seemed.   In
some cases, kolkhozniks who were officially members of two
and sometimes three separate kolkhoz households, in fact lived
as one family, consisting of a married couple, their children
and their parents. or an incomplete family where one of the
couple or parents was missing.   In reality they all live on
the same farm, run their affairs communally, have a common
budget and a common table.

This artificial division of the family usually reflected the
wishes of those who had, until recently, been individual
owners and wanted to strengthen their personal position
within the agricultural artel (artel = the Soviet co-operative
system. T.D.).   We meet with this especially frequently in
the first years of collectivisation, when a section of the peasantry, influenced by enemy agitation about the so-called in-
stability of the kolkhoz system, tried to organise their agriculture on an individual basis.   (46)   Many families were
split up at this time for other reasons: the elderly parents'
fear of placing themselves in an economically dependent position in the family, or their adult children's desire to free
themselves from their obligations to support their elderly
parents.

The tendency to an artificial division of the family, which
occurred at the beginning of collectivisation, did not meet
with decisive counteraction from the raion party and Soviet
organisations, or from the kolkhoz activists at the time.   In
the following years, when the raion organisations devoted
serious attention to this, it was already far more difficult to
liquidate the false divisions permitted earlier.   Today,
judging from materials published in the raion newspapers,
'divided' families continue to exist, though there are very few
of them.

The analysis of the results of the family questionnaire
reveals another phenomenon, which appeared in the transitional period in three-generation families.   Cases where the members of the kolkhoz were representatives of the third, older
generation, while the able-bodied members of the family (i.e.

the representatives of the middle generation) worked else-
where, were relatively common.   Characteristically, in the
vast majority of cases, this occurred in the families of weal-
thier peasants who had not gone to work outside the farm
earlier, before collectivisation.   It is not difficult to guess
that the circumstances here were similar to the ones described
above.   In some cases the artificial division of the family was
done to gain additional profit from the kolkhoz.   In other
cases, the family made a conscious decision to stay together,
so that they would be able to take as much advantage as possible from the kolkhoz - the right to a personal plot, to keep
livestock, etc. (since the elderly parents were members of the
kolkhoz) - while considering themselves free from any obligation to the kolkhoz.   In the first years of collectivisation,
local party and Soviet organs did not pay enough attention to
the inadmissibility of such a consumerist attitude to the
kolkhoz.   Today, such cases are now the exception, and meet
with determined opposition from the kolkhoz activists.

The new life, by its fundamental difference from the old,
gave rise to a series of completely new and positive phenomena
in the family.   Thus, data collected by us on the marriage-
rate after 1940 showed that the implementation of the Soviet
land reform coincided with the rapid formation of new families,
especially by the former hired labourers and the landless
peasants who received land from the Soviet regime.   Characteristically, in the first years of Soviet rule, i.e. until the
beginning of collectivisation, marriages were still conditioned
by the former social system (former hired labourers as a rule
married former hired labourers) - later, with the consolidation
of the kolkhoz system, this phenomenon disappeared.

A comparison between data on the marriage age in the years
of the bourgeois dictatorship in Latvia and earlier to 1917,
and the data for after 1940 shows that the marriage age remained high in the first years after the establishment of Soviet
power.   In later years it fell considerably: to 24-5 for men,
and 21-3 for women.   In the kolkhozes we studied, we found
no evidence of marriages between people of different ages,
whereas there are cases of the younger party instituting
divorce proceedings in unequal marriages concluded earlier.

The data on the number of children shows that childless
couples are now an extremely rare phenomenon.   In recent
years, according to the data collected by us in the above
raions, the number of families with many children has increased.

A study of the contemporary kolkhoz family cannot, of
course, be limited to the data provided by questionnaires.
The personal observations of the ethnographer, the question-

ing of informants, etc., have also a part to play.   Using this
method, the author collected information on other aspects of
family life, in particular material on changes in relations within
the family.

The establishment of the kolkhoz system led to fundamental
changes in the mode of inheritance and the property rights of
members of the family.   The division or the sale of the property can take place only with general consent.   In addition,
the main source of income is no longer the personal plot, but
participation in the social labour of the kolkhoz, and this virtually guarantees each member of the family an equal, economically independent position.   Favourable conditions are thus
created for the extirpation of the private-property psychology
which lay at the basis of relations within the families of the
'peasant-individualists'.   This is a complicated and gradual
process, since it is connected with changes in human psychology and with the destruction of the old ways and traditions -
but its results are already apparent.

Thus, the custom of concluding written contracts between
parents and adult children has completely disappeared.   In
the vast majority of cases we saw, the elderly parents (or one
of them) peacefully live out their lives in the families of their
married children, who show them every care and attention.

There are exceptional cases, however, when the adult children, who have families of their own and elderly parents
(usually the mother) living with them as well, consider it a
burden to support them, although they are not in any financial difficulties, and demand that the kolkhoz take over the
job.   Such cases are direct survivals of the relations between
parents and children which existed under the capitalist system
and give rise to universal condemnation.

Relations between brothers and sisters are now formed on a
new basis.   The consciousness of the fact that no one in the
family is any longer in the privileged position of the future
heir and that the others will not, therefore, have to leave the
parental home, leads to durable and disinterested relations
between relatives.   We have seen many families in which the
younger generation represents a cohesive collective, in which
all are concerned for the well-being and interests of each
member.

The family attitude to the son-in-law has completely changed.
The concept 'iegnatis' (primak) has lost its previous meaning.
The conditions of kolkhoz production mean that it is in the
interests of the family that its members should not leave home
when they marry.   The son in-law who joins the family is
therefore joyfully received and treated with respect.

One reminder of the dependent position primaks occupied in
the recent past is the fact that many kolkhozniks regard different people as the head of the family and the head of the
household.   The head of the family is always a man (except
in a family of widows), whereas it is often a woman who is
regarded as the head of the household.   This is explained by
the fact that, under the individual system of agriculture, the
husbands were primaks.   When they join the kolkhoz the
wives try to keep their former positions as head of the farm.
In later years this problem has no longer arisen.

There has been a fundamental change in the position of the
peasant woman.   The fact that the economic equality of women
was guaranteed was very important in attracting people to the
kolkhoz during the period of collectivisation.   Most of the
peasant women of Latvia very soon valued the advantages of
the kolkhoz system.   They occupied a prominent place in
social labour and in individual spheres of kolkhoz production,
and this, in turn, gave them an entirely new standing in the
family and in society.   The kolkhoz system developed a whole
pleiad of remarkable people, many of them women.

The everyday relationships between peasants underwent
great changes with the establishment of the kolkhoz system.
Private property and the specifics of labour in individual
farming isolated people;   collective ownership of the means of
production and social labour weld them today into a friendly
collective.   Very friendly relations exist between kolkhozniks
(members of field-brigades, workers on livestock farms) since
they are continually rubbing shoulders at work.

The everyday meetings of the kolkhozniks were a great en-
couragement for the emigration from farms to kolkhoz villages
in Latvia.   Now, as we have seen, no one any longer expresses surprise or alarm at the visit of a neighbour or other
kolkhoznik.   He is welcomed, invited to come inside, to sit
down and to chat.   Those kolkhozniks who have radios, and,
more recently, televisions, are delighted to invite their neighbours to listen to concerts or to watch programmes.   The
selection of guests for family celebrations is now conducted
very differently.   For example, the whole brigade is usually
invited to a wedding.   The president and secretary of the
village soviet, who register the marriage, are also honoured
guests.   It is done for guests to come on name-days (and
birthdays) and to see newborn babies (without a special invitation, as it was earlier).   The members of the brigade in
which the father and mother work come to see the mother and
child and bring them presents.

The establishment form of address has become 'comrade'
(biedris) or 'friend' (draugs), but most often people call each

other by their first and second name, especially if they belong
to the same generation.   At meetings the surname is sometimes added....   (The author notes the influence of the
Russians, Bieolorussians, and Ukrainians who have settled
there.   Before Soviet rule they were only in the Eastern part
of Latvia, but now they have increased and moved everywhere.
This is a deliberate nationalities policy. T.D.)

The changes in the family life of Latvian peasants are also
reflected in family rituals.   Under Tsarism and under the
bourgeois regime, the family rituals of the peasants had a
religious character.   The Catholic and Lutheran churches
demanded strict observance of the religious forms of these
ceremonies, both under the Tsars and during the bourgeois
republic.   It must be said, it is true, that the church played
a relatively small role in Latvia under Tsarism because of the
comparatively high level of culture of the peasants.   Latgaliya, where the population was predominantly Catholic and
which was set apart from the rest of Latvia by its economic
and cultural backwardness, was an exception.   Under the
bourgeois dictatorship, in spite of the formal separation of
the church and the state, the priesthood and the state administration worked together to strengthen the influence of the
church.   They had considerable success, and the peasants'
compliance with religion increased, though chiefly in the
formal observance of rituals.

The twenty years following the establishment of Soviet power
in Latvia were remarkable not only for vast reformation in the
economic and cultural life of the republic, but also for the
fundamental changes which took place in the manner of life
and the outlook of the population.   This, in particular, was
manifested in the growth of atheism and the development of
new forms of observance.   Both the town and country population of Latvian SSR made a clean break with religion and the
church.   It was shown most obviously by the sharp decline
in attendance both at ordinary church services and at special
ceremonies.   We observed that very few people now attend
the ordinary Sunday service, and these are usually very old
women.   The majority of churches are even empty on the two
major church holidays (Christmas and Easter). (47)

The lack of parishioners has meant that most Lutheran and
Catholic churches have begun to hold services much more infrequently.   There are many churches where services have
not been held for years.   In the last three years several
churches have been shut on the initiative of the local population.   In a number of parishes the church committees, or
'twenties', have long been inactive or broken up.   One hears
more and more often of cases of village citizens publicly
leaving the twenty.   The younger members of the twenty

(and there are now very few such) are usually people who
hold no position of authority and enjoy no respect among the
local population and whose consciousness, as I have more than
once found, is clouded with other harmful survivals of the
past (private-property instincts, nationalism, extreme individ-
ualism, etc.). The population is gradually abandoning the
religious rituals connected with the human life-cycle, and confirmation services and religious wedding ceremonies are dying
out especially fast. The consciousnesses of most young
people are free from religious survivals.... (The author
points to the fall in confirmations and church weddings. T.D.)

The christening ceremony is still observed by a considerable
number of kolkhoz families. However, these are fewer and
fewer each year, especially among the former Protestant population.... (The author continues to show that fewer christenings are taking place and that when they do the grandparents are blamed for it. T.D.)

Religious funerals are also still quite common in Latvia.
According to church statistics, in 1959 approximately half the
total number of funerals were religious. A sample shows that
the vast majority of these are held in the eastern raions.
However, the research carried out by the author over a
number of years in villages all over Latvia, shows that this
religious ritual is gradually losing its former importance.
This can be seen both from the way in which it is being simplified and from the increasingly common replacement of the
religious ritual by the civic.

Until recently, all ceremonies connected with the remembrance of the dead in Latvia were entirely in the hands of the
church. Only three years ago, the church held prayers in
memory of the dead twice a year in all village cemeteries in
Latvia. One of them, 'kapu svyatki' (the festival of the
graves), was held in summer, the other, 'mirusho diena' (the
day of the dead) or 'ovetsishu vakars' (Candlemas), in late
autumn in the so-called time of souls ('velyu laika'). On these
days, a large number of people of various ages and social
positions gathered in the cemetery. Theoretically, the whole
family including the children used to go. However, our
materials show that in later years older women usually predominated at these ceremonies. The graves were carefully
cleared of grass and decorated with fresh flowers beforehand.
On the day of remembrance everyone came with candles and
bunches of flowers. The ritual included a service in the
cemetery. On 'Candlemas' the prayers were held at dusk.
Large numbers of candles were lit on the graves (sometimes as
many as thirty to forty). It seems to us that the population
had a two-fold attitude to these religious days of remembrance
of the dead. Some, until recently the majority, accepted the

ceremonies as a viable tradition, and condemned those who did not attend the ceremony on the day appointed by the church or who did not tidy the graves in preparation. Others, at first the minority, but one which included the progressive members of the village society, were hostile to the rituals. Although some of the latter visited the cemetery on the day of prayer, they openly expressed the opinion that the initiative for these days of remembrance should be taken out of the hands of the church. In this way, as atheism spread, even the attitude to the most strongly entrenched religious rituals, such as funerals and commemoration of the dead, began to change.

Parallel with the refusal to participate in the above religious ceremonies went an active process of formation of new customs and rituals, and of new traditions, in Latvia. Before describing them, two general features should be noted: the desire of the Latvian population, especially the peasants, to give the new rituals and festivals a national colouring; and the tendency to transfer these festivals or rituals from the family to the social sphere.

We will begin by describing the rituals connected with the birth of a child. News of such an event flies round the kolkhoz, and especially round the brigade where the mother and father work. The kolkhozniks express their congratulations in an oral and sometimes in a written form. People sometimes also send telegrams or special birthday cards, especially if the baby is the couple's first child.

The visitors begin to arrive soon after the mother and baby come back from the hospital. They come from near or far on their own initiative, without invitation, to see the baby and wish him, his mother and the whole family well. These visits are called 'raudzibas'. The circle of people who come to see the baby has now considerably widened. It includes not only relatives and close acquaintances but also members of the kolkhoz on which the mother and father work. These visits, one after the other, often go on for a month, or even longer. The people who come bring presents, usually pies, cakes, etc., and wine. The hosts in their turn should be prepared to feed any number of guests.

In the last three or four years a new custom of social 'baptism' and of formally accepting the new member of society into the village collective has become quite common in the republic. This ceremony has been given the name 'vardu dogianas diena' (namegiving day) or 'bernibas svyatki' (the festival of childhood). Especially many such ceremonies have been held in Kuldigs raion, in the House of Culture of the raion and also in the machine repair workshops of some

kolkhozes there.   These festivals have also been well organised in Tuskums raion, especially in the fishing kolkhoz
'Selga' and also in many kolkhozes and sovkhozes of Balks,
Ergl's, Rsesis, Autss, Ruiens, Ekabpils, and other raions of
the republic.   Festivals of childhood are held at different
times of the year, but preferably in summer.   In many raions
it is timed to coincide with Children's Day, 1 June.   The festival is held in honour of children born in the previous year,
but since it was introduced very recently, children born
earlier are also invited to participate in many parts of the
republic (especially in the places where it was introduced
first).

The idea of 'godparents' - people who, on the parents' request, take the newborn child under their guardianship - is
preserved in the civil form of christening.   The godparents
are invited to the festival as well as the parents and their
children.

The organisers of the festival pay great attention to the
decoration of the building in which it is held.   They usually
choose the village club, or sometimes the school.   The stage
and hall are decorated with greenery, flowers, and posters on
which are written verses and quotations from Latvian poets
and writers, or folk songs appropriate to the festival.
Special chairs, usually garlanded with greenery or flowers,
are set aside for the children's parents and godparents.
They are greeted with music when they enter the hall -
amateur members of the collective play a special repertoire
(e.g. lullabies and nursery rhymes).   The festival usually
begins with the congratulation of the parents by representatives of the kolkhoz, village soviet, school, etc.   They wish
them success in bringing up their children to be valuable members of socialist society and promise that the collective will
give them all possible help in this.   They also usually turn to
the godparents and call on them to take an active part in the
upbringing of their godchildren.   The central moment of the
ceremony is when the parents are presented with special,
beautifully bound commemorative books, in which the child's
name, the date of the festival and the name of the collective
which organised the ceremony are written.   No less important
is the moment when the child's name is inscribed in the book
of the kolkhoz or village soviet (depending on who organised
the ceremony).   The president of the village soviet (or
kolkhoz) usually calls both the parents and the godparents to
his table for this, and their names are written in the book
opposite the name of the child with the fact that they are
taking on responsibility for his upbringing.   If the child was
born only a short time before, the official registration of birth
also takes place during the festival.   The presentation of
commemorative gifts usually ends the official part of the cere-

mony. The festival carries on with a short concert, given
by artistic amateurs. In some collectives, where the number
of people is comparatively small, refreshments are also provided. My personal observations, and the accounts of many
people who have taken part in these festivals, show that the
'namegiving days' are already very popular and widely accepted by the village population. For example, in places where
festivals of childhood are organised at irregular intervals or
not at all, the local inhabitants, led by the mothers, have
made insistent requests for the village Soviets and social
organisations to arrange them. It also seems to be true that
where these festivals are held, they play a very positive role
in eliminating religious christenings among the peasantry.
The statistics show this, and the kolkhozniks themselves speak
of it.

The coming-of-age festivals ('piligadibas'), introduced quite
recently, are even more popular and more generally accepted
by the workers of Latvia. These youth festivals, initiated
by the Central Committee of the Komsomol of the republic,
were first celebrated in 1957, and, in the short time since
then, the majority of the youth of Latvia has taken part in
them. Let us quote some figures. In Ekabpils raion, for
example, the coming-of-age festivals were first held in 1958
when 175 boys and girls took part; in 1959 in the same raion
600 people were involved; while in Dobel's raion in 1960 there
were 800 participants, and only 12 of those eligible did not
attend the festival. These figures show that the young have
been liberated from the influence of the church. The new
social festival in honour of coming-of-age is ousting the religious ritual, and is representative of the youth of today -
boys and girls who have consciously broken with the church.

The coming-of-age festival is held in the summer and is
usually timed to coincide with the Day of Soviet Youth, which
is observed throughout the Soviet Union on the last Sunday of
June. In this case, activities are organised not just for the
18-year-olds but for all the young people. However, the 18-
year-olds are the centre of attention. In many raions of the
republic it has become a tradition to invite the young people
who will be 18 that year to a camp at the raion centre, several days before the festival. There the young men and
women hear lectures on various topics - the rights and obligations of the Soviet citizen, communist morality, how young
people should behave in society, the principles on which a
healthy life should be based. They also learn new Soviet
mass songs and dances. Sports and competitions are organised for them. Often while they are at the camp, the young
people are introduced to old revolutionaries, leading members
of the kolkhoz and industrial enterprises, writers, painters
and actors. The camp programme also includes organised

excursions around the district and to the tourist centres of
the republic, and visits to the theatre and opera.   These
preliminaries to their coming-of-age attract the youth to the
festival and the vast majority of them await it with great im-
patience.

On the day, if it is held on a raion scale, the ceremony
begins with a solemn procession of the young people from the
camp to the place where the festival is held.   All the local
inhabitants come out to watch the brightly coloured column of
young people, headed by the president of the raion Komsomol
organisation.   At the entrance to the raion House of Culture
the procession is met by the pioneers, older komsomoltsi,
guests and parents.   After the opening ceremony one of the
directors of the festival congratulates the 18-year-olds sitting
at the front of the hall.   Then the ceremony of presenting
the coming-of-age certificates begins.

The coming-of-age certificate, introduced into the republic
on the initiative of the Central Committee of the Komsomol, is
a beautifully bound commemorative booklet in which is written
the name of the young man or woman, the date of his or her
coming-of-age and various good wishes, usually in verse.
The 18-year-olds are often given other presents as well as the
certificates, usually books.

When the ceremony of presenting the certificates ends, the
youths are congratulated by representatives of the social
organisations, the pioneers and their workmates, friends and
relatives, and they are given masses of flowers.   It is an extremely merry and joyful occasion.   The orchestra plays folk
melodies and Soviet youth songs.   Those taking part in the
festival sing mass songs such as 'My country is a wide country', 'The hymn of the democratic youth', etc.   A big concert, carnivals, games, torchlight processions, walks in the
parks and other amusements follow - in some cases immediately
after the official part, in others, after a break.

The coming-of-age festivals are held not only in the raion
centre but also in many village soviets, where they are organised by the collectives of the enterprises, kolkhozes and
sovkhozes, and also the educational establishments of the
raion.

The coming-of-age festivals organised by the kolkhozes or
other productive collectives are almost exactly the same as the
raion ones.   Many people come to them from neighbouring
kolkhozes and schools, from Riga or other towns and villages
of the republic with which the collectives have economic or
social-cultural connections.   The kolkhoz festivals are particularly friendly and enjoyable because all those taking part

know each other well and are members of a single unified
working collective.   These festivals usually include a supper
at which the young members of the collectives are congratulated on the attainment of their majority and toasts are drunk to
them.   Coming-of-age is also always celebrated within the
family.

Both the rural population's attitude to marriage and the form
of the wedding ceremony have undergone fundamental changes
in contemporary conditions.   If earlier marriage was the private affair of a small circle of relatives, today it is an event
of social importance in Soviet and kolkhoz life, and all the
members of the village collective in which the marriage takes
place are involved in it.   They see (if necessary) to the
creation of the essential material conditions for the life of the
young family (that they have jobs and somewhere to live),
take an active part in the preparation and organisation of the
wedding, often taking all the arrangements on themselves.
These are called social or komsomol weddings.

The wedding rituals practised by the kolkhozniks have now
been greatly simplified.   Matchmaking and dowries have died
out, and the wedding is no longer held in two different places
as it was before (first in the bride's parents' house, then in
the bridegroom's parents' house), but in one - the place
where the newlyweds are going to live.   The organisers of
the wedding and the guests always try to ensure that some of
the older popular traditions are observed, in combination with
the new ones which have appeared in recent years.

In the vast majority of cases the registration of marriages
takes place on the day of the wedding and is an integral part
of the wedding ceremony.   However, in the kolkhozes of
Davgapils raion we came across another well-established
system.   In this, the registration of marriage takes place not
less than two or three days before the wedding, and is seen
as a sort of betrothal, after which the bride and bridegroom's
families officially announce the forthcoming marriage.   Meanwhile, the young people do not begin their married life, but
merely consider each other engaged and go on living in their
parents' families until the wedding.   They are not considered
married until the wedding celebration has taken place.

Weddings can be held at any time of the year but they most
often take place in autumn and spring.   Saturday is the favourite day of the week.   They begin in the evening.   When
the wedding and the registration of marriage are held on the
same day, the ceremony begins with the trip to the ZAGS.
The wedding procession sets off for the village soviet, where
the ceremony of registering the marriage is performed.   The
president and secretary of the village soviet come to the

village soviet specially dressed up (sometimes in national costume); the building is often decorated in honour of the occasion - birch or fir trees are placed by the door and garlands
of greenery are twined round the chairs destined for the
newlyweds.

The newlyweds come to register their marriage with their
sponsors, a large group of young people and sometimes musicians. Cars are now usually used instead of carriages for
the wedding procession. Taxis are usually hired from the
nearest town for the young couple and their sponsors, or
they borrow someone's private car. All the rest travel in
the kolkhoz trucks. The cars are decorated with birch (in
winter, with fir). The bride and bridegroom are usually
already dressed in their wedding clothes: the bride in a
white dress with a veil, the bridegroom in a black suit, white
shirt and light-coloured tie. If the wedding is held a long
way from the place of registration the guests congratulate the
young couple on the spot in the village soviet; the musicians
play a flourish and the hosts provide glasses of wine and cake
for the young couple and their guests. Sometimes congratu-
latory telegrams and presents are sent to the village soviet
and given out after the registration.

The ceremonies which follow retain many traditional features.
The path of the wedding procession is blocked by locked gates
and similar obstructions, through which they have to 'buy'
their way. More obstacles are sometimes set up in front of
the gates of the farm the wedding procession is going to.
When they arrive at the bridegroom's parents' house (or the
house in which the wedding is to be held) his parents meet
them on the threshold with bread, salt and wine. Before the
young couple enter the house, they give presents to the
bridegroom's father and mother and his close relatives (in
some cases the presents are handed out later at the end of
the wedding feast). The wedding feast usually lasts for two
days - Saturday and Sunday.

At weddings where the old traditions are adhered to, they
perform the ceremony of 'michoshana' (in this the garland
is removed from the bride's head and replaced with a woman's
headdress - a scarf). Sometimes they pin flowers to her hair
instead. Contests of wit and songs between the bride's and
bridegroom's parties still occupy an important place at weddings. This is particularly widespread in Latgaliya.

It is interesting to see how the principle on which guests
are invited has changed in comparison with previous years.
The circle of people has widened to include comrades from
work (for example members of the brigade) and representatives of the kolkhoz and village society. One now often hears
such expressions as 'we have had a wedding in our brigade.'

There are also komsomol or social weddings.   They are
usually held in the kolkhoz club, the House of Culture, or the
school (if the kolkhoz has no club).   The komsomol wedding
ritual includes many old popular traditions, although it is here
that the youth have taken the greatest initiative in inventing
and practising various new ceremonies, chiefly of a gay light-
hearted character.   A very large number of people attend
such weddings - 'the whole kolkhoz celebrated it,' as one
often hears of komsomol weddings.

The ancient popular traditions and newly formed customs
are most closely interwoven in the funeral ceremonies.   It is
also here that local features are the most consistently preserved.   The dead man is immediately washed, dressed, placed
on a bed covered with a sheet until his coffin is made or
brought.   On the following day he is placed in the coffin.
From then on the custom varies.   In a large part of Latvia
the coffin is carried out of the house to one of the outbuild-
ings - a storeroom, shed or cellar.   The building is first
cleaned, cleared out and decorated with branches of fir.
The coffin is placed on a low stand (e.g. a stool), covered
with a homespun blanket, and the lid is shut.   The dead
man usually lies like this for not less than a week, while the
funeral arrangements are made.   All this time, practically no
one goes into the building and no honours are paid to the
dead man (this is just so that the body will not begin to de-
compose).   In the eastern raion of Latvia the dead man is
kept in the house, not left alone and always buried on the
third day.

It is customary for people only to attend funerals by invitation, and it is regarded as an honour to be given an invitation.   The kolkhoz musicians are invited to many funerals,
and sometimes a choir as well.   The funeral gathering begins
in the afternoon, and the actual burial takes place in the
cemetery at sunset.   All the guests bring flowers or wreaths
to the dead man's house, and place them on the coffin.   They
also usually observe a tradition called 'the last supper' after
which they all go out into the yard and go up to the coffin in
turn to say goodbye to the dead man.   The central figure of
the ceremony becomes from this moment the 'guide of the
dead'.   The relatives ask one of the most influential and eloquent of the local inhabitants, preferably a man (though there
are cases of women being chosen), to fulfil this honoured role.
The choice often falls on a teacher.   The guide makes a
speech before the procession sets off from the dead man's
house and another in the cemetery, before the coffin is
lowered into the grave.   On both occasions the speaker talks
of the dead man's achievements and his particular merits.

Trucks are now commonly used for the funeral procession.

However, the older people often insist on tracing the last road in the old way, on horseback.   The guide leads the funeral procession.   If they go to the cemetery in cars, he sits in the front seat of the car which carries the coffin. On their arrival at the cemetery the coffin is again opened for a ceremonious leave-taking of the dead man: the guide says his last word, some of the guests make farewell speeches, the choir sings funeral hymns, the orchestra plays. The guide invites everyone to take leave of the deceased, and the coffin is then lowered into the grave, which is decorated at the bottom and sides with branches of fir and covered above with a blanket.   Everyone present then throws three handfuls of earth onto the lid of the coffin, saying 'Have a good journey.'

After the burial of the coffin the funeral guests bring wreaths up to the grave, say more warm words of farewell to the dead man and lay the wreaths on the grave.   The relatives then offer the guests bread and wine with the request that they should remember the deceased.   The guests then go back to the dead man's house where the traditional wake takes place.

The new burial customs include civil funerals, organised by the village soviets, the kolkhoz administration and the social organisations.   This is the form of burial used for those who have done outstanding revolutionary, social or productive service.   Here the coffin is left in the village House of Culture, a guard of honour stands watch by the coffin, and funeral meetings are held there.   A large number of the local inhabitants take part in the funeral - the members of the local kolkhozes, the rural intelligentsia, the school children.

To conclude our description of contemporary customs and rituals, it only remains to acquaint the reader with the new civil ceremony of commemorating the dead.   We have already mentioned the growing desire of the village population that the custom of visiting the graves of the dead on a particular day should be freed from its religious associations.   In response to those wishes, some village soviets and social organisations of the kolkhozes of Latvia decided to take the initiative into their own hands and organise a day of remembrance of the dead.

The preparations for this day were made by the deputies to the village soviets, the representatives of the party and komsomol organisations of the kolkhoz, and teachers.   The initiative taken by the village organisations found a wide response among the workers, kolkhozniks and the rural intelligentsia. The local inhabitants were notified beforehand of the new day of remembrance of the dead.   Long before the appointed day

they tidied up the graves of those dear to them, planted
flowers, and sprinkled the paths with sand.   A large number
of people gather at the cemetery on the day - far more than
for the religious service practised in previous years.

In the last two or three years the civil rituals dedicated to
the commemoration of the dead have been held in many village
cemeteries.   One can predict that not many years from now,
the old church ritual of commemorating the dead will have
completely died out.

The process of the reconstruction of the family life and outlook of the kolkhoz peasants of Latvia has great prospects for
future development.   The guarantee of this is the certainty
of victory for the socialist means of production, the scale of
cultural construction and the growth of political awareness of
the population of the republic.   Latvian agriculture is ad-
vancing.   The output of animal produce, the main branch of
agriculture, and of crops, is growing from year to year.
The vast majority of the peasants of Latvia now live prosper-
ously.   The continuous growth of the material wealth of the
kolkhozniks, their certainty of the future, will lead to the
disappearance of many of the traditional features of family life
left over from the capitalist period.

The kolkhoz peasantry today takes an active part in the
political life of the country.   Many kolkhozniks are deputies
of village soviets and some of them are deputies of republics
and higher organs of Soviet power.   The tendency of the
leading section of the peasantry to join the Communist Party
is a clear indication of the growth of their political maturity.
Every kolkhoz in the republic already has its party organisation.   The membership of the kolkhoz komsomol organisations
has significantly increased.   The kolkhozniks display an
active interest in national and international events.

The successes obtained in a comparatively short time in
raising the cultural level of the Latvian peasantry are of equal
educative value.   Universal 7-year education was introduced
in Soviet Latvia several years ago.   The transition to 8-year
education is now under way.   Many young people carry on
with their education after finishing their 7 or 8 years at
school.   Most of them take up some agricultural profession
and stay in the village where specialists are greatly needed.
As well as specialists, the number of teachers, doctors,
workers in clubs, houses of culture and libraries has greatly
increased.

The new features of family life appear above all in families
(especially young ones) whose members include representatives
of the progressive section of the village population described

above.   There is also a completely new and comparatively
widespread practice of marriage between members of the rural
intelligentsia and the peasantry.

   The growth of political activity of the peasantry, the raising
of their cultural level, and the changing composition of the
village population contribute to a break with the old customs
and encourage the creation of the new Soviet family, the formation of a progressive outlook and a new Soviet morality.

NOTES

1 The author has materials relating to the second half of the
   nineteenth century, but does not make use of them in the
   present work.
2 The northern and central part of Latvia (Liflyandiya) was
   joined to Russia first (in 1721, under the Treaty of Nish-
   tad);   the eastern districts of Latvia (Latgaliya) were
   gained by Russia in 1772 after the first partition of
   Poland.   Kurland province was formed from the Duchy of
   Kurland in 1795.
3 The emancipation of the peasants from serfdom took place
   in these provinces almost half a century earlier than in
   the interior provinces of Russia (in Liflyandiya in 1817;
   in Kurland in 1819) through a settlement by which the
   peasants were also 'emancipated' from the land.   The land
   became the property of the German landowners and the
   peasants rented it from them for large amounts of money.
   The peasants of Liflyandiya and Kurland provinces were
   given the right to buy land in the 1860s, but the majority
   of them were unable to take advantage of this until the
   1880s and 1890s.
4 The German conquerors began a forcible liquidation of the
   communal type of settlement as early as the fifteenth-six-
   teenth centuries.
5 The splitting up of the countryside into farms was begun
   under Stolypin and continued by the bourgeois dictatorship (for more about this see below).
6 See V.I. Lenin, 'Collected Works', vol. 3, p. 205.
7 For example, in 1910, 19.4 per cent of farmers in Liflyandiya and Kurland Provinces had mechanical ploughs;   in
   other provinces of Russia, 3.4 per cent.   In these provinces, there was one seeding machine per 18 farmers;   in
   others one per 70 (for more about this, see S.A. Udachin,
   'Land Reform in Soviet Latvia', Riga, 1948, p. 31).
8 In the Baltic provinces, as has been said, there was one
   seeding machine per 18 peasant farmers, in Latgaliya, one
   per 20 (see 'A History of the Latvian SSR', vol. 2, Riga,
   p. 367).
9 S.A. Udachin, op. cit., p. 23.

10   Ibid., pp. 21, 30.
11   Ibid., p. 70.
12   Ya. Krastin, The Peasantry of Latvia under the Yoke of the Plutocracy, 'World Economy and World Politics', 1940, no. 9, p. 56.
13   For more detail, see S.A. Udachin, op. cit., pp. 93-7.
14   Ibid., p. 124.
15   Ibid.
16   In 1935-9, between 16,000 and 23,000 agricultural workers left Latgaliya each year to work in other parts of Latvia, not including the large number of peasants who went to work in the towns.
17   Valuable materials on the large undivided Latgaliyan family and the process of its disintegration can be found in the synopsis of L.S. Efremova's Candidate thesis, 'The Family and Family Life of the Latgaliyan Peasants in the Second Half of the Nineteenth Century and early Twentieth Century', Riga, 1960.
18   There were ten people in P. Lezdins's family, himself, his wife and his eight children (five sons and three daughters).   As the will shows, he appointed as his heirs to the farm and the whole property, not one, but two sons.   They were put under the obligation of paying a certain share to the remaining three sons and of providing dowries for their three sisters, Materials of the Central State Archives of the Latvian SSR, Collection 1536, vol. 25, folio 13992, line 6.
19   Ibid., Collection 1450, vol. 25, folio 14009, line 12 (obverse).
20   Ibid., Collection 1450, vol. 25, folio 13998, line 16 (obverse).
21   Taken down by the author from the testimony of one of the sons (Jania Leisavnieks) of the aforesaid peasant (Archive of the Institute of Ethnography of the Academy of Sciences of the USSR, Collection of the Baltic Expedition).
22   Materials of the Central State Archive of the Latvian SSR, Collection 1606, folio 561, line 2.
23   Materials of the Central State Archive of the Latvian SSR, Collection 16, folio 561, line 7, 7 obverse, line 8, 8 obverse.
24   Ibid., Collection 1606, folio 599, line 1 obverse.
25   'Ankambar' is one of the rooms of the dwelling house.
26   Materials of the Central State Archive of the Latvian SSR, Collection 1536, vol. 25, folio 14001, line 18.
27   For more about adopted children, see below.
28   Materials of the Central State Archive of the Latvian SSR, Collection 1606, folio 588, line 1.
29   Ibid., line 11.
30   Archive of the Institute of Ethnography of the USSR Academy of Sciences, Baltic Collection, 1961.

31 K. Marx and F. Engels, 'Communist Manifesto', Moscow, 1948, pp. 49-50.
32 This was done, for example, by a peasant of Friedrich-stadt District, M. Mezmalis, in 1914.   The owner of the document, Ya. Mezmalis, allowed the author to make a copy of it; it is kept in the Archive of the Institute of Ethnography, the original is written in Russian, with a Latvian translation attached.
33 Materials of the Central State Archive of the Latvian SSR, Collection 1606, folio 561, line 2.
34 Ibid., folio 589, line 5.
35 Ibid., folio 566, line 4.
36 Ibid., Collection 1536, vol. 25, folio 13998, line 3.
37 Ibid., Collection 1606, folio 597, line 1 obverse.
38 Ibid., folio 535, line 15.
39 Ibid., folio 532, line 31 obverse.
40 Ibid., folio 589, line 5, 5 obverse.
41 Ibid., folio 566, line 4.
42 J. Kengis, Giminese Laukstradnieki Musu Merkis, 'Jekab-pils Vestnesis', 2 February 1939 (in Latvian).
43 Archive of the Institute of Ethnography of the USSR Academy of Sciences, Baltic Collection, 1956.
44 Here we should remember the low birthrate in the Bour-geois period.
45 Women who lost their husbands in the great Patriotic War at the front are relatively few.
46 This is confirmed by comparison with the results of the family questionnaire naming groups of manual and white-collar workers living in the village soviets.   The percentage of three generation families in this group is significantly higher, as there were no economic incentives to divide the family.
47 Thus, in 1960, only 23 people gathered for Easter Matins in the Lutheran Church in Davgavpils and only three of them were aged 23-5, the rest being considerably older (Materials of the Davgavpils Pedagogical Institute).

Part IV
THE CAUCASUS

INTRODUCTION

Georgia, Armenia and Azerbaijan form the trans-Caucasian republics, but also included in this area are the north Caucasian territories, which are part of the Russian Soviet Federation of Socialist Republics, containing a mosaic of peoples speaking up to fifty different languages and dialects. Chechen-Ingusheti, Daghestan, Kabardia and Circassia and northern Ossetia are among the largest groupings and form autonomous republics within the RSFSR. Ethnographers there train mostly in Russia although some have come to Georgia where an established school has existed since the 1930s, founded by G. Chitaya and V. Bardavelidze. There are now two large departments at the University of Tbilisi and the Georgian Academy of Sciences.

The anthropologists in the three trans-Caucasian Union republics publish mainly in their own languages. The north Caucasians publish in Russian, but it is difficult for the Western scholar, so far, to visit at least two of the main centres of learning there since Maykop and Nalchik, two of the regional capitals, are closed to foreigners. A perusal of available literature from there gives one the impression that a major interest of north Caucasian ethnographers is in material culture, and another interest is in linking the history of their people's customs to those of other ancient peoples and well-known historical events. There are some forays by Russian ethnographers from the Moscow Institute's Caucasian Sector into the Caucasus to do fieldwork, mainly with the help of interpreters, and their work is published centrally and readily available in the West. Georgian, Armenian and Azeri Turkish are not easy languages to learn which precludes most other scholars from appreciating some of the best standards of anthropological writing there ever were, or of being aware of the sheer volume of works published on all aspects of anthropology, from ethno-musicology to new methods in physical anthropology.

Vera Bardavelidze's paper on sworn brotherhood centres on the relations between mountain and valley peoples in the past. They share most features of the Georgian people: the Georgian state was one of the first to convert officially to

Christianity in circa AD 337, and although the integration of
Greek Orthodox Christianity into the native religions of the
mountain peoples has always been less complete than in the
valleys, they share much of the idiom and imagery.   Geor-
gians recognise cognatic descent, although clan surnames and
main allegiances are patrilineal.   You may not marry anyone
to whom you are related through ancestors up to seven generations back, and this strict exogamic rule is adhered to
even today in the most urban circles as well as the countryside.   To create relationships of trust and mutual aid with
non-kin there are two options – to form a marriage alliance,
or to form a link of spiritual kinship.   This paper illustrates
both the historical depth of this still lively tradition, and also
some of the special political uses to which one form of spiritual
kinship was put, which, in contrast to its other uses, became
obsolete with the end of the Georgian monarchy in 1802.

9 The institution of 'modzmeoba' (adoptive brotherhood): an aspect of the history of the relations between mountain and valley populations in Georgia
*Vera Bardavelidze**

There is evidence of the existence of three customs of sworn brotherhood among the population of Georgia in ancient times:

(a) The two parties to an oath of brotherhood met, accompanied by their relations, in front of a sanctuary ('khati', literally 'ikon', but the term is also used to describe the sanctuary or shrine dedicated to it. T.D.), or in a 'jvari' (literally 'cross', but means 'shrine' in this context. T.D.), to which one of them brought a sheep, a calf or other animal for sacrifice. A prayer was offered for the sacrifice, after which the governor of the valley, chief priest of the sanctuary ('khevisberi', literally 'elder of the valley', elected by valley residents. T.D.) slew the beast and sprinkled its blood on those who were taking the oath. At the same time they swore, once or more, brotherly loyalty and love and laid a curse on either of them who should break the oath or betray his sworn brother, i.e. his 'modzme' (fraternal comrade. T.D.) or 'dsmobili' (adoptive brother. T.D.). (1)

(b) Those who took an oath of brotherhood, usually at a wedding or other festive gathering of a large number of people, would cut the little fingers of their right hands, making the incision in such a way that the blood from both wounds mingled together. At the same time they pronounced a vow of brotherly loyalty and love towards each other.

(c) The ceremony known as the Oath of Silver was performed with food and drink; each of the participants dipped the silver part of his weapon in a vessel of wine, beer, 'araqi' (home-brewed vodka. T.D.), or, more rarely, milk, and uttered the ritual oath: 'Your father is my father, your mother is my mother, your brother my brother, your sister my sister, your wife my sister-in-law, your enemy my enemy.' Then the sworn brothers drank together once or twice. When they began the meal, the 'khevisberi' pronounced a blessing in the following terms: 'May the Father Lord (i.e. God. T.D.) not sever your brotherhood; love each other until death: neither let your grandchildren hate each other after your death.' Through popular belief, this verbal formula of sworn brotherhood was preserved as an adage from generation to generation.

* First published in 'Matsne', the Journal of the Georgian Academy of Sciences, 1971.

There was another custom of sworn brotherhood, which was a combination of the last two: those taking the oath pricked the little finger of their right hands, pressed out the blood into a vessel of wine or 'araqi', offered it to each other and drank, then incised the fingers, once more mixed their blood together and at this time uttered the above formula.

After the oath-taking ceremony both parties drank a toast to each other from a drinking horn of 'araqi', after drawing lots to decide who was to drink first.   Next, they gave each other valuable presents - such as a silver-mounted dagger, silver rings, etc. - after which for the rest of their lives they behaved to each other in the strictest accordance with their vow, in adversity as in prosperity, always aiding each other with a devotion which often went to desperate lengths.

The mutual dependence and obligations of sworn brothers have been well described by an old man in the following words:

> Sworn brothers were always together, in sorrow as in joy. When a community 'themi' (sub-tribe.   local group in pre-industrial society, in the Marxist understanding.   T.D.) was preparing for an attack on their enemies, one of the sworn brothers would address the other in these terms: 'Together we stand and together we fall, but if one of us should perish the other shall not abandon the dead.'

Our informant also relates how, when one of them suffered a material loss, his sworn brother divided his own possessions in half - whether it was a flock of sheep or a herd of cattle - and gave one part to his deprived sworn brother.   In building a house, sworn brothers would give each other the same assistance as natural brothers.   If one of them fell ill and had no one to work on his land, the other would bring out his plough, harness his sworn brother's oxen and plough his fields as if they were his own.   When one sworn brother who had a mortal enemy went to visit the shrine ('khati') the other would accompany him, to defend him from his enemy.   If one was mortally wounded he would leave his sworn brother this charge: 'Make peace with my enemy if you can;   otherwise - avenge me.'   And indeed his sworn brother would pursue his enemy and take revenge on him as he would for his own brother's sake.   The same speaker relates:

> There is a story with us that one Pshav killed another, but no one could discover who was the slayer.   The dead man's sworn brother searched for him seven years.   At last he slew a Kisti, but when he reloaded his gun, blood flowed from the bullet.   That was a sign that the Kisti was not his brother's killer, that is to say, he had been in too much

haste, he had not taken enough pains to find his brother's
killer. (Pshav = inhabitant of the Georgian mountain
province of Pshaveti. Kisti = neighbouring, non-Georgian
tribesman. T.D.)

It was a rule of sworn brotherhood that those who took the
oath should have exogamous relations (i.e. they and their
descendants should not intermarry. T.D.). For all the
latter part of their lives they would give each other fraternal
aid, but when one sworn brother died his kinsfolk would
invite the other to meet before the 'khati' where the children
and grandchildren of both brothers together discharged the
'spiritual debts' of the deceased. It is interesting to note
that a man would take as much care of his sworn brother's
wife as if she had been his own sister-in-law.

Relations of sworn brotherhood and sisterhood were established in just the same way between parties of different sexes.

Thus, we see that although the oath of brotherhood and
sisterhood was taken between individuals, nevertheless it
united in an adoptive relationship not only those who swore it
but the families on both sides.

Often people of the same village formed an alliance through
an oath of brotherhood for the purpose of taking concerted
action against a common enemy. In this way the population
was united; for instance, a village of Khevsureti was hostile
towards the Ghlighwis (Galgais) in Khadu, who had carried off
their cattle.

As has been observed in Khevsureti and Mtiuleti, the institution of sworn brotherhood was also made use of when enemies
were reconciled. (2)

Pshav and also Kisti valley governors often settled their
quarrels by an oath of brotherhood, the procedure of reconciliation between the two parties being completed by the ceremony of the Oath of Silver. (3)

Likewise, the oath of brotherhood was often used in the
Pshav institution of brotherhood and sisterhood, which formulated the special, established customary law on intimate relations between young men and girls. As soon as the young
people had performed the ceremony with silver coin, they gave
no outward sign afterwards of the bond between them except
to persons who knew about it.

The practice of sworn brotherhood took place between Georgian mountain dwellers and their neighbours of foreign descent
- Kistis, Chechens, Ghlighwis (Galgais) and Ossetes. It is a

point of interest that the sworn brothers regarded it as their
sacred duty to help each other in every way in the event of
one of them needing aid against his fellow-villagers. (4)

There is ample evidence of the existence of sworn brotherhood and sisterhood among the people of the Caucasus as a
means of establishing an adoptive kinship relationship between
individuals, and through them moreover between the families
of both parties.   It was widespread also among many peoples
outside the Caucasus.   Furthermore it existed at various
social and economic periods of the class-based social order,
not only in traces from the distant past, but as an active
judicial institution serving to establish social and political
alliances both within the Caucasus and beyond its borders.

It is mentioned first of all by the ancient classical writers
Herodotus and Tacitus.   In the words of Herodotus, 'when
the Lydians and the Medes concluded a treaty, the representatives of both sides cut the skin of their hands and their
blood was mingled' (Herodotus I, 74, tr. W. Beloe).   In the
words of the same writer, the Arabs in their negotiations dyed
the rocks designating a boundary with the blood of the two
parties.   Finally, Herodotus informs us that in Scythia the
parties to a settlement would drink their own blood mixed with
wine and dip their weapons in it. (5)   Information is found
in Tacitus concerning sworn brotherhood as a judicial institution.   When Tacitus tells us about an Iberian king, the boy
Pharsman, led by Rhadamistus, King of Armenia, into working
evil against Mithridates, he is emphasising an event that is
strongly in contrast to a characteristic feature of the Georgian
popular custom of sworn brotherhood - the sacrificial offering
to the 'khati':   when King Mithridates came to the place
appointed for concluding the treaty, he followed Rhadamistus
'into a neighbouring grove where he assured him that the
appointed sacrifice had been prepared for the confirmation of
peace in the presence of the gods.'   Later, Tacitus gives a
description of the means employed by the kings of Georgia
and Armenia to confirm the conclusion of a peace treaty:

It is a custom of these princes whenever they form an alliance, to unite their rights hands and bind together the
thumbs in a tight knot: then, when the blood has flowed
into the extremities, they let it escape with a slight punc-
ture and suck it in turn.   Such a treaty is thought to have
a mysterious sanctity, as being sealed with the blood of both
parties (Annals, XII, 47, tr. Church and Broadribb).

Sworn brotherhood as a political institution of uniform
character having the force of law, was regarded of old among
Georgian mountain dwellers as the sworn brotherhood of their
communal deities.   The act of sworn brotherhood, again as

between the parties to an alliance, was actually performed in
the name of the deities of the community by their chiefs who
at the same time represented the servants of the principal
cult of the community's 'khati' or 'jvari'. The explanation of
this practice must be sought from the point of view that the
shrine represents in itself the unity of the community of which
it is held to be the highest governor and protector. (6)   It
is natural, therefore, that on all this we should have abundant material concerning the union between deities through the
institution of mutual sworn brotherhood and sisterhood (alliances between communities stabilised through this institution),
in religious forms and ceremonies, and especially in the texts
of those who served cults in the mountain population of eastern Georgia.   Thus, for example, certain texts of highland
'sadidebelthai' (benediction prayers) mention the oath of
brotherhood between the god-hero Kopala and an angel, the
deity of the homestead, and similarly the sworn brotherhood
of the deity Sharaveli with the angel (7) of the peak of
Maghatzal, etc. (8)

     The sister- brotherhood deities representing the different
sexes is well illustrated in the religious beliefs of the Khevsurs (inhabitants of the Georgian mountain province of
Khevsureti. T.D.).   For example, Samdzimari, the Khevsur
goddess of fertility, was generally regarded as the sister of
the communal deity Giorgi of Hakhmati; but the 'Mother of
God of Likoki' (a fusion between local and Christian beliefs
characteristic of the Georgian mountain peoples.   T.D.) was,
on the one hand, the communal deity of Likoki at the sanctuary of Karatis Jvari, and, on the other hand, she was also
the adoptive sister of the deity of all Khevsurs at the Gudani
sanctuary.   At the same time, on the one hand their own
Khevsur 'Likoki Mother of God', and Nakharela, the Mother of
God of the Kistis, were sworn sisters, and, on the other
hand, the Kistis and the Gudanis shared Nakharela as their
own Mother of God.   Now here as regards sworn brotherhood
between deities of the male sex, there may be seen no less
clearly, set beside the corresponding Pshav material, the
social roots of this institution.   In accordance with Khevsur
religious beliefs, the following were sworn brothers: the
Shrine of the Chains (Jachvis Jvari) of the Ochiauri clan was
linked to the Shrine of the Fields (Mindoris Jvari) of the
Chabakauri patrilineage, who had joined the Narozauli clans.
As we know, these communities were component cells of the
Akhiela local lineage. (9)   The Shrine of Iron (Rkenis Jvari)
of the lineage of Amghi, which was at the same time the Shrine
of the Tsiklauri Amghi lineage, was linked in the same village
to the 'pillar' of the deity Iakhsar of the Chinglat patrilineage.
Two deities of the Chirdili local community were regarded as
each other's sworn brothers, and were called by Christian
names: St George and the Mother of God;   at the same time

these deities were 'sworn brothers' with the local community's
valley shrine of the Uken Akho Angel.   They were likewise
linked to the valley deity at the Arkhoti shrine and to the
deity Michael the 'Next-door Neighbour', protector of the
Gaburs of the community in Chimghi village.   The Arkhoti
shrine, the mountain deity Veshagi of the Tsiklauri clan's
village of Akhieli, the deity Kvirae of Barisakho and the
Kivivae of Atabe, 'George the White', also at Atabe, and
Kopala the Angel of Ungi (both protectors of the Burduli kin
group), were all sworn brothers.   The shrine of Tsqalsikit
Pass at Didgori and the Shrine of the Archangel of the Roshkel clan of the Tsiklauri lineage were linked.   Also Didgori
and Juta (Ghalangur St George, protector of the local community at Artkhmo, in the district of Kazbeg), were likewise
interconnected.   This kin group consists of the father of the
Bichinaguri (a clan name of Arabic origins) and Roshkel of
the Tsiklauri clan, of Khevsur origin.   Likewise the Didgori
shrine and Iakhsris shrine of the Salikoko valley community
are sworn brothers, and finally the Khevsur deity of Gudani's
Holy Cross Shrine and the Karati shrine of the local community of Salikoko.

If we envisage circumstances in which sworn brotherhood
and sisterhood between deities represented an actual alliance,
such as existed between a variety of social groups, while
these groups were represented ideologically by the cults of
their own protective deities, then on the basis of such traces
of material as have come down to us we can establish that
alliances existed between the following Khevsur communities.

(1)   Within the same village, between a clan organisation and
a patrilineal organisation, and between the local clan-based
community in one village and the patrilineal clan.

(2)   Within the same valley, between a village and another
village community situated within the bounds of one valley
and between the valley community as a whole and the clan-
based organisations of other villages.

(3)   Between the village communities of different valleys and
a particular valley community and between a whole valley community and patrilineal communities living in other villages.

(4)   Between one valley community and another, and between
a particular valley community and those of Khevsureti in
general.

It may be said that we can see social alliances of this kind,
strengthened by the institution of sworn brotherhood, most
clearly in the case of the Pshavs.   Pshav society was constructed on the same principles as societies in other mountain

districts of Georgia, especially Khevsureti, but until our time
its structure took a more complete and self-contained, more
centralised, form.   Pshaveti consisted of twelve valleys, each
of which possessed its own supreme protector, while this protector ('Khati') had his own sanctuary, within the region, and
religious attendants.   The elders ('khevisberi') of the twelve
valleys embodied the general community of the Pshavs in their
worship of the war god common to them all, the Lasharis
Jvari, and likewise, to some extent, the Pshavs' goddess of
healing and female fertility, who was known by the name of
'Tamar Akim Dedopali' (literally Queen Thamar the Doctor
('hakim' = Arabic: doctor); Queen Thamar of Georgia
reigned 1184-1212. T.D.).   In popular ideology, however,
this union which, although it was voluntary, was indispensable
for the self-defence of the Pshav community as a whole, and
was explained as union through the oath of brotherhood of the
deity of each valley with the deity common to all the Pshavs.
Accordingly, the liturgical texts uttered by the Pshav elders
at the communal festivals, the so-called 'benedictions'
('sadidebelthai') included such formulae as: 'May his adoptive
sister and brother be blessed with victory!' This formula
was addressed to the deity of the valley in which the word
'sister' referred to Queen Thamar, and 'brother' to the deity
of Lasharis Shrine.

Thus it appears that alliances may have existed also between
groups of different social composition, through the sworn
brotherhood of mountain and other Georgian tribal deities -
alliances which were brought into being by the theocratic
power of Georgian communities.

The obligations imposed by the oath of brotherhood through
this institution on the parties to an alliance are defined in the
liturgical texts of the Georgian highlanders as follows.   A
Pshav benediction ended with the formula: 'Glory to Thee
again, great Mother of God, and to God's son and all who up-
hold you, all adopted brothers and sisters and those who are
in accord with the holy angels.' (10)

In a Mtiuleti benediction we find: 'God bless and prosper
the sovereign St George, the glory of Akhaltsikhe, his adoptive brothers and the angels his supporters.' (11)   Here,
notwithstanding the conjunction 'and', the 'supporter' is likewise a sworn brother (the angels), as we find indicated in the
text of another Mtiuleti benediction in which these two words
are found occurring twice, in both cases joined by a hyphen -
'modzme-momkhre', 'modzme-' (adoptive brother) 'momkhre'
(ally, supporter).   'God bless also the angel of the peak of
Maghana, our Pshav "modzme-momkhre"', (12) so that among
the Georgian highlanders sworn brotherhood, as a social and
political institution, laid on the sworn brothers an obligation
to remain on peaceful terms and to give each other aid.

The primary obligations between sworn brothers are clearly
seen among the Georgian feudal nobility of the twelfth century, as is so well exemplified in Shota Rustavel's immortal
poem. (13)

From documents of the early eighteenth and nineteenth centuries in our possession, it appears probable that a similar
understanding existed between kings (and likewise overlords)
and their sworn brother Lasharis Jvari in whose name probably the 'all Pshav' elders - who were no doubt the actual
rulers of the unified community - conducted their affairs.
We have retained these documents - for the analysis of char-
ters of benefice ('tsqalobis sigelebi'), books of accounts and
historical manuscript material - which are kept at the Keke-
lilze Institute of Manuscripts. (14)

I must record at the beginning that in late feudal times
also, tribal self-government in the mountain districts of
Georgia was apparently fully accepted in administrative circles
of the Georgian kingdom.   It was admitted by the authority
of the king, who endeavoured to treat it in the same way as
a united kingdom, to suit his own purposes.   From the earliest times, through the philosophy of dependency and over-
lordship, the king of Georgia was regarded as a ruler in the
likeness of God, God incarnate, the son of God.   He was related by adoption to the deity of the mountain community as
like to like, and was called 'modzme' (adopted brother, and
sworn brother), for all of which there is ample evidence in
documents of the eighteenth and nineteenth centuries.

King David (called by Mohammedans the Iman Quli-Khan)
calls the Lasharis Jvari 'our brother', sometimes 'our
"modzme"'. (15)   The second son of Erekle I, King Constantine, also refers to Lasharis Jvari as 'our "modzme"', in this
case the shrine of the Pshavs - 'all Pshavs, friends of
Lashari Shrine'. (16)   There is evidence of the same influence in several deeds of benefice ('tsqalobis sigelebi', deed of
noble title or freeing of serfs) of George XII.   He addresses
the Lasharis Jvari and refers to it as 'our "modzme"', adoptive
brother. (17)   In one of these, King George calls Lashari
Shrine itself 'our "modzme"', but addresses the Pshavs with
the words 'our treasured vassals, subjects, "qmani".' (18)
There is no doubt that by this form of address the king
wished to assure the Pshavs that he distinguished them especially among his other subjects as particularly close to him and
privileged.   In order to understand the significance and the
effect of this form of address, which must have made an impression on the Pshavs, it is necessary to consider the social
standing of the so-called 'treasured subjects'. (19)   Not only
kings, but princes of the blood called Lasharis Jvari 'our
"modzme"'.   In the above-mentioned documents it was referred

to in these words by the royal prince Pharnavaz and
others. (20)   The phenomenon of the royal family being
'artificially' related by the oath of brotherhood to the tribal
deities in general was widely known and admitted, both among
the feudal nobility and throughout the population.   In a
document dated 1741, the Grand Chamberlain Grigol Choloqash-
vili speaks of the King as 'modzme' of Lasharis Jvari and the
Pshavs as 'his [the king's] subjects'. (21)   (Qmani – from
'Qma', the Georgian word for 'slave'. T.D.)   The same phrase
occurs in a document of 1800 in the name of the peasants of
Mareiisi. (22)   In a document of King Constantine we read:

> Then we returned to our dwellings in Georgia, we and the
> children of King Shahnavaz.   We made war on each other,
> we were never separated from you and went through many
> campaigns, you fought in advance of us.   Again when the
> Urumians invaded Georgia, we made war on them, we fought
> with your soldiers under your banner, with you our
> 'modzme', beside all the Pshavs.   When we went to battle
> you slew many Urumians before us;   and when there was no
> longer a dwelling place for us in Georgia, nor a place for
> us in the quarters of the army commanders, since the Uru-
> mians had taken those places, then our 'modzme' would not
> abandon us, but directed us to his own place and sent his
> own Pshav soldiers and fellow subjects to meet us, whom
> you loaded with our baggage and carried it on your backs
> and shoulders, and we offered you the dwelling of our Pshav
> 'modzme' as a place and you did me great service, just as
> you served our 'modzme' loyally, and we his 'modzme';   but
> since there were not so many services to be performed for
> you we did not exert ourselves to make gifts and perform
> services for our 'modzme', St George, or grant favours to
> you, but we offered a sacrifice to Lasharis Jvari, and also
> bestowed favours on you and granted for his subjects, the
> Pshav people half of Othar's share of Marilis, with the ex-
> ception of Garsevan Mouravis and the part of Alaverdi which
> would belong to Othar in his native land of Marilis, and we
> gave to Lasharis Shrine and to your Pshavs a vineyard and
> a cellar. (23)

In the earliest of all these records, the voluntary nature of
the oath of brotherhood between a king and the deities of a
community is quite clearly seen, a bond which obliged the two
parties to render each other aid and service of every kind.
Thus, for example, when King Constantine enumerates in his
'charter of grants of aid' ('tsqalobis tsigni', literally 'letter of
mercy') the services performed by the Pshavs to his forebears, he is thinking of his own flight to Pshaveti (when his
defeat was brought about through treachery in a battle against
the Turks).

King Constantine attaches great importance to the mutual
obligations imposed on voluntarily sworn brothers: under the
guidance of Lasharis Jvari, the Pshavs as a people fought
inseparably beside the king in the many wars in which he
defended the kingdom of Georgia against enemies both within
and without;   they were prepared individually to lay down
their lives for the king;   they closed their ranks to go before
him in battle and many of them perished at the hands of their
foes.   Lasharis Jvari would not abandon them at the gravest
moment of their lives, and it guided them and caused their
soldiers to lead them to take refuge in the country of their
native land.   There, it was of service to them in every way.
The king considered it unthinkable (in his own words, 'it
could not happen') that he should not put himself out for his
sworn brother and the latter's subjects and make generous
gifts to the Pshav people and their Lasharis Jvari of arable
land, vineyards and other movable and immovable property.
At the same time, an important circumstance clearly emerges –
namely that rulers by divine right must ensure that through
the oath of brotherhood just such a mutual bond be established between the subjects of those who were party of the
oath as the rulers had with them.   'You have done me great
service, just as you serve our "modzme" loyally, and we
serve his "modzme"' – thus spoke the king of the Pshavs.
But as for their divine sworn brother the rulers had to treat
the people reciprocally, i.e. each of them must treat his
sworn brother's subjects as the sovereign did his own people.
It is obvious that, on the basis of such an interpretation of
the obligations of sworn brotherhood, the sovereign executive
power not only tacitly admitted self-government in mountain
districts but gave it official recognition whatever differences
there might be in their social order from those of so-called
'free' societies.   With the aim of turning this to advantage
against the enemies of the Georgian kingdom, King Constantine
specially enumerates in the above-mentioned document, in a
precise and strict sequence, the strata of population affected
through the initiative of his relationship in the Lasharis Jvari,
the appointments of persons and all the people of Pshaveti to
whom he had given presents and objects for sacrifice:

> we bestow on you undamaged gifts and sacrificial offerings
> and you shall make sacrifice wholly to the glory, wholly in
> praise of the warrior god, our 'modzme' St George of
> Lasharis Jvari, and further you shall give presents to the
> subjects, the high priests, prophets and all the Pshav
> people.

King Giorgi XII in one of his deeds of benefice, as mentioned above, calls the Pshavs his favourite subjects and
throughout his short reign assiduously defends them from the
insurgence of the native valley population;   he forbids the

ordering of impracticable services to be performed for the
Pshavs (with commands particularly directed against the
nobility, who appropriated to themselves gifts of land made to
the shrines ('khati'), by former kings); renews the
Pshavs' ancient deed of benefice and punishes his own servants who illegally seize the property of the Pshavs; finally,
by formal decree, he lays down the Pshavs' rights to retal-
iate against their oppressors. (24)

The Georgian highlanders, for their part, brought fame to
the royal house by their loyalty to the Georgian kingdom at
the times of its greatest trials. One such period was in the
last centuries of Georgia's existence as an independent state.
At that time the Georgian mountain dwellers played a part
more active than any of the Georgian people in their numerous
battles against the Persians, Turks and other invaders. In
the middle years of the seventeenth century, it was precisely
these highlanders who held them back, especially the Persians.
At the same time the Pshavs, Khevsurs and Tushis privately
swore an oath of allegiance to Teimuraz I, and declared their
readiness to go to war against Georgia's enemies. When the
governor of Kakheti, who was appointed by the Shah named
Khan Selim of Ganja, and who faithfully carried out the
Shah's directions, had for about two years been moving the
Turkish nomads out of Azerbaijan who had taken possession of
Bactrioni, Alaverdi and other strategic points, the Daghestanis
(a non-Georgian neighbouring tribe. T.D.) alone continually
streamed into the villages, pillaged, took prisoners and behaved as it pleased them. Then, like an avalanche from the
mountains the Kakhetians, Pshavs, Khevsurs and Tushis came
down as conquerors and delivered their native land from the
Turks, in 1569. (25) After Agha Mahmud Khan's penetration
of Tbilisi's defences 300 volunteers declared themselves for
King Erekle, sacrificing themselves to give the king a means
of retreat. Later moreover, Aragveli soldiers blocked the
Aragvi gorge and successfully repulsed an enemy attack. (26)

King Constantine of Kakheti assembled together the Kakhetians, Tushis, Pshavs and Khevsurs and marched into Kakheti
to drive out the Turks. At that time traitors were giving
aid to the Turks and saving them from defeat. Constantine,
who had hardly established Shanshe as governor at that time,
fled to Pshaveti with his brother, Teimuraz, and the nobles of
Kakheti. He stayed there the whole year, as, during that
period, Kakheti was suffering under the Lesghi mountain
tribesmen. Pshaveti was a reliable place of refuge later also
for Georgian kings and princes of the blood. The same
Teimuraz, Constantine's brother, fled a second time to
Pshaveti, in 1731. On a third occasion, in 1735, when he
had become king of Kakheti, he went into hiding there in
order to escape punishment by Nadir-Shah of Iran. (27) In

general, the highlanders represented reliable support for the
kings of Georgia, especially at times in their innumerable
wars when the king's power was weakened, as it was in a
period of turmoil both from without, in battles against the
enemy's countless hordes, and from internal strife with the
feudal nobles and princes.

On account of the mountain dwellers' high merit in the sight
of their country, their boundless devotion and self-denying
loyalty to the royal house, Georgian kings, princes and those
in their entourage made generous donations to the highlanders'
'khatebi' (ikons.   'Khatebi' = pl. of 'khati'.   T.D.).   Thus,
for example, after the Turkish nomads had been driven out of
Kakheti, according to a legend that survives among the mountain population, the king gave the plain of Alaverdi to the
Tushis and presented the vineyards in Akhmeta to the shrines
with holy icons of the Pshavs, under whose banners they had
taken part in that campaign.   Then the Pshavs, Khevsurs
and other Georgian highlanders, according to their fathers'
and grandfathers' custom, came out against the enemies of the
Georgian mountain peoples, under the banners of their own
respective 'khati', then also the common deity of the Pshavs,
Lasharis Jvari of the Kisti deity Iakhsar, as well as under
banners of other valleys, while the Khevsurs were united
beneath the banner of their holy Gudani Jvari.   The details
of their exploits are legendary.   It is thought that the king
of Georgia had asked the highlanders who had played a part
in gaining the victory what they wanted as a reward for their
heroism.   The Tushis requested the plain of Alaverdi for
their winter quarters, while the Pshavs and the Khevsurs said
to the king:

We are mountain dwellers and we cannot bear the heat of the
lowlands.   So that we may commemorate these great vic-
tories, and proclaim your greatness, give us vineyards and
we will labour in them, and the wine and money we obtain
from them we will devote to the shrines, where we will
drink the sacrificial wine at popular festivals, glorify our
sacred icons and remember the warrior heroes who have
fallen in this war.

The king granted their request, giving the plain of Alaverdi
to the Tushis, while he dedicated vineyards in Kakheti, in
particular Akhmeta and those in Khodasheri to all the great
'khatebi' of Khevsureti and Pshaveti whose banners had done
so much to drive the enemy out of Kakheti.

Thus, in late feudal times there was a relationship between
the Georgian kings and the contemporary community organisations which was regulated by the oath of brotherhood between
the participants on both sides.

To summarise the data set out above, we will draw the following conclusions. The oath of brotherhood (and sisterhood) represents the oldest legal institution through which
the rulers of more or less independent social organisations
having a tribal character in the local community organisations
on the one hand and kings on the other established social
and political alliances with each other. The oath of brotherhood imposed on the participants and on their underlings and
subjects, the obligation to remain at peace with each other
and give each other mutual support, adherence, self-sacrifice
and loyalty. In the interests of a sworn brother, they were
prepared to sacrifice themselves in battle against his enemies.

NOTES

1 This custom has been witnessed among mountain people.
2 I will give an instance of it from a mountain region.   An
   inhabitant of the village of Qvelaani, Michael Kvelaidze,
   and one from the neighbouring village of Gonauri, Andrea
   Obgaidze, swore brotherhood to each other in the following circumstances: Kvelaidze's father and Obgaidze's
   uncle mortgaged three acres of land (acre in the original
   sense of as much land as can be ploughed by one team in
   a day), for which they obtained 240 roubles.   Several
   years later, Kvelaidze wished to buy back his land and
   made the following statement to Obgaidze: In successful
   years he (Obgaidze) had made a profit of 480 roubles out
   of the land.   He ought therefore to repay to Kvelaidze
   both the land and 240 roubles in cash.   Obgaidze refused
   both the first and second of these demands and from that
   time onwards they treated each other as enemies.   When
   they met each other once on a social occasion, Kvelaidze
   could scarcely restrain himself from starting up a quarrel
   with Obgaidze, but unexpectedly the latter went up to
   him and begged him to become his sworn brother.
   Kvelaidze was delighted and after they had taken the 'Oath
   of Silver' in the presence of several people, according to
   the custom, Kvelaidze declared before witnesses that on
   account of the oath of brotherhood he would make Obgaidze
   a present of 240 roubles and the land with which the
   quarrel had begun.   Obgaidze for his part gave a sheep
   to his sworn brother's wife.   In this way, a fraternal
   relationship was established between them which continued
   uninterrupted throughout their lives.   When they went to
   visit each other on feast days, each would give his sworn
   brother's children presents of money.   Andrea, his cousins and relations were the owners of a flock of sheep, and
   at shearing time they would give Kvelaidze the same share
   of the wool as the members of their own family had received.   Once, in their presence, a certain Gudamaqreli

picked a quarrel with Kvelaidze, and just as his dagger
was about to strike, Obgaidze came to Kvelaidze's defence
and struck with all his might, while Kvelaidze himself
would do nothing to aid the Gudamaqreli or to rescue him
from his sworn brother.   Then, when Kvelaidze realised
that his sworn brother was in danger of death, he immediately went to his aid and saved him from death at the
hands of his enemy.

3   Among the Kistis this was usually performed by touching
weapons in a vessel of honey or milk.

4   Out of the wide variety of forms of sworn brotherhood
among Georgian mountain dwellers and their neighbours, I
have taken as an example the oath of brotherhood among
the Pshavs and Kistis.   The Lesghis killed a Kisti who
was the sworn brother of a Pshav, Gamikhardi Thvarelashvili.   He killed two Lesghis and sacrificed their dead
bodies at the grave of his sworn brother.   The Lesghis
then slew Gamikhardi himself.   Then Thvarelashvili's
son, who was called Boigari, and his cousin, sought vengeance for the death of their uncle and father and slew
two more Lesghis.   The Pshav Boigari, for his part, was
the sworn brother of a Kisti, Baghathur, a man of the
Lamuri clan.   Baghathur had killed a fellow villager
Mithkhoeli and had been in hiding from his mortal enemies
for two years with his son in Boigari's house.   When the
Lamuri warned him of danger to his only son, who was
threatened by his enemies, Boigari Brigar reassured him in
the following terms: 'Have no fear - what do I need my
"khirmi" (gun) for?'   Two years later, those at feud with
him made peace with Baghathur's fellow villagers, through
a second oath of brotherhood.   It is a fact of interest
that the reconciliation took place only after his sworn
brother, who had consulted with the Kisti, had brought
the Lamuri secretly into the house of his mortal enemy and
personally introduced him to the hearth wrapped in a felt
cloak.   When the heads of the household came across him
there they were obliged, for the honour of their house
and by the laws of hospitality - since their mortal enemy
had now to be reckoned as their guest - not only to be
put out on his behalf, but even to consent to a reconciliation, which was effected and confirmed as usual through
the institution of sworn brotherhood.

The facts cited are extracts made at my request from
material collected in accordance with a questionnaire
which I composed, by the sisters Th. and D. Ochiauri in
Pshaveti and M. Kedeladze in Mtiuleti.   In addition, I
have drawn on material from the Georgian Ethnographic
Archives Section of the Department of Ethnography of the
Institute of History, Archeology and Ethnography of the
Academy of Sciences of the Georgian SSR: A. Ochiauri's

1941 ms., 'Testaments in Khevsureti', N. Baliauri,
'Adoptive Sisterhood and Brotherhood'; 'Tsatsloba in
Pshaveti', and 'Stsorphroba in Arkhoti Valley in Zvner
Khevsureti'.*

In a private letter, dated 12 September 1943, V.I.
Abaev gave us the following information about sworn
brotherhood and sisterhood among the Ossetes:

Sisterhood and brotherhood taken as one. This was a
phenomenon of common occurrence between participants
of different sexes. Those taking part swore the 'oath
of silver'; they dipped some silver object (a coin, a
ring, etc.) in a glass of beer or araqi, they both drank
from the glass and swore an oath of eternal friendship.
Within my mother's memory, no mixing of blood took
place.

On all important occasions in life, sworn brothers
behaved as the persons nearest to each other; they pro-
tected and aided each other in every way, were prepared
to make every kind of sacrifice, etc. They were bound
to seek vengeance on each other's account 'but not for a
sworn brother's kinfolk'.

Between a sworn brother and sister every kind of inti-
macy was permitted which did not overstep the bounds of
a natural brother and sister relationship.

It was a feature of the relationship that one would often
give presents to, or perform services for, the other. An
adoptive sister would look after her sworn brother's
hood, leggings and gun-case, stitch his coat and tunic
and embroider them with gold and silver. An adoptive
brother on his side would give the head of his sworn
sister's household assistance in his affairs, send presents
for the most part obtained from a town: headbands,
dress material, etc.

An adoptive brother was called 'oefsyoer-gond', 'one who
has been made a brother', or 'ordxord', 'sworn-brother',
if the solemn oath was accepted among them. An adoptive sister was called 'xo-gond', 'one who has been made a
sister'.

* 'Tsatsloba' among the Kelans and 'Stsorphroba' in Khev are
the names of 'an institution whereby a young girl and boy
who may not marry but enjoy each other's company, swear
an oath of sister-brotherhood'. (T.D.)

I have confined myself to accessible published material
on the Georgian institution of sworn brotherhood, and I
think it is more or less sufficient to illuminate that aspect
of sworn brotherhood which I have studied here.   At the
same time, it appeared to me that it would be of use to
give concrete examples which would bring this material
within the sphere of attention of those specialists who are
making full use of similar material data in the Caucasus
for a monograph study of the institution of adoptive
relationships.

5   The Greek writer, Lucian Samosateli, in his novel,
    'Tokaridi or Friendship', refers to the existence of the
    institution of sworn brotherhood among the Scythians.
6   On ancient Georgian communal deities and communal theo-
    cratic rulers, see my paper, The Khevsur Community,
    'Proceedings of the Academy of Sciences of the USSR',
    vol. 13, no. 10.
7   V. Bardavelidze, Sacred Texts of the Georgian Mountain
    Dwellers of Eastern Georgia, 'Georgian Ethnographic
    Material', vol. 1, 1948, p. 35.
8   Ibid., pp. 12, 17, 31-4.
9   V. Bardavelidze, The Khevsur Community.   The Struc-
    ture and Institution of 'Jvarisqmoba' (Devotees of a
    Shrine), 'Proceedings of the Academy of Sciences of the
    Georgian SSR', vol. 13, no. 8, pp. 495-502.
10 V. Bardavelidze, Sacred Texts of the Georgian Mountain
    Dwellers, p. 34.
11 Ibid., p. 34.
12 Ibid., p. 35.
13 See N. Marr's article in his The Opening and Closing
    Stanzas of Knight in the Leopard Skin of Shota of
    Rustava, 'The Cult of the Woman and Chivalry in Nozma',
    St Petersburg, 1910, no. 5, pp. 23-30.
14 Copies of these documents were furnished by my academic
    colleague in the Department of the Academy of Sciences
    of the Georgian SSR, R. Kharadze.   I have compared them
    with corresponding material.
15 Sd 2344.
16 Sd 2990/5100.
17 Sd 2945/4162, 2946, 2942, 2349.
18 Sd 2949.
19 See V. Bardavelidze, The Khevsur Community, pp. 495-
    502.
20 Sd 2950, 2958.
21 Sd 2941.
22 Sd 2942.
23 Sd 2940/5160.
24 See Sd 2949, 2942, 2952, 2945/5162, 2946.
25 N. Berdzenishvili, I. Javakhishvili and S. Janashia,
    'A History of Georgia', vol. 1, 1946, pp. 370, 372.
26 Al. Orbeliani's notes, edited by S. Kakabidze.
27 N. Berdzenishvili et al., op. cit., p. 15.

Part V
SIBERIA

INTRODUCTION

With the return of the anthropologists who had been exiled to
Siberia by the Tsarist authorities and also the academic interest of Lenin and other leaders in the minorities there, the
tribes of the far north received attention from the earliest
Soviet period, with a special commission set up for studying
them in 1924. These peoples, such as the Eskimos, were
hunters and herders who occasionally traded with the Russians, but to whom it would be difficult to demonstrate the
relevance of Soviet government and doctrine. Over the
decades they have been slowly absorbed into the system, and
regular air services during the summer permit anthropologists
from centres such as Yakutsk and Novosibirsk and from large
departments in Moscow and Leningrad to make annual visits to
them.

I have selected Popov's work on the Dolgans because it is a
classic, unique in its kind. It is one of the only Soviet
anthropological papers that attempts to give an account of the
life cycle of the family as a whole, and could hardly have been
omitted from our selection. Fainberg's work, in contrast,
focuses on a specialised, hypothetical subject very typical of
Soviet studies where ethnographic data are used for historical
reconstruction. The polemics surrounding the origins of the
Siberian peoples never cease to fascinate Soviet folklorists and
ethnographers and it is a recurring theme in many of their
works. Unfortunately it has been until now very rare for a
Western scholar to do field work among any of the peoples
there because most areas are closed to foreigners. It is
therefore to be hoped that the study of kinship and marriage
and the family will elicit more interest among the Soviet anthropologists to whom the region is accessible.

10   The family life of the Dolgans
A.A. Popov

I

In 1930 I was sent by the Museum of Anthropology, Archaeology and Ethnography to conduct an ethnographical study of the Dolgans in Taimyrsky Nationalnyi Okrug (Krasnoyarsky Kray) (Nationalnyi Okrug and Kray are both Soviet regional administrative divisions. T.D.)   I intended to use this material for a book on the life of the Dolgans.   This intention has for a number of reasons remained unfulfilled and only part of my materials have been published in a series of separate essays, mainly in journals. (1)   There is almost no ethnographical literature on the Dolgans.   The present work will partly fill this gap by describing the family life of the Dolgans.

The Dolgans consider it a blessing to have many children and a misfortune to have none (the man is usually blamed for this).   A barren woman, just like a barren reindeer, is called a 'bangai'.   Deformed children are thought to be the product of marriages between close relatives.   The Dolgans think that girls are carried in the mother's womb a day longer than boys.   The craving that a woman gets to eat particular foods in the final months of pregnancy is called 'syuryaktya-tyar'.   This word is also used to describe the exhaustion which men feel for several days after their wife gives birth. It is not considered necessary to hide pregnancy.   On the contrary, pregnant women willingly visit the shaman and ask him to predict the sex of the child and the date they will go into labour.   These predictions take place in public, and many people are involved in the ritual magic.

As soon as a woman is known to be pregnant she is put under various bans and taboos.   This applies in particular to certain sorts of food which it is thought will cause physical deformities in the child.   She may not eat duck, in case the baby is born with flat feet;   hare's head, in case it has pop-eyes or buck teeth;   hare's heart, in case it's a coward;   and unskinned burbit (a fish), in case it has a pock-marked face. She is also forbidden to eat poor quality food or drink vodka. A pregnant woman may not step over a rope, in case her child becomes entangled in its umbilical cord, or cross behind

* First published in 'Sovetskaya Etnografiya', 1946, no. 4,
   pp. 50-71.

another woman's back in case her child is born feet first.
Pregnant women are never put together, as it is thought that
the one whose baby is due first will have a difficult birth.
From the moment the first signs of pregnancy appear, women
are considered unclean.   They must not cross the road from
the south (sunny) side, the side along which the household
gods ('saitan'ov') and shamanite charms are transported.   To
do this would be to profane the spirits who would send the
woman a difficult birth, or cause her child to be born dead as
a punishment.

As the date of the birth approaches, the shaman performs
more magic rituals and a separate hide or bark tent is built
for the expectant mother.   The Noril'sk Dolgans place two
young larches with pieces of wood inserted crossways through
them (called 'turu', which means pole) at either side of the
entrance to the tent.   These are a symbolic representation of
the idea which plays an important part in the shaman religion
as practised by the Dolgans - that wood, the 'turu', is linked
with the life and soul of man.   The Dolgans believe that with
the help of the holy 'turu' wood, the woman's soul will rise up
after birth and return to life.   Dogs are kept on a leash
during the birth, in case their barking should scare away the
child's 'aiy' (good spirit).   All other pregnant women are
kept away from the one giving birth in case they imitate her
and give birth prematurely.

Before going into the special tent, the expectant mother
takes leave of all her acquaintances, but does not touch them.
They reply: 'God bless you' ('Buok lastabi') and wish her
good luck, but never say 'goodbye' since this might be taken
to mean that they did not want her to come back.

Before the actual birth, all rings and belts are taken from
the mother to prevent them getting in the way.   The woman
gives birth standing up, holding on to a horizontal pole, one
end of which is attached to one part of the framework of the
tent, the other to the pole which stands in the middle of the
tent.   The pole the mother holds on to is always attached on
the left side of the entrance, and a wooden anthropomorphic
image made of fox or rabbit skin is hung above it.   This is
known as 'the protector of women'.   If a shaman charm has
been said over the skin, it is handed down from generation to
generation and used at all future births.   If a shaman charm
has not been said over it, it is made into a blanket for the
baby.

The expectant mother's tent is considered unclean and only
three people are allowed into it - the expectant mother, the
midwife and one other woman.   The latter tends the fire,
prepares the food and washes the dishes, since both the

midwife and the mother are considered unclean and cannot
touch fire until the umbilical cord is cut from the baby.   The
women who bring food or come to ask after the mother's health
do not have the right to enter the tent and their conversations and the handing over of the food take place through the
open door of the tent.

The Dolgans, like other peoples of Siberia, believe the pain
of birth can be relieved if the father's name is known. When
the midwife has delivered the baby, she usually asks the
mother to name her lover if this is permissible;   only if the
woman is a widow may this not be done.   If this does not
produce the desired results, they turn to the shaman.   The
shaman puts on his costume and performs his magic just outside the tent.   This consists of an image of the women's protectress ('nyadzhi') and pronouncing the appropriate incantations over it.   The image is then placed by the woman in
labour.   If the woman recovers, she must keep her image
and use it in future births.   At meal times, she 'feeds' her
'protectress' by throwing it small pieces of food.

When the child is born, its umbilical cord is tied with string
and cut with a pair of scissors.   After this the midwife holds
the child over a basin and washes its mouth out with water.
If the baby does not show signs of life, the midwife takes a
metal tube and drops a thread through it.   She covers the
child's ears, nose and mouth with her hand, places one end of
the tube over its anus and blows down the other end.   This
is seen as the process of transmitting life to the child, and it
is then expected to revive.   It is said that a child born in a
'sorochka' (shirt) will be happy.   The 'sorochka' is sewn up
inside the tent covering or a cloth which someone carries
about with them to bring luck.   They believe, for example,
that a 'sorochka' in your pocket will bring you an acquittal in
court.   Birth marks are thought to be made by mice.   The
Dolgans believe that after the person's death the mouse will
recognise its mark and eat his corpse.

If the child is born prematurely, in the seventh or eighth
month, he is placed in the stomach of a reindeer specially
killed for this purpose, and kept there for between one and
two months.   This is an extremely expensive regime, since,
according to the elders, the stomach must be changed no less
than nine times a month, i.e. nine reindeer must be slaughtered each month.   If the child's parents cannot afford to kill
so many of their reindeer, their relatives come to their aid.
A child born just a few days early is kept warm by being
wrapped up in a foxskin which is then hung from a pole sus-
pended horizontally over the fire.   (This pole is normally
used for hooks for hanging pots from.)   The baby is never
wrapped in foxskin unless it is premature as they believe this

will give the child sharp teeth like the fox's with which he
will bite his mother's breasts.

The cradle is made in advance.   A dog is put in it first
and rocked to sleep there with the idea that any unclean
spirits in the cradle will enter the dog and not the child.
They are afraid of the newborn baby's remembering and yell-
ing out the evil spirit's name ('abasy').

The mother is given the very best food - 'sooshki' (round
crackers) and white rusks, and a plump young deer is killed
for her.   If she is unmarried, her father demands that the
man responsible give her a reindeer, saying 'Let him send his
child its food' ('egotun mininya yttyn').   With this the
father's responsibilities for his illegitimate child cease.   This
reindeer is killed and a feast held on the third day after the
birth.   This is also the day the mother gets out of bed and
goes through a ceremony of purification.   The midwife fumi-
gates herself, the mother, the child and their assistant and
everything they have touched with the smoke produced by
placing juniper wood or light wood resin in a bucket of hot
coals.

Shortly before this a cone-shaped tent ('dzhukanan'), made
of sticks, is erected some distance away.   In it, on the morning of the purification ritual, the midwife hangs the placenta,
wrapped up in the mother's clothes and the reindeer hide on
which she gave birth.   This is done to prevent the placenta
being eaten by the 'carnivores' ('asylaktar') - dogs, wolves
and foxes.   If this happens, the woman will have no more
children.   The Dolgans believe that if a stone is put on top
of the placenta the woman will have no more children until it
is removed.   Many women who don't want to have children
resort to similar 'contraceptive measures'.   The Dolgans call
the placenta the child's mother ('ogo inyata').

The first time the mother enters her tent after the purification ritual she is given a small piece of food so that 'her
breasts don't dry up' ('emiye karya dien').   On the third day
there is a feast and dancing in the open air.   The friends
and relatives give the child a 2-year-old reindeer and other
presents.   These gifts are called 'nyagzhima', and are afterwards regarded as the inalienable property of the newborn boy
or girl.   After the feast the mother pays her first visit to
her nearest neighbours.   When she enters the tent, they
offer her a tiny piece of food (meat, fish or cake), with the
words: 'The mice have been at our stores!' ('Nyokyubyutyui
kutuiaktar siektyarya').   The mother's first visits are called
'tabyskyr'.

In spite of her 'purification' the woman remains under

various taboos for another two weeks.   For example, she
cannot touch fire until the umbilical cord falls, and
she dare not cross the road from the south side used for
transporting the household gods.   If she fails to observe
these customs, her child could fall ill or die, and she herself
become barren.   If she does break the taboo, she summons
the shaman and asks him to ward off her misfortune by pro-
pitiating the offended spirits with his charms.   The guilty
woman and her child are cleansed with the smoke produced by
placing reindeer or fish grease in a bucket of hot coals and
passing it three times under her armpits.   A woman who sits
in a sledge which has carried the shamanite attributes will also
become barren.   The sterility that results from breaking
these taboos can also be treated by fumigation.

The Dolgan midwife is greatly respected, especially by those
she has brought into the world and who call her grandmother
('ebe').   For first children she is usually paid a doe reindeer, for succeeding ones dress lengths, pieces of scented
soap, and, each time, a large copper ring symbolising the
female sex organs.   Poor families pay the midwife what they
can afford.   Even if they do not give her anything, she has
no right to complain or refuse them her services in the future.

If the baby looks like one of his dead ancestors, it is said
that his spirit has passed into the child and the child takes
his or her second name.   Although the Dolgans officially
regard themselves as Orthodox, most of them have non-religious names.   This is especially true of the Dolgans of the
Noril'sk raion.   When Dolgans do have religious names, they
are usually found in their diminutive form;   for example Limka
(Philemon), Van'ka, Fil'ka, etc., although the owners of these
names may be seventy or eighty years old.

The non-religious names of the Dolgans have an apotropaic
meaning.   For example, boys are given the name 'Dapsibul',
which comes from 'dapsi' - the bone plate which protects the
arm from the lash of the bow string.   This name is supposed
to protect its bearer from illnesses caused by evil spirits.
The name Turubul comes from 'turu' - the shamanist pole
which symbolises the mythical sacred wood which harbours the
child's soul.   People whose names do not bring them happiness can change them after the appropriate shaman ritual is
performed.   Thus, for example, if a child is often ill the
elders will say 'Your name is your enemy' ('esigi sychoyokyo-
gyut'), and give them a dog's name in place of their own.   It
is usually girls who are given these names, Basyrgas, Bialka,
Sukachan (from suchka, twigs), etc.   (The mistress of the
tent in which I lived for a summer in Noril'sk raion was called
Sukachan, which didn't prevent her from being the wife of
one of the most honoured and respected of the Dolgans.)

People keep these names for their whole lives. The Dolgans believe that when an evil spirit comes to eat children who have the names of dogs, it will go away again thinking it has found not a child but a dog.

Dolgan children are raised solely on their mother's milk. They are breast fed until they are four or five years old. If the mother has no milk, the child is given to a foster mother. It is agreed that the child will either stay with the foster mother until he reaches a certain age, or permanently. In the first case, the foster mother is paid when she returns the child. She is regarded as close a relation to the child as his own mother. The foster mother's sons and daughters cannot marry their foster brothers or sisters.

II

With the birth of their first child, the parents stop being called by their own names and, instead, as a mark of respect they say, 'the father or mother of so-and-so', e.g. the father of Poduo (Theodosiya), the mother of Spiri (Spiridona). They keep these names even if their firstborn dies, as a way of preserving his memory. Dolgan boys are called after the custodians of the holy relics; girls, after people from other settlements. The Dolgans are fond of all children, regardless of their sex or parentage. Small boys are nicknamed 'kyusya' (master, from the Russian word 'khozyain'), little girls 'kychai' or 'kyusyauka' (mistress). Parents rarely punish their children, and never in company, in case this gives the guests a bad opinion of them.

The children are sheltered in every possible way until they come of age. Among the Dolgans of the Dongot kin who live on the left bank 'beyond the river' (beyond the Enisei) the mother does not let her children leave her side until they are capable of going about on their own, and even takes them with her when she goes visiting. This is to prevent a stranger coming between her and the child. To protect the child from the evil spirit, the Dolgans hang a wooden or iron bow and arrow on the left side and a wooden knife in a scabbard on the right side of the boys' cradle; just a wooden knife is hung by a girl's cradel. Families who have had children who died try to protect those who survive by persuading an elderly female relative who has raised many children of her own to make a fictitious purchase of them for a nominal sum. The 'buyer' goes to the parents' tent, lights a candle in front of the ikon and says: 'I am an old woman who has brought up many children. God, give me this child so that he will be with children of his own age.' The child who has been 'bought' stays on in his parents' tent. The parents use the 'fee' received for the child to buy candles and incense.

If a child seems disturbed for some reason, his parents
attribute it to the evil spirit visiting him at night.   To drive
it away, the shaman makes a wooden idol, 'the children's
friend' ('ogo dogoro'), which is tied inside the cradle.   The
shaman makes no incantations at this time.   But if the child's
condition remains disquieting, if he cries continuously, and
loses weight, he is thought to be under the influence of a
more powerful spirit, 'devki abasy' (the evil spirit).   If it is
a boy, the Dolgans believe that the 'devki abasy' disturbs
him at night because it wants to have sexual intercourse with
him.   The shaman used to be summoned to charm it away.
He would make an image of a woman from rotten wood and
suck the 'devki abasy' from the lips of the child into his
mouth and breathe it into the image.   He would then pretend
to have sexual intercourse with it, and then banish it to the
underworld.   After the magic ritual the female image is
buried in the ground.

The Dolgans forbid anyone to place their hands on a child's
head, in case this stunts its growth;   they also consider it a
sin to hold a child up higher than his head and to kill the
'dalbaki' bird, which is called the spirit of children.   When
children reach six or seven years old, the ears of both sexes
are pierced with a needle and a thread of human hair is
passed through the hole.   The Dolgans believe that on a
person's death the evil spirit looks at his ears, and, if they
have not been pierced, he cuts them off and uses them as
spoons.   The evil spirit will not touch pierced ears, since a
spoon with a hole in it is no good for eating with.

The bow and arrow are the most notable toys of Dolgan
children.   They differ from real ones only in size, as I described in my previous work on hunting and fishing among the
Dolgans.   They also have dolls made from reindeer bones
wrapped up in rags or paper.   You can tell the female dolls
from the male by the sort of scarf they have wrapped round
their heads.   'Reindeers' are made either from broken matchboxes or from slivers of wood turned up at right angles, and
the raised parts splintered to look like a reindeer's branched
antlers, or the model of a whole animal is carved from a piece
of wood.   Sometimes the children use reindeer ankle bones or
large stones to represent reindeer;   smaller stones are placed
on top to represent riders and their loads.   They use the
dolls and model reindeer to form long 'argishi' (caravans) on
the ground, with matchboxes serving as sledges.   Toys made
from splinters of wood are very popular with the Dolgan children.   There are two sorts.   A 'pipik' is a disc with two
holes in it, through which they pass a cord and then tie the
ends together;   they wind the rope up tightly from both ends,
then pull it out, making the disc in the middle rotate.
'Tyali-yngyrar' (summoning the wind) is a piece of wood with

a long cord attached at one end; taking the free end they twirl the wood round and its toothed edges cause it to make a humming noise. The top's strange name derives from the fact that the noise it makes spinning round sounds like bad weather coming up, and children are therefore often forbidden to play with it.

They also have children's games very similar to our own. 'Kabylyk' (throwing and catching wooden sticks); and hitting the 'lomour', a wooden cylinder, 6 or 7 centimetres long, with a piece of reindeer hair and hide inserted in its split end. The players have wooden bats about half a metre long with which they hit the 'lomour' up in the air, and try not to let it fall to the ground. This game is also played by adults.

In winter the children, in particular the boys, play a game which teaches them how to lasso reindeer. They set a number of reindeer skulls up in a row and throw the lasso at their antlers. The astonishing accuracy and dexterity with which the Dolgans catch reindeer is thus a skill acquired from childhood.

There is also the lake game, 'kyuyol' onnyu'. Two reindeer lassos are placed in circles on the ground at some distance from one another. Between them stands a 'wolf' who catches the children who are pretending to be reindeer as they run from one lake to the other. When the 'wolf' catches a 'reindeer' he 'blinds' it by putting his hand on its face, and it then helps the 'wolf' to catch the other 'reindeer'.

In addition to the games we have mentioned cat's cradle (making different shapes with a piece of string tied round the fingers) is very popular with Dolgan children, and can be used to depict the pattern on the back of a woman's coat, the legs of a partridge, fishing nets, and scissors. Other rope games include, for example, tying up one's fingers ('bysar'), cutting things up with scissors ('kantyiy tasarar') and 'suffocation' ('mongunnarar').

Childhood ends very early among the Dolgans. Children of eight or nine are already considered grown-up and have their own reindeer to ride. At ten or twelve boys are allowed to hunt wild reindeer on their own, and participate in the general conversation and all family gatherings on a level with adults. Girls of ten or twelve help with the housework, prepare food and make clothes for their parents. They are also permitted to smoke at this age.

Dolgan children always treat their parents with great respect. Every day the adolescents go to them to be blessed after morning and evening prayers. If children refuse to

help their aged parents, which happens very rarely, they are
obliged to do so by the court of elders.   Sons or daughters
who treat their mother badly are reproached with the words
'Think how your mother carried you for nine months.'   If the
elder son treats his father with respect during the time that
they live together, his father will allow him to organise their
herd of reindeer as he thinks best, except for the reindeer
which were received as gifts and belong to other members of
the family.   But if his son turns out to be a spendthrift and
a gambler, his father will not only refrain from granting him
this right, but may even deprive him of his inheritance.
This, however, rarely happens.   Instead, the father, in the
hopes that his son will settle down, marries him off and gives
him a number of reindeer with which to set up on his own.
If his son squanders these reindeer, too, his father will give
him five or six more out of the goodness of his heart, after
which his son has no further claims on him.   A favourite
son, on the other hand, who knows how to please his parents,
remains the object of his parents' concern even after he's received his inheritance, and they will always help him.

III

The young Dolgan men and women meet and get to know each
other at the dances which take place either on the days of the
former Christian holidays, or at family celebrations (marriages,
namedays, etc.).   The young man sends a woman, 'suorumdzho', to ask the girl of his choice to give him her ring.   If
the girl returns the young man's feelings, she fulfils his request, but sometimes she tells the 'suorumdzho': 'If he really
has his eye on me, let him come and ask for himself.'   The
young man then has to go himself to ask the girl for a token.
When the girl gives him her ring, she says to him (or tells
him through the 'suorumdzho'): 'Let him pay me back at such
and such a time.'   At the appointed time the young man
gives the girl something of greater value than the ring she
gave him.   The gift of the ring means that the girl gives the
young man permission to visit her at night.   If it happens in
summer, the lover goes to his girl's tent during the daytime,
supposedly just for a visit, and notes how far the tent pole
by which the girl sleeps at night is from the entrance to that
tent.   At nightfall the lover creeps up to the tent, either
alone or with a friend.   If he comes by reindeer, he tethers
them some way away from the tent.   He wears his boots with
the fur on the outside to avoid making a noise.   The lover
creeps up to the tent, removes the peg, and removes the soil,
holding down the skin at the spot where the girl lies, and
thus crawls into the tent.   His friend stays outside and puts
the clods of earth back in their original place.   In winter,
when the Dolgans live in sledge tents, the young man tries to

lie next to the girl when he stays the night. If she sleeps
in a separate 'balok' or sledge tent, the lover comes to her
secretly and undoes the hook of the lock from the outside
with the blade of his knife. The girl gives herself to her
'guest' of her own free will, her lover may not possess her
without her consent.

Lovers usually go to their girl when everyone has gone to
bed and is in the first and deepest part of their sleep. As
morning approaches, the girl sometimes decides to send her
lover away in case the others wake up. This is usually just
a pretence, since in most cases her parents close their eyes
to it all. But occasionally, her father acts otherwise and
confiscates the trapped lover's reindeer strap and belt and
even one of his reindeer. Public opinion condemns such
behaviour. Cases of it are found most often in Noril'sk
raion. In the east they treat such matters more indulgently.
But even in Noril'sk raion, parents who notice the lover's
presence during the night often wait until morning to say,
'You should have fulfilled your needs in secret,' and confis-
cate his reindeer and his harness. However, some jealous
parents in Noril'sk raion protect their daughter from her
lovers by making her sleep next to them.

Sometimes, the young girl refuses to allow her lover to
spend the night with her in spite of the mutual exchange of
gifts. This prompts some lovers to ask for their gifts back.
The society does not encourage young people to behave in
this way.

The fact that young people sleep together in no way obliges
them to get married. A girl who has children out of wedlock
has no problems getting married, and her illegitimate children
are usually left with their grandfather on the mother's side.
I encountered Dolgan girls who had two or three such children, and who made no secret of their lovers' names. One
respectable young Dolgan girl, in the presence of her husband
and a large number of guests, even said with a certain amount
of pride that she had borne three children before her marriage, and that they were a great help to her. A girl's
pregnancy is only condemned when it is revealed after her
betrothal. It is considered wrong for either men or women
to have lovers after their marriage, but this does not stop
such romances occurring.

The following story, which was told me by a Dolgan, Pavel
Yarotsky of Krys stanok (settlement), Pyasin raion, shows
how far free love may be considered normal among the Dolgans.

Once upon a time, there lived two maidens, both very rich.
One believed in free love and lay with all God's people, (2)

young or old - whoever asked, she refused no one, and
gave them all that was in her power.   The other girl lived
very chastely and did not allow men to visit her.   She
asked the free-loving girl 'Why do you behave so shamelessly,'   The free-loving girl replied 'I warm the people who
lie with me.   How can I refuse them?'

    Soon after this, the free-loving girl died.   After her
death, she saw two roads, a light one going upwards, and
a dark one going down.   She wanted to take the light
road, but it was blocked up with bones and scales.   'How
can I get to the higher world?' the girl asked sadly.   'It
must be my bad luck,' she thought.   From behind her a
voice said 'Where are you going?   Have you lost your way?'
'I can't find the way to the after depth.'   'Just look at my
side!   Did you use to throw away the bones and scales
when you cleaned fish?'   'I did.'   'That's a sin,' said the
voice, 'but all the same it is a minor sin.   Perhaps you've
lost your way because of your other sins?' said the owner
of the voice.   The girl said 'What other sins did I commit?'
The voice replied, 'I created you to be childless.   Meanwhile you lay with men and you probably gave warmth to
many of them.   Don't you understand that's good?   Please,
look above your head.'   The girl looked and saw the
brightly lit sky above her and in it the sun, sending down
rays of light, like three shining ropes, 'Here is the good
you've done changed into threads connecting with Aii' (the
good deity. A. Popov).   Then the voice said, 'Did you
give yourself to those around you?'   'I did,' answered the
girl.   'Look what has become of your generosity.'   When
she looked up, many coloured threads were descending.
And so it happened that the girl was taken up to the land
of Aii.

    The chaste girl also died.   After her death, she too lost
her way at the crossroads.   A voice behind her said,
'What sins have you committed to get so lost?'   She replied,
'I have committed no sins.'   'Did you clean fish properly?'
'I did,' she replied.   'I intended you to raise children, why
did you keep your vagina closed?   Why didn't you give
yourself to anyone?   Not every child has a legal father,
and there is nothing wrong in a child being born illegitimate,
this is your great sin.   Well, did you give anything to mankind?'   'I once gave some thread to an old woman.'
'Where is this thread of yours?'   'Where can I find it?' the
girl wondered, looking round, and lo and behold her thread
lay on the man's shoulders.   The man took the thread and
said, 'It seems you have very little good in you.   All the
same, let's try and see if the thread will hold you.'   The
girl held on to the end of the thread and an attempt was
made to raise her up on it.   How could the thread hold out?
It snapped and the girl fell down into the underworld.

Two literary sources confirm that the so-called 'hospitality hetaira' did exist among the Dolgans. In Tretyakov we read: 'Girls sometimes agreed without a murmur to sacrifice their chastity to a passing guest whom his host wanted to honour.' (3) The second reference occurs in Latkin: 'In the old days, even this century, a father often sold his daughter or sister to the guest who promised to pay well for such hospitality, or even gave her free if it was particularly in his interests to please this guest. Today this custom has died out completely.' (4)

IV

Until very recently it was considered a great sin (an'i) for a man or woman to remain single. After their death 'their souls became heretics' ('dzheretinnik'), and would not go to the land of the dead but stay on earth near their grave to frighten the living. The soul of an unmarried mother, however, did not become a 'heretic'. It is also considered a sin for a widower to remarry, or for married Dolgans to get divorced. A man is guided by the good spirit in his choice of a wife - she has been destined for him from birth. If, after his wife's death, a widower married again, he will lose the Aii's (good spirit's) favour ('aiytyn eietya aragar'). The Aii chooses one not ten wives for each man. Second marriages therefore take place not according to the will of the Aii but to the will of the individual man. When a man who has had two wives dies, he is united with his first wife in the life after death. His second wife goes back to her relatives on the mother's side. A man who marries a third time has fallen under the influence of the evil spirit ('abasy') and is committing a great sin. When he dies, he and his wives belong to the 'abasy'.

Just as it is considered a sin for a widower to marry a second time, so it is forbidden for a widow to remarry. It is not thought wrong for a widow to have children, only for her to have them by her dead husband's relatives. The fact that remarriage is forbidden, but not extra-marital relations, indicates that the ban is of later origin, and possibly due to the influence of Christianity. The very word 'dzheretinnik' is nothing other than the Russian word 'heretic' known also to the Yakuts.

The Dolgans often marry very young. Two male friends 'marry off' their young children. The boy's father adopts his friend's daughter and the young boy and girl are brought up as brother and sister until they are nine or ten, after which they are married to each other. Sometimes the fathers agree on the marriage of their children soon after their birth.

The fathers swear an oath that their children will later become
man and wife.   The bridegroom's father gives the bride's
father a reindeer and a coat of fox fur as an advance on the
bridewealth ('til bastingata', the beginning of the compact).
The children live apart, each with their parents, until they
are ten, then marry.   If the girl dies before she reaches a
marriageable age, her father has to return the bridewealth he
has received in advance.   If he refuses to do so they resort
to the judgment of the elders.

Unequal marriages also often take place.   For example, a
pretty and hard-working girl of about fifteen or sixteen may
be married to a boy of seven or eight.   The bride lives in
the boy's tent in the capacity of a ward until her fiancé grows
up.   The boy's parents do this so as not to lose the pretty
and domesticated bride.   The social and economic position of
the older bride or bridegroom also plays an important part in
unequal marriages.

Children are married in turn, so that as the elder children
leave home, they lose their right to the inheritance.   This
means that they will not be able to prevent their younger
brothers receiving their share on their father's death.

The Dolgans usually allow marriages only between relatives
in the fourth generation on the mother's or father's side, but
there are many exceptions to this rule.   For example, in
Noril'sk raion, if a widow has no son, she can marry her
daughter to the son of her younger brother, saying that she
'returns her bones' ('unguokpun tyonnyoryobyun').   If a
domesticated, hard-working girl is born on the father's side
before the fourth generation, one of her mother's relatives
will marry her, saying that they used to take their wives from
this kin in the past.   There is a general tendency among the
Dolgans for there to be marriages among the descendants of
brothers and sisters, after the third generation, when they
are no longer kin 'so that the kinship is re-established in that
generation'.

The marriage of cousins and levirate should also be treated
as survivals of group marriages.   Both these phenomena have
been met with very recently in the Noril'sk raion.   According
to the custom of levirate, the younger brother married his
elder brother's widow.   If there are several younger
brothers, the one who manages to propose first marries her.

Marriages between foster brothers and sisters are forbidden,
natural and foster fathers are regarded as relatives.   But an
adopted son is allowed to marry his foster father's niece, and
vice versa.   Closeness between relatives lasts only to the
fourth generation.   Relatives in the male and female line from

another kin are considered distant - 'sydzhan'.   The closest
relatives, the 'syuryk uru' (heart relatives) are: (a) for the
grandfather and grandmother, their grandson and granddaughter, (b) between themselves, sons (or daughters) and
brothers and sisters (see the list of relationships at the end
of this chapter, pp. 215-19).

When they've picked out a girl for their son to marry, the
bridegroom's parents ask the bride's relatives in a roundabout
way about her virtues and vices.   The bride's relatives often
deceive the bridegroom's parents by attributing non-existent
merits to the girl and subsequently justify themselves by
saying 'Birds are many-coloured on the outside, people on the
inside.   How were we to know about her faults?'   The
bride's relatives also gather information about the bridegroom.

Before the marriage of their sons or daughters, parents
consult the father's close relatives, except for his married
sisters who are considered outsiders.   If, at the family meeting, the majority is against the marriage, it will be called off.

The relatives try to pick an available bride from the kin
from which their ancestors most often take wives.   The
parents take no account whatsoever of their children's wishes
in their choice of a bride or bridegroom.

The matchmaker ('suorumdzhu') has to be an elderly and
respected man, a good talker, not over-sensitive and with
great powers of endurance in case the bride's father wants to
try his patience.   There are few such professional matchmakers and they are known far afield and sent for from as far
as 100-200km away.   It is considered unlucky for a betrothal
to take place at the end of the day.   If the matchmaker
arrives late, he will postpone discussion of the object of his
journey to the next morning.   Before he sets out to see the
prospective bride, the matchmaker comes to an agreement with
the bridegroom's father on the sum of bridewealth to be put
forward as a basis for negotiations.   However, the stubborn-
ness of the bride's father often forces the matchmaker to step
up the amount of the bridewealth.   When this happens, the
bridegroom's father has to pay the price promised by the
matchmaker without any objections, no matter how high it may
be.

In the raion of the eastern tundra, when the matchmaker
arrives at the home of the bride's parents, he goes into the
tent, crosses himself in front of the ikon, shakes everyone by
the hand and remains standing and says,

I have come for your child, in accordance with the law.
May God bear witness to what is said today.   This man

with such and such a name [he names him] bows down
before God and begs that it may please him to put our
children in one bed.   I put this before you as a beginning
[literally, as an opening] and ask you with a pure heart.

He then takes 10 roubles from his purse and lays them on the
table.   The Dolgan Onufriya Porotov says that the matchmaker sometimes put a coat of fox fur on the table as well as
the money.   If he was, in Dolgan terms, a respectable
person ('many') he would say, 'It would be wrong to act so
quickly.   Let us talk without this [the money].'   The
matchmaker shakes his head and thanks him.   However,
sometimes the bride's parents do not say a word in reply to
the matchmaker, and do not return the money.   The matchmaker leaves at once.   If, on the matchmaker's second visit,
the money and fur coat are placed outside the door, this indicates a refusal.   If they agree the money will be on the
table as before.

According to Stepan Durakov, when the matchmaker reports
back to the bridegroom's father, he says, 'They are silent' -
which means that the negotiations can continue.   The matchmaker then goes back to the bride's parents with gifts of ox-
skin for the bride's father, a wolf-skin for her mother, and
either a fox- or wolf-skin for her eldest brother.   On his
arrival, he goes into the tent and says, 'Well, old man and
woman, let us have your heartfelt opinion.   I give you these
gifts with all my heart to help you in your decision.'   If the
bride's parents are against the marriage, they throw the skins
on the floor.   If they do not do this, the matchmaker goes
back to the bridegroom's father without saying another word
and waits there for several days.   If, in this time, the
bride's parents do not reject the proposal by sending the
money and skins back through a third party, the matchmaker
goes back to the girl's parents once more.   Immediately he
enters the tent and asks, 'What have you decided?'   The
bride's parents remain silent.   The matchmaker then says,
'From the time the world was the size of a reindeer skin, men
have lived, taking wives and lighting fires.   These people
began others and multiplied and endured from century to century.   Such is the destiny of man, he takes a wife and goes
on living.   Therefore, I beg you: though you never think
or speak again, decide!'   If they remain silent, that means
they agree and the matchmaker takes gifts from his bosom and
gives the father a fox-skin and the mother a she-wolf's.
The bride's father then turns to the matchmaker and says,
'If you really beg with all your heart and soul, then I don't
know.'   The matchmaker sits down and says, 'Old man and
woman, perhaps I forgot something - if there is anything you
want to say, say it, even if it is only one word.'   The
father replies by turning to his wife, 'What can I, a man,

say?   You speak!'   The mother answers, 'What do I know?
I was only born yesterday.   You know, you're a man.   You
have frozen and suffered many times for her sake.'   With
this the discussion ends.

However, the matter is not always settled so quickly.   The
bride's father may begin to say that he has not given his
consent and, if there were any grounds for expecting a positive answer, that was because the matchmaker, in his simplicity, had interpreted him wrongly.   Such situations demand
great patience and diplomacy on the matchmaker's part – his
skill means that things almost always end up in his favour.
In Noril'sk raion, a stubborn father will finally give in, with
the words, 'So be it, give me your best reindeer.'   The
matchmaker agrees.   Sometimes the bride's father remains
silent and forces the matchmaker to 'open his mouth' by
giving him a fox-skin.   Sometimes even this does not help.
Then it is up to the matchmaker somehow to provoke at least
one word from the bride's father, to draw him into conversation.

Once agreement has been reached, they embark on business
discussions about the bridewealth.   These again require
great diplomatic ability on the matchmaker's part.   The
bridewealth ('sulu') is divided into two parts: (1) the 'first
bridewealth', 'bastyky sulu', so called because it is paid in
advance, which usually consists of goods and a few reindeer;
(2) 'black bridewealth', 'kara sulu', the main part which is
made up entirely of reindeer.   There are no consistent norms
for this – the amount of the bridewealth is determined by
special agreement and varies according to the bride's lineage,
her beauty, her parent's greed, etc.   I wrote down the following examples of bridewealth:

A large sum.   First bridewealth – a choice of 4 bulls, 4
heifers, one broken-in reindeer, 'manshchik' (trained for
hunting);   for the bride's mother – 2 reindeer, one front and
one trace for a sledge 'so that she can ride with them until
her death';   3 wolf- or she-wolf skins, 4 fox-skins, 2 blue
fox-skins and one sable, 2 summer skins (tent coverings), 5
coats and a blanket of blue fox fur including one coat for the
mother and a woman's wolf-skin headdress, a good dress for
the mother, a copper cauldron and a rifle.   The black bridewealth – 60, 80 or 100 reindeer.

A medium sum.   First bridewealth – 3 sledges (for the
bride's father, mother and eldest brother), each with harness
and 3 reindeer, making 9 reindeer in all;   4 women's coats of
wolf or blue fox fur, 2 fox-skins, 1 she-wolf skin, and from
60 to 100 roubles in money.   The black bridewealth – 60
reindeer.

A small sum.   First bridewealth – 10 or 12 choice reindeer,
2 wolf-, 2 she-wolf- and 2 fox-skins;   the better-off families
add vixen's skins and blue fox-skins and 5 or 6 ordinary
polar fox-skins.   The black bridewealth – 40 or more reindeer.

In the past a valuable payment of bridewealth would include
a copper cauldron and a flint-lock rifle worth a large sum.
While the youngest and best reindeer are handpicked for the
first bridewealth, the black bridewealth is made up of reindeer
of medium quality.   If the first payment is ready, it is
handed over on the day after the agreement is reached;   if
not, it is delayed to an agreed time.   If the payment of the
bridewealth is stretched out over a long period, this creates
obstacles to the marriage.   When most of the first bridewealth has been paid, the bride is free to marry, and if her
bridegroom later refuses to pay the rest, the marriage will
not be dissolved.   The bride's parents usually console themselves with the fact that if their son-in-law is an honest man,
he will pay them in the end.   In fact, cases of non-payment
occur very rarely.   However, if 60 reindeer are agreed on
as bridewealth and only 40 are handed over, the bride will
have 3 sledges as her dowry, instead of the usual 5.   The
first items of the bridewealth to be paid are 8 reindeer, reindeer skins, fur coats, other animal skins and money.   When
the first bridewealth has been paid, they agree on the date
on which the reindeer which make up the black bridewealth
will be handed over;   this is always the first day of the wedding.   When the reindeer are handed over their ropes are
given back to the bridegroom's father together with one reindeer 'so that the lassos don't go back empty'.   After the
betrothal, restrictions are placed on the freedom of both the
bride and bridegroom;   they can no longer take part in the
meetings of the young.   If the bride's relations ('kyngattar')
see the bridegroom dancing with the girls and find out that he
is still exchanging gifts with them, they condemn him with the
words, 'Once he's given his word, he should restrain himself.'

On the day of the wedding the tents of the bride and bridegroom's fathers are placed near each other.   In each tent, 4
or 5 reindeer are slaughtered to feast the guests, depending
on the financial situation of their owners.   The bridegroom
himself kills another reindeer and sends its meat to the bride's
father.   Then the bridegroom and his friends catch the reindeer for the black bridewealth.   Meanwhile, the young people
gathered at the bride's tent catch the reindeers required for
the dowry.   The bride dances in the open air with the young
men and girls.   When the reindeer for the black bridewealth
have been caught, they tie them up in one long string with
the matchmaker's sledge at the end, and he goes ahead of the
bridegroom, driving the reindeer.

When the matchmaker and the bridegroom arrive at the
bride's tent, they drive three times round it sunwise. Then
the matchmaker goes into the tent alone (without the bridegroom) and says: 'Your son-in-law has come.' Meanwhile
the guests drive the reindeer into a special enclosure made
out of lassos tied round trees and upturned sledges. A
large number of guests accompany the bridegroom. Outside,
the matchmaker takes the bridegroom by the hand to the
bride's father, the bridegroom leading a doe reindeer on a
rope, which he presents to his future father-in-law ('nyald-
zhin'). The bridegroom and his guests then stay outside
until the feast is ready and the bridal bed made (by one of
the bride's female relatives). While the guests await the
feast outside, the matchmaker runs backwards and forwards
from the bride's tent to the guests, and gives them hilárious
accounts of what is going on inside the tent. Meanwhile,
the bride's father receives the reindeer of the black bridewealth. In the eastern tundra raion the reindeer are usually
accepted unconditionally, but in Noril'sk raion, the bride's
father often rejects some of them and sends them back,
demanding others in their place. If the bride's father is
exacting, this can go on until late in the evening.

The guests meanwhile have to stand and freeze in the open
air. When the feast and bed are at last ready and the black
bridewealth transacted, the matchmaker and the bridegroom go
into the tent together and pray before the ikons. The bride
joins the bridegroom in his prayers. After this the matchmaker turns to the bridegroom and says: 'Bow down to your
father-in-law and ask him for her hand.' The bride and
bridegroom bow down to the ground and ask the bride's
parents and her elder relatives for their blessing. The
latter bless them, give them their hands to kiss, and wish
them every happiness. The matchmaker gives the bride's
father 10 roubles and her relatives lengths of cloths and
scarves. In Noril'sk instead of money the matchmaker gives
the bride's father a fox-skin and her mother a polar fox-skin
or coat. These gifts are called 'yunyo' - the prayer or plea.
On receiving them, the bride's relatives stand up and shake
hands with the bridegroom, but not his guests. After the
ritual blessing the bride and bridegroom sit behind the curtains of the bed and only then are the guests allowed in, in a
strictly predetermined order. The bride's relatives go outside and lead the guests in by the hand - the adults lead the
adults, the children lead the children - and show them to
their seats. Close relatives, special guests and foreigners
(Yakuts, Russians, Tungusy) are led in first. To prevent
mistakes, the bride's relatives ask their friends which of the
guests has the first right, before they start to bring them in.
Also at this time, two 'fortune tellers' ('ypkyordyoryordzhon')
are chosen for their talents of improvisation, one by the

bride's relatives, the other by the bridegroom's. This, however, is not always done.

When the guests of honour are seated, the bride's father
turns to them and says: 'Guests! What do you have to
say?' The matchmaker replies, 'We have a word or two.'
Then the man chosen by the bridegroom's side makes an elab-
orate and flowery speech, describing how the young couple
will live in peace and harmony, talks about the number of
children they will have, their future wealth, etc., and ends:
'My speech is over, now it's your turn.' The man chosen by
the bridegroom's side then makes a similar speech. They
judge whether the bride or the bridegroom will be the happier
in their married life according to which of the two speeches
was better. After this the bride's female relations pour tea
for the guests and organise the food. All the guests go outside again after the 'first course', and do not begin eating
until the table is spread ('ostuolu asyagar iniger'). The
young people dance until the second course is ready. Meanwhile the ceremony of dividing out the bridewealth takes place
('sulu tuttarar').

If the bride's father is too poor to provide the agreed
dowry, he asks his close relatives to contribute something
towards it, e.g. a fur coat, a cauldron, etc., and promises
to repay them with reindeer from the bridewealth. If the
bride's father is wealthy he gives the reindeer from the bridewealth to his close relatives, saying: 'Here is my gift to you
on the christening of my child.' The relatives who are given
reindeer pay back the newlyweds with goods of greater value
within the year. On receiving the reindeer they immediately
cut their personal marks in the animals' ears, and harness
them to their sledges. The guests then go back into the
tent. The bride and bridegroom come out from behind the
bed curtains and sit with the others. After the first lot of
guests has eaten, a second shift of less important guests is
fed. It is said that the guests are only allowed into the tent
in two shifts so that the guests of honour and the strangers
may have the pick of the food ('bastyng asy dzhosun kisi,
omuk kisi koluoktak'), but it is really due to the size of the
tents.

In some families in the eastern tundra region the bridegroom
spends his wedding night in the bride's tent and does not
take her away for three days. In Noril'sk raion the bride
rides on a reindeer which one of her respected and elderly
female relatives leads by the bridle, leaning on a wooden hook
for hanging pots from (this hook she herself keeps). A
woman supports the bride on each side.

The marriage bed is transported to the bridegroom's tent

before her arrival.   The wedding procession is led by the
matchmaker followed by the bridegroom and then the bride,
leading the reindeer loaded with her dowry.   The bride
wears two cloth coats ('sontap') and an embroidered fur coat
('ardaidakh sangyiakh').

In Noril'sk raion the matchmaker settles the amount of the
dowry.   In other places, this is not done, as the dowry
depends on the size of the bridewealth.   Where the bridewealth is 60 reindeer, the dowry will be 45.   A rich dowry
would consist of 60-70 picked reindeer, of various ages, none
broken in, none old.   There should be not more than 2 or 3
calves.   As well as reindeer the dowry includes, in rich
families, 7, in poor 5, sledges pulled by the best-riding reindeer (in pairs in rich families and singly in poor ones).   One
of these sledges is a sledge tent, pulled by 4 reindeer.

The sledges are filled with polar fox-, wolf- or reindeer
skins (in rich families enough to make a whole tent out of, in
poor, half a one), 15 or 16 ladies' and transport saddles, a
winter harness with straps of coloured cloth embroidered with
beads, a woman's riding crop, with an iron hook with patterns
on it, a samovar, a teapot and other crockery, saddle bags,
ornaments, etc.   All this should be new, well-cared for, or
at least clean.

The dowry includes two fur coats, one of which the bride
wears;   each should have a separate cloth coat over the top,
the hem of which is embroidered with coloured ribbon or
beads.   The dowry clothes also include a woman's fur shoes,
embroidered with beads, and wolf-skin kneecaps.   Before the
items of the dowry are packed into trunks, they are filled
with small change, so that each of them 'has an inside'.
Each of the sledges in the dowry has to carry a load, however small, as it is considered disgraceful for them to arrive
empty.   In Noril'sk raion a piece of meat from a specially
killed reindeer is put on each of the dowry sledges.   This is
called the maintenance sum ('matanga isya').   The sledges of
dowry are covered with reindeer skins and tied round with
ropes.

When the wedding procession reaches the bridegroom's
tent, the matchmaker goes and tells the bridegroom's parents
that they have come.   On their arrival, they drive three
times sunwise round the tent.   In Noril'sk raion, the bride
herself drives round the tent, but if she goes into it, someone
else drives her reindeer.   This ritual is called the introduction to the home ('sarany bullarar').   An old woman, never a
relative, leads the bride into the bridegroom's tent.   The
bride and bridegroom pray before the ikon, then bow to the
ground before his father and mother, ask for their blessing,

and kiss their hands. The bridegroom's parents bless them
and wish them happiness. The bride gives them money or
valuable furs. These gifts have to be of greater value than
the bridegroom's presents, as the bride's father wants to show
off in front of the bridegroom's father. The guests are again
fed in two shifts in the bridegroom's tent. In the past, the
shaman used always to be asked to the wedding. Before the
feast, dressed in his ordinary clothes, not his ritual costume,
and leaning on the bride's reindeer crop, he called on the
good deities and spirits to wish the newlyweds a long and
happy life. After this, the first shift of honoured guests
sits down to the meal.

Afterwards, the bridegroom's father goes out to look at the
reindeer in the dowry, and decides which to give to the
people who helped him in paying the bridewealth. When the
feast is over, the ritual inspection of the dowry takes place,
except among the Noril'sk Dolgans. The bridegroom's father
goes outside, opens the trunks and meticulously inspects their
contents. If they turn out not to be worth as much as the
bridewealth, this arouses general disapproval. The bride's
father usually tries to include valuable objects in the dowry,
so as not to bring disgrace on himself. Here the Dolgan
wedding rituals end. The guests spend the day eating,
playing games and dancing and go home in the late evening.
The bride's father and mother stay at the bridegroom's for
three days. The bridegroom's father gives the bride's
parents one reindeer ('ogo keryoryu') on their departure, in
place of their daughter. This reindeer will be especially well
looked after. On the morning of the third day the young
bride pours out tea. While they drink it, her father reads
her a lecture: 'From now on you must obey your husband
rather than me. You must look on your mother-in-law as
your own mother, your father-in-law as your own father.
Respect them and obey them, do not quarrel with them.'

Among the Noril'sk Dolgans, the young bride does no work
in the tent for three days, neither preparing food nor tending
the fire. Only on the third day does she cook the meat she
brought with her. From then on she has to obey her father-
in-law rather than her own parents. There are certain
taboos affecting the relations between the daughter-in-law and
her husband's parents. For example, a daughter-in-law may
not drink from her father-in-law's cup, or her father-in-law
from hers. The father-in-law may not sit on his daughter-
in-law's bed.

The wedding of an orphan is arranged by the father's kin
and the dowry is always 5 sledges.

V

The husband and wife call each other 'Eidno!' ('O friend') instead of their real names. When a husband refers to his wife, he says 'my old woman', when a wife refers to her husband, 'my man'. They do occasionally use their real names, but this is considered bad manners and a sign of the couple's lack of mutual self-respect. The Yakutsk word 'oiakh' - wife - is hardly ever met with among the Dolgans, especially those of Noril'sk raion, and is replaced by the word 'dzhaktar' - woman. The man says 'my woman', not 'my wife'. The man's main job is hunting and looking after the reindeer. If the family is short of food the man is to blame. The woman does all the housework. A good wife's tent should be warm and clean, and all holes in the reindeer skins should be patched. A housewife is judged by the state of her tent.

The reindeer are regarded as the husband's property, with the exception of the ones his wife received as presents from her relatives ('nyad-hyma') or from guests ('yallaty taba') and also those which draw her sledge and carry her property (crockery, clothes and small household articles). Reindeer given to their children by relatives are also excluded. The crockery, skins and money brought as dowry is regarded as the wife's property, and she has the right to dispose of it at will. Some husbands raise objections to this, but such behaviour is regarded as a violation of the law. Women also have the right to dispose freely of the money they receive from the sale of their property. The reindeer which come in the dowry are thought to bring luck and some families will not sell them for three years. Some of the family's fox snares and traps may belong to the wife, or the sons and daughters. However, this is usually a fictitious possession, since trapping foxes is regarded as the father's preserve. It happens for the following reason: if animals stop falling into the snares, the father of the family, their owner, thinks that perhaps this is because his luck is out, and that perhaps the luck of other members of the family is in. He then makes a fictitious division of the traps among the other members of his family. However, when a daughter marries, the traps which are theoretically hers, remain in her father's possession.

Divorce is very rare among the Dolgans. Causes of divorce are: the infidelity of the husband or wife, or other family troubles. If the wife's guilt is confirmed by the court of elders, she has to return half the value of her bridewealth to her husband; if the husband is pronounced guilty, he has to return half the value of the dowry to his wife. If the dowry was worth more than the bridewealth or the bridewealth more than the dowry, nothing is returned. On divorce a woman

returns to her parents or relatives, who are obliged to support her without touching either her reindeer or her other
property; she is regarded as a full member of the family and
helps in the housework. Her children usually stay with their
father.

Although the Dolgans disapprove of a widow's remarrying
(see p. 203) a wedding celebration is held if she does get
married. If she marries without the consent of her dead
husband's parents, they take the children and half of the
property left on her husband's death. If the widow has
three children, her husband's relatives will only take two of
them. If the mother doesn't want to give up her children,
the relatives may agree to wait until they come of age. In
this case she keeps most of the property and only a small
portion passes to her dead husband's brother. If several
relatives claim the widow's children, the court of elders allots
all the children to one of them, so that they will not be separated. Half of the dead husband's reindeer are given to the
guardians. The guardian has to preserve them and later
gives them and their offspring to his wards. If the guardian
treats the children badly, they are placed in the care of
another relative. If the children are left without father or
mother, they are brought up by their father's relatives.
Relations in the mother's line only take the children in if
there are no relations in the father's line present at the death
of the father or mother. Later, when they hear about it,
the father's relatives collect the children, not wanting to leave
them with other kin.

If a widow marries a relative, she keeps her dead husband's
property. If she marries into another kin group, she keeps
a small, arbitrarily decided amount and the rest goes to her
husband's kin, it being considered inadmissible to transfer
property to strangers ('bai omukka barara tyukteri').

Before his death, the father divides his inheritance between
the children living with him. He also gives his closest
friends a reindeer each, and asks his children to treat them
with respect for his sake. The children who live on their
own do not inherit anything, since they will have already
been given a share in their father's lifetime. The heirs are
the younger sons, who live with their father right up to his
death. The traps and snares are transferred with the rest
of the inheritance. One of the relatives is given free use of
the traps until their owners come of age.

If the dead man has an adopted son who was not taken from
among his brothers, or chosen without their consent, the
adopted son gets only half of the inheritance and the other
half is divided among the deceased's other sons. If the son

was adopted with the consent of the dead man's brothers, the
whole inheritance passes to him.

A widow usually lives with her younger son.   If there are
no children from the marriage, half of the property of her
dead husband passes to his brother.   But if the widow is
able to say that most of the reindeer are the offspring of the
reindeer which came in her dowry, she has the right not to
give anything away.   After her death, the property goes to
the wife of the son she has been living with.   This daughter-
in-law, according to my observations, has to give her husband's sisters something to remember their mother by.   They
often do not get what they want and get very cross about it.
However, the matter does not usually go as far as the court
of elders.   The sisters complain to their brother about their
sister-in-law and he makes her give them the things they
want.

On the death of a childless widow her personal property
(mainly her dowry) goes to her brother.   But if a wife dies
in her husband's lifetime all her property goes to him.   The
dead man's son or widow is responsible for his debts.
Creditors usually feel it indelicate to press for payment immediately after his death, and are content to wait a year.

A LIST OF DOLGAN KINSHIP AND AFFINAL TERMS

This list of Dolgan kinship and affinal terms does not reflect
kinship relations in the past, as all the terms are Yakut.
They have obviously formed in place of the previous ones as
a result of Yakut cultural influence.   Unfortunately, it is not
possible to compare the Yakut with the Dolgan kinship terms,
because of the lack of detailed records of the latter.   Such a
comparison would be of great interest, since, as far as we
saw, some of the Yakut terms have taken on new meanings
among the Dolgans.   (The list is in alphabetical order according to the Cyrillic equivalent, with a few addenda when the
author deemed necessary.   T.D.)

'Aga' - father.
'Amiran' - stepfather.
'Balys' - younger brother (younger than me), (5) younger
sister, my sister's son, the wife of my sister's son, my sister's daughter, the husband of my sister's daughter, the son
of my father's brother (younger), the son of the son of my
father's sister, my brother's daughter (younger), the daughter
of the son of my father's sister (younger), the son of the
daughter of my father's sister (younger), the daughter of the
daughter of my father's sister (younger), the son of my
father's father's brother (younger), the daughter of my

father's father's brother (younger), the daughter of my husband's brother.
'Baltym uola' - my brother's son (younger).
'Dzhaktar' - wife.
'Iie' or 'inya' - mother.
'Iieren' - stepmother.
'Kinit' - the wife of my brother's son (younger), the wife of
the son of my father's brother (younger), the wife of the son
of my mother's brother (younger), the daughter of the son of
my mother's brother (younger), the daughter of my mother's
sister (younger), the wife of the son of my father's father's
sister (younger), the wife of the son of my mother's sister
(younger), the wife of my son, the wife of my husband's
brother (younger), the wife of my wife's brother (younger),
the brother's wife (younger), the sister of my brother's wife
(younger).
'Kyutyuyo' - the husband of my brother's daughter (older
than me), (6) the husband of the daughter of my father's
brother (older), the husband of the daughter of my mother's
brother (younger), the husband of my mother's sister (elder),
the husband of the daughter of my mother's sister (older),
the husband of the sister of my mother's father, the husband
of the sister of my father's mother (older), the husband of
my father's sister (older), the husband of my sister (older),
the husband of the daughter of my mother's brother (older),
the husband of the daughter of the brother of my father's
father (older), the husband of the sister of my brother's wife
(older).
'Kyutyuyot' - the husband of my brother's daughter (younger),
the husband of the daughter of my father's brother (younger),
the husband of the daughter of my mother's sister (younger),
the husband of the daughter of the brother of my father's
father (younger), the husband of the sister of my father's
mother (younger than my father), the husband of my wife's
sister (younger), the husband of the sister of my wife's
father (younger than my wife), my sister's husband (younger,
I may be a man or a woman), my daughter's husband, the
husband of the daughter of the sister of my father's father
(younger), the husband of the sister of my brother's wife
(younger, I am a man).
'Kylyn' - the husband of my wife's sister (older), my wife's
brother (older), my wife's father, the son of the brother of
my wife's father (older than my wife), the brother of my
wife's mother, the husband of the sister of my wife's mother,
the son of the sister of my wife's mother (older than my
wife).
'Iie kylyn' - my wife's sister (older than my wife), the wife
of my wife's brother (older), the wife of the brother of my
wife's father, the daughter of the brother of my wife's father
(older than my wife), the sister of my wife's father, my wife's
mother, the wife of the brother of my wife's mother, the sister

of my wife's mother, the daughter of the sister of my wife's
mother (older than my wife).
'Ulakan kylyn' - the brother of my wife's father (older than
my wife).
'Kuchchungui kylyn' - the brother of my wife's father
(younger than my wife).
'Kodogoi' - the sister of the wife of my father's brother, the
sister of the wife of my husband's brother, the sister of my
sister's husband (I am a man), the sister of my brother's
wife (I am a woman), the sister of my husband's sister (I am
a woman), the sister of the wife of my wife's brother.
'Kotun' - the wife of my husband's brother (older than my
husband), my husband's mother.
'Kyurya balyo' - my wife's brother (younger than me), the
son of my wife's brother, the daughter of my wife's brother,
the son of the brother of my wife's father (younger than my
wife), the daughter of the brother of my wife's father
(younger than my wife), the son of the brother of my wife's
mother, the daughter of the brother of my wife's mother, the
son of the sister of my wife's mother (younger than my wife),
the daughter of the sister of my wife's mother (younger than
my wife), my wife's sister (younger than my wife).
'Kys' - my daughter, the daughter of the brother of my husband's mother (younger), the daughter of the sister of my
husband's mother, my husband's sister (younger than my
husband).
'Ogo' - my brother's grandson, my brother's granddaughter,
my sister's grandson or daughter, the daughter of the son of
my mother's sister, the son of the daughter of my mother's
sister, the son of the son of my mother's sister (younger),
the daughter of the daughter of my mother's sister, the son
of my husband's brother (younger), the daughter of my husband's brother (younger), the son of my husband's sister,
the daughter of my brother (younger than me), the daughter
of my husband's sister (younger), the daughter of the sister
of my husband's mother (younger), the son of the sister of
my husband's mother (younger), my stepson, my stepdaughter.
'Ogom uola' - granddaughter.
'Ogom kysa' - granddaughter.
'Sangas' - the wife of my brother's son (older), the wife of
my father's brother (younger), the wife of the son of my
father's brother (older), the wife of my mother's brother, the
wife of the son of my mother's brother (older), the daughter
of the son of my mother's brother, the daughter of my
mother's sister (older than me), the wife of the son of the
brother of my father's father, the wife of the son of the sister
of my father's father (older), the wife of the son of the sister
of my mother's mother (older), my brother's wife (older, I am
a man), the sister of my brother's wife (older, I am a man),
the wife of the brother of my mother's mother (if the brother
is younger than my mother).

'Sien' - the son of the sister of my father's father, the daughter of the sister of my father's father.
'Syrdzhum' - the son of the son of my father's brother (younger, I am a woman), the son of the son of my father's sister (younger, I am a woman).
'Sygan' - the son of my father's mother's sister, the daughter of my father's mother's sister.
'Tai' - my mother's brother, the son of my mother's brother, the daughter of my mother's brother, the son of the son of my mother's brother, the son of the daughter of my mother's brother, the daughter of the daughter of my mother's brother, the son of the brother of my mother's father, the daughter of the brother of my mother's father, the sister of my mother's father, the brother of my mother's mother, the son of the brother of my mother's mother, the wife of the son of the brother of my mother's mother, the son of the brother of my father's mother, the daughter of the brother of my father's mother.
'Kat tai' - the husband of the daughter of the brother of my mother's mother, the son of the sister of my mother's mother, the daughter of the sister of my mother's mother, her husband, the daughter of my mother's brother (older).
'Toion' - my husband's brother (older).
'Tyungyur' - the brother of the husband of my mother's sister, the husband of the sister of my brother's wife (I am a man).
'Ubai' - the son of my father's brother (older), the daughter of my father's brother (older), the son of the son of my father's brother (older), the son of the son of my father's sister (older), the daughter of the daughter of my father's sister (older), the son of my mother's sister (older), the son of the son of my mother's sister (older), the son of the brother of my father's father (older), the daughter of the brother of my father's father (older), the son of the daughter of the sister of my mother's father.
'Uol' - my son, my husband's brother (younger than my husband), the son of the brother of my husband's mother (younger than my husband).
'Uru' - the son of my wife's sister, the daughter of my wife's sister, the daughter of the sister of my wife's father.
'Ebe' - grandmother, the wife of my father's brother, my mother's sister, the wife of the brother of my father's father, the sister of my father's father, the wife of the brother of my father's mother, the wife of the brother of my mother's mother, the wife of my father's brother, the wife of my husband's brother (older), my husband's sister (older than my husband), the wife of the brother of my husband's father, the sister of my husband's father (older than my husband), the wife of the brother of my husband's mother, the daughter of the brother of the brother of my husband's mother (older than my husband), the sister of my husband's mother, the daughter of

the sister of my husband's mother (older than my husband),
my husband's mother.
'Ebem uola' - the son of my husband's sister (older), the son
of the sister of my husband's father.
'Ebem kysa' - the daughter of my husband's sister (older),
the daughter of the sister of my husband's father.
'Edzhy' - the daughter of my father's brother (younger), the
daughter of my mother's brother (younger), my mother's
younger sister, the husband of my mother's sister (younger),
the son of my mother's sister (younger), the sister of my
father's mother (younger than my father).
'Er' - husband.
'Eeya' - grandfather, my father's brother (older), the husband of my father's sister, the brother of my mother's father,
the brother of my father's mother, my husband's brother
(older), my husband's father, the brother of my husband's
father, the brother of my husband's mother, the son of the
brother of my husband's mother, the husband of the sister of
my husband's mother, the son of the sister of my husband's
mother (older than my husband).
'Esyam ogoto' - the son of the brother of my husband's father,
the daughter of the brother of my husband's father.
'Ynara ebya' - the sister of my mother's mother
'Ynara esya' - the husband of the sister of my mother's
mother.

NOTES

1 In the journal 'Soviet Ethnography': Materials on the Kinship System of the Dolgan, 1934, no. 6; Reindeer Breeding among the Dolgan, 1935, nos 4-5; The Technology of
  the Dolgan, 1937, no. 1. In Collected Papers Dedicated
  to V.G. Bogoraz, Hunting and Fishing among the Dolgan,
  also separately published in 'Dolgan Folklore', Leningrad,
  1937.
2 The Dolgan call people 'God's people', in distinction from
  the 'abasy', evil spirits.
3 Tretyakov, 'The Turukhan Territory, Its Natural History
  and Inhabitants', 1869, p. 406.
4 N.V. Latkin, 'Eniseisk Province, Its Past and Present',
  St Petersburg, 1892.
5 In future, the term 'younger than me' is indicated by the
  abbreviated 'younger'.
6 'Older than me' we indicate by 'older'.

11   The kinship terminology of the Nganasan as a historical source
*L.A. Fainberg**

The Nganasan, one of the small peoples of northern Siberia,
live in the Avamsk and Khatangsk regions of Taimyrsk
Nationalniy Okrug (one of the Soviet subdivisions for the
territories of small nationalities).

The archaic and distinctive culture of the Nganasan, which
sets them apart from neighbouring peoples, and the complex
question of their origin, have long aroused great interest.
However, serious research into the Nganasan only began after
the October Revolution.   A.A. Popov and B.O. Dolgikh
described the Nganasan economy, solved the question of
ethnogenesis, and also studied various aspects of their culture
and social structure. (1)   However, light has yet to be
thrown on many aspects of Nganasan ethnography, in particular the history of their social structure and the nature of
their cultural life.

In the present article we will attempt to describe the kinship
system of the Nganasan, to analyse it as a reflection of their
social structure and to compare it with the kinship systems of
the Entsi, Nentsi, Evenki, and the Yukagir, i.e. all the
peoples with which the Nganasan are known or thought to
have been genetically connected in the past.

I

B.O. Dolgikh's study of archival sources, Nganasan folklore,
toponymy and vocabulary, economy and daily life established
that the Nganasan were formed in the following way. (2)   The
fundamental and most ancient component of Nganasan nationality was the ancient hunters of the wild northern reindeer.
Ethnically, they may have been some of the ancient Yukagir
tribes.   In the region between Taz and Enisei and the Pyasin
Basin, this ancient aboriginal population was assimilated by the
Samoeds, who penetrated from the south.   This led to the
formation of the Samoed-speaking groups of the 'Vorons' and
the 'Orls'.   Later, but still before the arrival of the Russians,

* First published in Museum of Anthropology and Ethnography
  of the Academy of Sciences of the USSR, 'Collected Works',
  vol. 78, Moscow, 1962, pp. 226-37.

the Tungus (Evenks) penetrated the region between Lake Pyasin and the River Avam and assimilated the 'Vorons' and the 'Orls' and formed the Samoed-speaking Tidirisy group. The Paleoasians who lived in the Khatanga and Anabar Basins were originally absorbed by the Tungus.   Later, they moved west to the Rivers Taimyr, Kheta and the lower reaches of the Khatanga and Anabar.   There they were assimilated by the Samoeds and formed the Tavgi group.

During the second half of the seventeenth and the beginning of the eighteenth century, the 'Orls' (Eagles), 'Vorons' (Crows), Tidirisy and Tavgi merged to form the tribe of the Avam Nganasan, with a unified Samoed culture and language.   The Paleoasians, occupying the south-west of the lower reaches of the Khatanga, were first assimilated by the Tungus and then by the Samoeds to form the tribe of the Vadeevsk Nganasan.

In the nineteenth century, the Nganasan were increased by the addition of the separate kin of the Oko, or Dolgans, which was formed at the beginning of the nineteenth century from the descendants of Oko from the Dolgan tribe of the Tungus, which had been assimilated by the Nganasan.

The culture of the Nganasan bears most resemblance to that of the tundra Enets, who are also probably Paleoasians assimilated by the Samoeds.

In distinction from the Nenets, the main branch of the Nganasan economy in the eighteenth and nineteenth centuries remained the hunting of wild reindeer on foot - a characteristic inherited from their Paleoasian forebears.   At the same time, the practice of breeding reindeer, which the Samoeds introduced from the south, gradually spread among them. By the end of the nineteenth century, the Nganasan were the richest of all the reindeer peoples of the Taimyr.

After the October Revolution, 'soviets' (councils. T.D.) were organised in the kin groups, then in the nomads' camps and finally as village soviets.   In the 1930s the Nganasan joined kolkhozes.   By 1957 there were three kolkhozes with Nganasan members, two in the Avam and one in the Khatanga regions.

Great changes have taken place in Nganasan culture since the advent of Soviet rule.   Earlier, none of them could read or write.   Now the Nganasan children are educated in boarding schools.   Social newspaper readings are organised within the reindeer-breeding and hunting brigades, and films are shown in the settlements.   However, the Nganasan still preserve some of the old ways - in particular their kinship divisions. All the Nganasan are members of kin groups; the Chunanchera (Chunanchar), the Linancheras (Turdaginy), the Ninonde or Falysyada (Porbiny), the Ngomde (Momde), the Ngamtusuo or Kula (Kosterkiny), the Kokory (Kokore), the Ngaibuo (Maibu), the Asyandu, the Kupchik, the Lansakha and the Oko (Yarotsky).

The first five clans listed belong historically to the tribe of the Avam Nganasan, the next five to the Vadeevsk, and the last one (the Oko), as has already been said, to neither tribe.

The Nganasan clans are patrilineal but preserve some features of the matrilineal kin, especially in religious survivals. The custom of exogamy is strictly observed to the present day.

The common forms of marriage are as follows. For men, marriage is usually with the daughter of their mother's sister or brother. For women, marriage takes place with the son of their mother's sister or brother. That is to say, the Nganasan have the custom of marriage between cross-cousins, which, as M.O. Kosven has shown, is historically connected with dual exogamy and a matrilineal kinship system. (3) This means that the Nganasan often take wives from their mother's kin.

It is forbidden for a Nganasan to marry the daughter of his father's sister, although she belongs to another clan according to the patrilineal view of kinship. The ban on marriage with the daughter of one's father's sister is a widespread phenomenon in kinship societies. As M.O. Kosven remarks, (4) it arose in the period of transition from the matrilineal to the patrilineal kinship system, and is connected with the fact that marriage with the daughter of one's father's sister violated the matrilineal concept of kinship.

We will briefly touch upon some of the other marriage norms and customs and the survival of fraternal divisions when we come to describe the Nganasan kinship system.

II

The Nganasan kinship system is a classificatory system, although it does contain a small number of descriptive terms.

Members of the great-grandparents' generation are designated by descriptive terms, formed from the term for the corresponding member of the grandparents' generation and the word 'tagonta' (distant, great). For example - 'tagonta iri' = great-grandfather ('iri' = grandfather), 'tagonta imi' = great grandmother ('imi' = grandmother), 'tagonta idi' = great-grand-

father's brother ('idi' = the father's elder brother, our grandfather's younger brother, etc.).

In this generation no distinction is drawn between the patrilineal and matrilineal lines of kinship. The following terms
are used to designate members of the grandparents' generation.

'Iri' is the name given to all men of the grandparents' generation, regardless of whether they belong to the father's or
mother's clan. Here one must make the reservation that the
generations are merged in the Nganasan classificatory system.
Members of different generations are placed in the same class,
more precisely, the younger branch of one generation with the
elder branch of the next generation. Therefore, the younger
brother of the father or mother's father and the grandmother's
younger brother come into the same class as the father's elder
brothers and they are all called 'isi' (see below).

'Imi' is the name given to all women of this generation
except the younger sister of the mother's mother ('kotu).
The practice of giving the same name to members of different
generations means that the younger sister of the mother's
mother comes into the parents' generation, while her elder
sister remains in the grandparents' generation. Characteristically, no distinction between the patrilineal and matrilineal
lines of kinship is made in this generation either. The lines
of kinship are not separated in the elder generations even in
some kinship societies which otherwise very strictly delimit
both lines of kinship. This is because both these generations are regarded as too old to marry and therefore there is
no need to separate the lines of kinship for the purposes of
exogamy. In the parents' generation, individual terms exist
for the father - 'dyasy' (the descriptive form) - and the
mother - 'nea' (also the descriptive form). The vocative
forms for the father and mother have a classificatory character. They are 'idva' ('idi') - father, father's elder brother,
the grandfather's younger brother.

The descriptive expression 'inidem idi' is also formed from
the word 'idi'. 'Inidem' means the elder sister's husband.
Taken together it means the husband of the father's elder
sister.

The term 'isi' is used to address the 'inidem idi' (on this,
see below). 'Aba' is the vocative form used for addressing
the mother and the younger sister of ego and the father's
younger sister. Two general terms are used for the other
people, whom the Nganasan regard as belonging to the
parents' generation - 'isi' for men, and 'kotu' for women.

'Isi' is the name given to the grandmother's grandfather's
younger brother in the patrilineal or matrilineal line, the
father or mother's elder brother, the grandfather's brother's
son (in the patrilineal or matrilineal line).   If he (the son)
is older than the father with regard to the affinal relations,
the term 'isi' includes the father of the sister's husband, the
husband of the mother's elder sister, the husband of the wife
of the elder brother of ego (if the latter is older than him),
the brother of the elder sister's husband (if he is older than
ego), the husband of the sister of his elder brother's wife.

The concept 'isi' thus embraces all men younger than the
grandfather but older than the father of ego belonging to the
father or mother's kin or to the kin into which women of ego's
kin married.   This term is not used in relation to his wife's
relatives.

The term 'kotu' designates women older than the father or
mother of ego belonging to the father or mother's kin or to
the kin from which the men ('isi') have taken wives.   It is
used for the father or mother's elder sister, the wife of the
grandfather's younger brother in the patrilineal or matrilineal
line, the wife of the grandmother's younger brother in the
patrilineal line, the wife of the son of the grandfather's elder
brother in the patrilineal line.   There is some evidence that
the wife of the son of the father's brother or sister and the
wife of the husband's brother were also given this name.
According to information received in 1957, the term 'kotu' in
addition applied to the younger sister of the grandmother in
the mother's line.

The kinship terminology (for one's own generation) is
worked out in much greater detail.   Here, too, people older
than ego and younger than his parents are placed in one category, and people younger than ego and older than his children, in another.   The members of one's own generation are
thus split up into two groups.   We will examine them in turn.

Men of his father's kin older than ego, but younger than his
father he refers to as 'niny', and addresses as 'oo'.   The
concept 'niny' therefore includes the father's elder and
younger brothers and parallel cousins in the patrilineal line of
all degrees of kinship, as long as they are older than ego.

Women of the father's kin older than ego but younger than
his father he calls 'nakhu', i.e. he uses this name for his
elder sisters, his father's younger sisters and his parallel
cousins in the father's line, if they are older than he is.

According to our informants, the term 'nakhu' is also used
to refer to the daughter of the father's sisters, i.e. elder

cross-cousins.   However, this assertion is open to doubt and
more evidence is needed.

The wives of the men who are 'niny' are also called 'nakhu'.
Men of the father's kin younger than ego are called 'nadya';
oddly enough, the same name is used with reference to some
categories of women.   A Naganasan uses the name 'nadya' for
his younger brother or sister, the son or daughter of his
father's brother or sister, if they are younger than him, the
son or daughter of his elder brother, if they are younger
than him and parallel cousins of all degrees of kinship, but
again, only if they are younger than ego.

The Naganasan calls the wives of his 'nadya' 'myai'.   This
term is also used to refer to other categories of wives where
the men are younger than ego.

The male members of the mother's kin are called 'tytyya',
independent of whether they are older or younger than ego.
Parallel cousins in the mother's line ('syomu') and those who
are his 'iri' or 'isi' are an exception.   The Naganasan will
therefore use the term 'tytyya' for his mother's younger
brother, the son of his mother's brother, the grandchildren
of his mother's brother or sister, the great grandchildren of
his mother's brother and the son of the brother of his
mother's father, if he is younger than ego; if he is older,
the Nganasan will call him 'isi'.   According to our informants
(in 1957) the term 'tytyya' is also applied to the son of the
father's sister.   This clearly refers to the case when the
father's sister marries into his wife's kin and her child thus
belongs to the kin of the mother of ego.

The children of two sisters are parallel cousins in the matrilineal line, and call each other 'syomu'.   Ego also uses this
name for the son of the daughter of the sister of his elder
brother's wife, and the wife of the son of his mother's sister,
if she (the wife) is older than him.   If she is younger than
him, he calls her 'myai'.

At first glance it seems unusual to use the same term for
the children of the mother's sister and the children of the
sister of the elder brother's wife.   However, this can be explained by the special features of the Nganasan kinship system.
Since the elder brother of ego and his father's younger
brothers belong to the same category, it can easily happen
that the younger sisters of the Nganasan's mother marry his
father's younger brothers and his elder brothers.   In this
case the children of the sister of the wife of the elder brother
of ego will also be the children of his mother's younger sister
and he, naturally, will call them 'syumu', just as they do him.

The Nganasan calls women of his mother's kin, of her own generation or younger than her, 'naga'. He also uses this name for his mother's younger sister, the daughter of his mother's sister, the daughter of the daughter of his mother's sister and the daughter of the son of his mother's brother or sister. He also calls the wives of his 'tytyya' 'naga', if the 'tytyya' is older than ego. If the 'tytyya' is younger than ego, ego will call his wife 'myai'.

A Nganasan calls his wife 'ny', and she calls him 'kodyumu'. He calls her kin 'ny khonka' ('khonka' = kin), and she calls his kin 'kodyumu khonka'. He calls those of his wife's kinsmen who are older than him 'ninaba', and those younger than him 'nado'. We will discuss the deviations from this general rule later. The wife also calls her husband's kinsmen who are older than him 'ninaba', and those younger than him 'nado'.

'Ninaba' is thus the name given to the husband or wife's father and mother, the brother and sisters of the wife's (husband's) relatives if they are older than ego, and the wife's (husband's) elder brothers and sisters.

'Nado' is used to designate the wife's (husband's) younger brother or sister, the son or daughter of the wife's younger brother, the brothers of the wife's parents if they are younger than ego, etc.

The term 'mondu', which literally means distant relative, is used for brother-in-law, and is often used in place of the terms 'ninaba' and 'nado' and other affinal terms.

'Mondu' can thus apply to the husband's parents, their brothers and sisters, the husband's elder brother, the husband's sister, the husband of the husband's sister, the brother of the daughter's husband, the wife of the brother of the husband's sister, the husband of the sister of the husband's father, etc. The husband's father and the wife's father, the husband's mother and the wife's mother usually call each other 'mondu'.

There are several terms which designate the brother-in-laws of the brothers and sisters of ego, and also the brother-in-law of the wife's (husband's) relatives.

'Inide' is the name given to the husbands of women who are older than ego. The Nganasan uses it to refer to the husband of his elder sister, the husband of the sister of his elder brother's wife, the husband of his elder brother's daughter, if she (the daughter) is older than him, the husband of the daughter of the father's (mother's) brother or sister, the husband of the daughter of the son of the mother's brother, and the husband of the daughter of the mother's sister.

The husbands of women of the corresponding categories younger than ego are called 'bini'. A 'bini' can be the daughter's husband, the husband of the brother's or sister's daughter, the younger sister's husband, the husband of the husband or the wife's younger sister, the granddaughter's husband, the husband of the mother's sister, if he is younger than ego, etc.

The husband of the wife's sister, the wife of the husband's elder brother and the husbands of the sisters of the wife's father or mother are sometimes called 'selu'. Exactly when 'selu' is used, instead of one of the affinal terms, we did not manage to discover.

All these terms are employed independently of whether ego is a man or woman. However, some terms, it is true, are used rather infrequently and do involve distinctions between the sexes.

A woman uses the name 'syuarma' (literally, 'comrade') to refer to the brother of her elder brother's wife, the brother of her elder sister's husband, and the sister of her elder brother's wife. A man uses it to refer to the son of the sister of his elder sister's husband.

A man calls the brother of his elder brother's wife and the sister of his elder sister's husband 'kheli' (5) (literally, 'relative'). He refers to his wife's kinsmen as 'khelini' (the plural of 'kheli') or 'ny khelema' (literally, 'my wife's relatives'). A woman calls her husband's kinsmen 'kodyumu khelema'. The name 'khelini' is also used to refer to the Nganasans' blood relations in general. For example, 'khelini' is used for the brother and sister of ego, 'mona khelema' means literally, 'my blood relations'. We will return to this term later.

The children's and grandchildren's generations are split up into the children of people older than ego and the children of people younger than him. The same terms are used for the latter as for his grandchildren.

The Nganasan calls his son 'nyo', his daughter 'kopta' (literally, 'little girl', 'girl'), and 'mona nyonya' means 'my children'. As we will see below, ego uses the same terms for his children as for the children of his relatives, i.e. 'nyo' and 'kopta' have a wider meaning than the children of a given person. The son of the elder sister's daughter is called 'manka'.

The sons of a man's relatives, and his brothers-in-law who
are younger than him, he calls 'nyuo' (literally, 'children').
'Nyuo' is the descriptive form.   The 'nyuo' are addressed as
'niju' (literally, 'little children').   Ego uses the name 'nyuo'
for his children's sons, the younger brother's son, (6) the
younger sister's son, the son of the wife's younger sister, the
son of the husband's younger brother.

The name 'nyuo' is used more rarely in relation to women.
It is employed for the younger sister of the son's wife, the
daughter of the wife's younger sister, and the daughter of
the husband's father.   The latter can also be called 'kopta'.

Various descriptive expressions are formed from the word
'nyuo' to refer explicitly to the different categories of grandchildren.   These are: 'nyuononyuo' (the son's son),
'koptanonyuo' (the daughter's son), 'nyonanyuo' (the child of
my children), 'nyuonokopta' (my daughter's son), 'koptanyuo'
(my daughter's daughter), 'togapta nyuo' (the son of a parallel cousin).   The plural of 'nyuo' - 'nyuonya' - means children, descendants.   'Nyuoty' means stepson, stepdaughter.

The Nganasan calls the daughters of his younger relatives
'kopta', i.e. he uses this name to refer to the daughter of his
younger brother or sister, the daughter of his father's son or
brother.   Women also use it for the daughter of their husband's brother or sister.

Women give the name 'nyo' to the children of their husband's
relatives as well as their own children, and, in particular, to
the son of their husband's brother or sister.

This completes the kinship terminology of the Nganasan.
What are the characteristic features of this kinship system, on
what principles is it based?

First, it is a classificatory system.   Most of the kinship
terms refer to entire categories and classes of relations rather
than to individuals.   The number of descriptive terms in the
Nganasan kinship system is very small.

Second, the patrilineal and matrilineal lines of kinship are
quite clearly differentiated: the father's brothers are distinguished from the mother's brothers, the mother's younger
sister from the father's younger sister, the children of the
father's brothers from the children of the mother's sisters,
the children of brothers from those of sisters.   The differentiation between the patrilineal and matrilineal lines of kinship,
between the children of brothers and the children of sisters,
is both an inevitable consequence and a condition of the
normal functioning of an exogamous kinship society.

This makes it possible to say that the kinship terminology of the Nganasan originated as a direct reflection of the kinship system of their ancestors. One might ask why a distinction is drawn between the mother's and father's younger sisters but not between their elder sisters. According to the marriage customs practised today, a Nganasan man can marry the younger but not the elder sister of his former wife. Today, it is true, soratorial marriage is not very popular among the Nganasan. However, it seems to have been fairly widespread in the past, and, as a result, it is reflected in the kinship terminology. It is natural that one should want to distinguish one's father's potential wife, one's possible 'second' mother, from one's father's sister. In addition, the Nganasan method of classifying generations means that one's mother's younger sister may also become the wife of one's elder brother. There is no such need to distinguish between one's father and one's mother's elder sisters since they came into the category of those whom one's brothers were forbidden to marry.

The theory that the custom of sororate (a custom that allows or requires marriage with a wife's sister. T.D.) and levirate were widespread among the Nganasan in the past provides a plausible explanation for another unusual feature of Nganasan kinship terminology. The Nganasan men differentiate between their elder and younger brothers but not their elder and younger sisters. On the other hand, a woman has different names for her younger and elder sisters but does not distinguish between her brothers.

According to the custom of levirate, a man has the right to the wife or widow of his elder (but not his younger) brother. He therefore needs to make a terminological distinction between people whose wives are potentially his wives, and people whose wives he is forbidden to marry. There is no reason for him to classify his sisters according to their ages. According to the custom of sororate, a woman has the right to the husbands of her elder sisters (a man does not have the right to marry his wife's younger sisters). Therefore she needs to distinguish them from her younger sisters. However, there is no reason for her to classify her brothers according to age. All this in no way alters the fact that this division is closely connected with the third principle or third characteristic of the Nganasan kinship system.

This is that the Nganasan place in the same category of relatives people who, in fact, belong to different generations, in particular the younger members of one generation, and the elder members of the next descending generation; for example, they use the same terminology for a man's elder brothers and his father's younger brothers. This way of classifying leads to the isolation of the terms father, mother, wife, husband, so that they preserve their purely individual meaning. This reflects the isolation of the family, in the narrow sense of the word, from the rest of the clan. The isolation of the individual family is a comparatively recent phenomenon. The Nganasan and similar kinship systems must therefore have developed later than the classic Turano-ganovsk kinship system, which reflects the family, not in isolation, but, on the contrary, as an integral part of the entire kin. The isolation of the individual family could not have occurred in a matriarchal kin, so the Nganasan and similar kinship systems must be the product of patriarchal kinship relations.

We therefore find it impossible to agree with A.M. Zolotarev (7) when he says that the custom of levirate is closely connected with kinship systems of this type. In our opinion, levirate and sororate are more ancient phenomena than the kinship systems of the Nganasan or of the Tunguso-manchzhursk type (for the latter, see below). Men have marriage rights to the wives and widows of their elder brothers, and women to the husbands of their elder sisters in many tribes and nationalities whose kinship systems do not mix the generations, and who belong properly to the Turano-ganan type (Aleuty, Eskimos, tribes of the Amazon and many others). Levirate and sororate have been found to exist among some of these peoples at a time when they had only just begun the transition from the matriarchal to the patriarchal kin (e.g. the Aleuty). It therefore seems obvious that the customs of levirate and sororate arise in a matriarchal kinship society considerably before the development of the Tunguso-manchzhur type.

As regards the causes of the origin of levirate and sororate we think that L. Ya. Shternberg (8) is right in seeing them in the necessity of guaranteeing the posterity of husbands and wives of two inter-marrying groups (Shternberg says 'the posterity of groups of brothers and sisters'), i.e. of the members of two matriarchal kins, connected by dual exogamous ties. The restriction which only allows the woman's younger sisters to use this right in relation to the husbands of their elder sisters, and only the man's younger brothers in relation to the wives of their elder brothers, is most likely explained by the fact that the younger brothers and sisters married later than the elder, and therefore it was they who suffered if there was a shortage of men or women in the inter-marrying kins.

The Nganasan custom of placing members of different generations in the same category shows that the practice of marriage between representatives of different generations has long been established among them. For example, the younger

sister of the Nganasan's wife might marry not only his
younger brother, but also his son. During our expedition in
1957, we discovered one very interesting custom connected
with marriage between members of different generations. As
our informant Dedyumo Yarotsky explained, if two Nganasans
belonging to different kins married two sisters, their relations
to each other became those of father-in-law and son-in-law,
with all the obligations that flow from this. The husband of
the younger sister calls the husband of the elder sister
'ninaba' - father-in-law - and the latter in turn refers to his
as 'bini' - son-in-law. They also avoid each other as is the
custom for the father and son-in-law among the Nganasan.
Our Nganasan acquaintances included Yure Turdagin and
Khindelyu Chunanchar whose marriages to the sisters Mutobi
and Mamelyu placed them in this relationship to each other.
If the sister's husbands are brothers, this does not happen.
This custom can be explained by the special feature of the
Nganasan way of classifying generations. It has already been
said that the kinship terminology indicates that sororate was
common among the Nganasan in the past, but that the same
name was used for the wife's younger sisters and the
daughters of the wife's elder sisters. The husband of the
wife's elder sister is thus a potential father-in-law, and so
the two men call each other, and behave to each other, as
father and son-in-law. However, this only happens if they
are not blood relations. If the sisters' husbands are
brothers, members of the same kin, the daughter of the elder
sister in the patriarchal type of kinship belonged to the same
kin as the husband of her younger sister and it was therefore
impossible for the husband of the elder sister to be the
father-in-law of his younger brother. Besides, all this evidence is superfluous in view of the fact that the custom described, and the kinship terminology resulting from it, are the
products of a patriarchal kin.

Traces of the previous practice of dual exogamy can also be
found in Nganasan kinship terminology. Our informant
Dedyumo Yarotsky told us that the word 'khelema' means not
only 'comparatively distinctly related', but also 'my half'.
'Khelema', in his words, 'is your own generation, and those
who are not "khelema" are the other half.' The 'khelema'
give each other presents, those who are not 'khelema' do not.
Our informant Atakai Turdagin said that those 'who are
"khelema" are one half, the relatives in the father's line, and
relations in the mother's line, are the other half,' but he
could not give a general term for this. This information
seems to prove the existence of two phratry in the patrilineal
view of kinship among the Nganasan in the past. (Phratry:
term fondly used by Soviet authors and taken from nineteenth-
century anthropology: tribal or kinship division among primitive races (OED, 1909), and here meaning a social organisation

where groups of brothers form the base unit or where, as
Westermark noted ('History of Human Marriage', 1894), the
Seneca tribe of the Iroquois was divided into two 'phratries'
or divisions, intermediate between the tribe and the clan.
T.D.)

We will go on to compare the Nganasan kinship system with
the kinship systems of neighbouring peoples. In comparing
the kinship systems of different peoples, we also compare the
social structures reflected in these systems.

III

In the introduction we remarked that B.O. Dolgĭkh established that the Nganasan are the descendants of the ancient
Paleoliths, possibly of the Prayukagir tribes, and were either
gradually assimilated by the Samoeds, or first by the Tungus
and then by the Samoeds. This raises the question of whose
kinship structure, whose marriage customs prevail among the
Nganasan, the Tungus, or the Samoed proper.

Kinship systems are, as is well known, very conservative.
Kinship terms are also a constant element of the vocabulary of
any language. Therefore a comparison of kinship systems as
they survive in the twentieth century can contribute to a
better understanding of the history of the Nganasan kinship
systems.

Jochelson, (9) who compared the kinship system of the
Nganasan with that of the Yukagir, at the end of the nineteenth century, concluded that there were no particular similarities. Some features of the Yukagir kinship system, it is
true, are the product of a later development and are connected with its transformation and decay. By the twentieth century, the Yukagir kinship system was still basically 'Turano-
Ganovan', but contained elements of the Malay kinship system.
This is especially clear from the fact that there is no distinction between blood relations in the father's and the mother's
line. By Jochelson's time, descriptive rather than classificatory terms were used for the descending generation. In
spite of this, if the Yukagir kinship system really is a prototype of the contemporary Nganasan kinship system, some of
their basic principles must still be similar. However, principles of classification of relatives such as placing the younger
members of one generation in the same class as the older members of the descending generation, e.g. using the same term
for the father's younger brothers and the son's elder
brothers, which are so important among the Nganasan, are
completely absent from the Yukagir kinship system.

Evidently, in the period of the formation of the Nganasan, the Tungus and the Samoeds coming from the south did not take over the kinship-tribal organisation of the Yukagirs, but, on the contrary, destroyed it, assimilated the ancient inhabitants of Taimyr and drew them into their own kinship-tribal organisation. This was reflected in their dropping the Yukagir kinship system for a kinship system typical of the Samoeds or Tungus.

Of course, there is a possible alternative – that the lack of resemblance between the Yukagir and Nganasan kinship systems is due to the fact that the ancient population of Taimyr are not Yukagir. Whether this was so, we will only know when the question of the origin and the area of settlement of the Yukagir has been finally settled. The Nganasan kinship terminology can also be compared with that of the Nenets. For this we must first give a brief description of the latter, as far as our information allows. (10)

The Nenets' terms for the grandparents' generation are: 'iri' = grandfather, father's or mother's elder brother; and 'khaba' = grandmother, father or mother's elder sister. In the parents' generation, the Nenets have individual terms for the father and mother: 'nisya' ('nesya' among the Yamal's Nenets) = father; 'nebya' = mother.

The Nenets give their father's younger brothers and sisters the same names as their elder brothers and sisters. 'Nika' or 'nineka' is the father's younger brother, the son of the father's brother (older than ego), the elder brother. 'Nyabako! is the father's younger sister, the daughter of the wife's elder sister, if she (the daughter) is older than ego. 'Neya' is the mother's younger sister, the daughter of the mother's brother. The son of the mother's sister is called 'syuny'. 'Myangg' means the son of the father's sister, the elder sister's son, the son of the wife's younger brother, the son of the husband's elder brother.

The Nenets call their younger brother and the son of their elder brother 'papa'. The descriptive expression 'papa ne' (literally, 'the younger brother's woman'), is used for the younger sister. In one dialect the younger brother is called 'pebya'. 'Nyu' is the name for the 'son', the younger brother's son, and the grandson. The descriptive expression 'ne nyu' ('ne' = woman; 'nyu' = son, child) is applied to the daughter, the younger brother's daughter and the granddaughter.

The Nenets call their wife 'ne'.

The names given to affinal relations are as follows: 'ngynab'

= the wife's father, the wife's mother, the wife's elder
brother, or sister, the husband's elder sister; 'nyaba' = the
elder brother's wife, the wife of the father's brother; 'meya'
= son's wife, younger brother's wife, wife of husband's
younger brother; 'ii' = the younger sister's husband or the
daughter's husband; 'ferenya' = the parents of the daughter's
husband or the son's wife; 'sel' = the term used as a form of
address between the husbands of two sisters.

What are the principles on which the Nenets' kinship system
is based? First, a clear distinction is drawn between the
patrilineal and matrilineal lines of kinship. The relatives of
the father and mother are only not differentiated in the grandparents' generation, where the distinction has no practical
meaning. Second, the system reflects the ancient dual exogamous division of Nenets' society. Traces of this can be
seen, e.g. in the term 'nyaboko'. This name is used both
for the father's younger sister and the wife of the mother's
younger brother. This is obviously a reflection of the custom
by which a woman's younger brothers took her husband's
younger sisters (of course, classificatory) as wives, i.e. the
men of each kin took wives from the kin or kinship groups, in
which they had placed their sisters.

Finally, the third principle of Nenets' kinship terminology is
the placing of members of different generations in the same
class. This proves that the Nenets' kinship terminology is
related to that of the Nganasan. The vocabulary of the kinship terminology of the Nenets provides a good deal of additional evidence. Both among the Nenets and the Nganasan,
the woman, the wife, is called 'ne'. Both call the grandfather 'iri'. The Nganasan call the husbands of two sisters
'selu', and the Nenets 'sel'. The Nenets' 'nyu' (son, younger
brother's son, grandchild) corresponds to the Nganasan 'nyuo'.
The Nenets' 'meya' (son's wife, younger brother's wife, wife
of husband's younger brother) corresponds to the Nganasan
'myai'. The Nenets' 'ngynab' (wife's father or mother) has a
phonetic resemblance and its meaning is the same as the
Nganasan 'ninaba'.

These parallels provide grounds for supposing that the kinship terminology of the Nenets and the Nganasan has a common
prototype, i.e. that they derive their terminology from common
ancestors.

Before we turn to an examination of its southern parallels,
the Nganasan kinship terminology properly ought to be compared with that of the Enets, a small people of the lower
reaches of the Enis, whose culture is in many ways similar to
that of the Nganasan. However, it is, at present, practically
impossible to undertake such a comparison. The kinship

terminology of the Enets has not yet been fully recorded.
Only individual terms are known, from which it is impossible
to get a general idea of the Enets' kinship system.

On the basis of the terms known at present, all one can
say is that the Enets' kinship terminology has a series of
phonetic parallels with that of the Nganasan and Nenets.
For example, the Enets have 'me', the Nganasan, 'myai';   the
Enets have 'kaza', the Nganasan, 'kotu';   the Enets have
'syuen', the Nenets , 'syuny';   the Enets have 'pribo', the
Nganasan and Nenets, 'iri'.

However, we do not know whether there is full semantic
correspondence between these terms among the Enets, on the
one hand, and the Nenets and the Nganasan, on the other.

The kinship system of the southern-most of the contemporary
Samoed peoples, the Sel'kups, is based on the same principle
as the kinship terminology of the Nenets and Nganasan, i.e.
the younger members of one generation are joined with the
older members of the succeeding, younger, generation. (11)
There are also some, though very few, parallels between the
vocabulary of the Sel'kup terminology and that of the Nenets
and the Nganasan.   For example, the Sel'kups call the
father's elder sister 'kot'yam', the Nganasan, 'kotu';   the
Sel'kups call the father's younger sister 'abzhan aba', the
Nganasan, 'aba';   the Sel'kups call the son of the husband's
elder brother 'manggam', the Nenets, 'myangg'.   A comparison
of the kinship system of the Sel'kups with the kinship system
of the Samodiisk peoples reveals a striking resemblance to the
kinship system of the Chulym Tyurok.   A.P. Dul'zon, who
has made a special study of this question, claims that the
Sel'kup kinship nomenclature coincides with the Chulym
Tyurok not only in general principles, but also in most of its
basic classifications, and differs from it only in having a large
number of synonymous terms. (12)

It has already been said that the ethnic elements involved in
the formation of the Nganasan include the Tungus.   It would
therefore be interesting to compare the kinship terminology of
the Nganasan with that of the neighbouring Evenk groups.
However, in view of the lack of adequate information about the
kinship terminology of the latter, we have to limit ourselves to
a comparison of the Nganasan kinship system with a kinship
system characteristic of the Tungus, as a whole, which has
been well studied, e.g. the kinship system of the Ul'ch.
A.M. Zolotarev wrote that the placing of two generations in
the same class is one of the important principles of Ul'ch kinship nomenclature and an important feature of all Tunguso-
manchzhur kinship systems. (13)   This is exactly the
feature that first strikes the eye on looking at the Nganasan
and Nenets' kinship systems.

Two conclusions can thus be drawn from a comparison of the Nganasan kinship system with that of the Yukagir, Nenets, Sel'kup and Tungus systems. First, after its formation, the Nganasan people did not preserve the kinship organisation of their ancient Paleoasian forebears, who were possibly the Prayukagirs; second, the question of whether the Nganasan developed within the framework of the Tungus kinship structure, or whether their kinship organisation was brought from the south by their Samoed-speaking ancestors, cannot be settled purely on the basis of a comparison of the principles on which the kinship systems are based. However, the presence of parallels in the vocabulary of the kinship terminology of the Nganasan and those Nenets who did not undergo assimilation by the Tungus, would suggest that the kinship organisation of the Nganasan comes from the Samoed proper. In either case, the similarities between the basic principles and the marriage customs of the kinship systems of the Tungus and the ancestors of the Samoeds would have facilitated their merging into a unified Nganasan nationality.

If there is any truth in the suggestion we made on analysing the kinship terminology of the Nganasan, that it is a product of a patrilineal kin, a third conclusion can be drawn, and we can say that the Nganasan were already members of patrilineal clans when their separate tribe was formed, and that the traces of matrilineal kin that can be found are survivals of the kinship organisation of their forebears.

NOTES

1 The Nganasan kinship terminology was recorded by B.O. Dolgikh in Taimyr in 1935. These notes, which B.O. Dolgikh kindly placed at the author's disposal, form the basis of the present article. During the author's and B.O. Dolgikh's expedition to the Nganasan of Taimyr in 1957, they were defined more precisely and some additions were made. The author expresses his deep gratitude to B.O. Dolgikh for giving him these materials and also for his valuable advice and guidance.
2 B.O. Dolgikh, The Origin of the Nganasan, 'Collected Siberian Ethnographical Papers, Works of the Institute of Ethnography of the Academy of Sciences of the USSR', New Series, vol, 28, 1957, p. 86.
3 M.O. Kosven, Avunculate, 'Soviet Ethnography', 1948, no. 1, pp. 24-5.
4 Ibid., p. 26.
5 The sister of the elder sister's husband can also be called 'kotu'.
6 He was sometimes called by the descriptive expression 'togonta nyo' (literally, 'distant son').

7 A.M. Zolotarev, 'The Kinship System and Religion of the Ulch', Khabarovsk, 1939, pp. 67-8.

8 L. Shternberg, The Social Organisation of the Gilyak, 'Family and Kinship among the Peoples of North-East Asia', Leningrad, 1933, pp. 100-7.

9 W. Jochelson, 'The Yukaghir and the Yukaghirised Tungus', New York, 1926, pp. 68-75.

10 The terms listed below are taken from 'A Shorter Nenets-Russian and Russian-Nenets Dictionary', by G.O. Verbov, Salekhard, 1937.

11 A.P. Dul'zon, 'Kinship and Affinity Terms in the Languages of Narym Territory and Chulym', Tomsk, 1954, p. 93.

12 Ibid., p. 94.

13 A.M. Zolotarev, op. cit., pp. 64-6.

Part VI
THEORETICAL ISSUES

INTRODUCTION

Kryukov and Girenko are familiar with Western literature -
both out of their interest in theory, and because Kryukov is
a specialist in Chinese, and Girenko in African, studies.
These two publications were, however, intended for a wide
Soviet readership so they refer to familiar authors, often
ones who appeared in Britain long ago, read in Russia before
isolationism set in. The issues discussed are not so familiar
to a Soviet readership who are concerned more often with historical analysis than the very important question of ethnocen-
trism in kinship annotation with which Kryukov deals and, for
those unfamiliar with the African monographs to which Girenko
refers, the possibility of using kinship terms as social categories. The papers demonstrate how these subjects can be
discussed in understandable terms for the wider anthropological community. On the other hand, the problem approached
by Kryukov has hardly been solved in Western literature.
At their weekly seminars, Soviet scholars who did the field
work presented in this volume no doubt have discussed the
two papers, as they do most innovatory topics published in
'Sovetskaya Etnografiya', although many colleagues would probably agree that the issues involved are far from new.

12 Towards a method of gathering field material on kinship systems

*M.V. Kryukov**

The study of kinship systems has long been accepted as a traditional branch of ethnography. It is now difficult to find a monograph on a people which does not include a speical section or at least a paragraph on its kinship terminology. (1) However, enough attention has not been paid to the question of the methods of gathering material on kinship systems in the field. It is indicative that the recently published 'Methods for Ethnographical Expeditions', by G. Gromov (Moscow, 1966), contains nothing on the method of gathering information on kinship systems: the author contents himself with brief recommendations which touch on only one practical question – the coding of the meaning of kinship terms. The programme drawn up by I.N. Vinnikov over 30 years ago remains the sole methodological guide for the ethnographer studying kinship relations. (2)

The 'programme' states that kinship systems can be studied in three ways:

1 by means of direct research;

2 by means of questioning;

3 on the basis of literary sources. (3)

In this, 'one should where possible combine the three methods, so that the materials gathered in different ways can supplement and be checked against each other.' (4)

Though fully upholding the recommendation to use different, overlapping methods and procedures for studying kinship systems, I will make the remark that the extraction of relevant data from literary sources, while an essential preparation for field work, has no direct connection with methods of gathering field materials. Some preliminary notes of a general nature must be made before we proceed to evaluate the merits and deficiencies of the two other ways of studying terminology, the most reliable of which I.N. Vinnikov considers to be the method of direct observation.

* First published in 'Sovetskaya Etnografiya', 1972, no. 4, pp. 42-50.

By a kinship system we usually mean a set of terms indicating the various kinship relations which function in a given society. A kinship term designates not a person, but a relationship (~) between two people: the speaker (Ego or E) and the named, the person who is referred to or addressed by the given term (Alter or A). The concept 'kinship term' (T) can thus be expressed by the formula T+E~A. The methods of gathering field material differ according to the component this formula takes as a point of departure, for the fixing of the kinship terminology of the people studied.

As is known, L. Morgan was the first scholar not only to establish the importance of kinship systems as a historical-ethnographical source, but also to work out a concrete method of conducting research in the sphere of kinship terminology. In 1859, Morgan drew up a 234-point programme for recording terms. One of the three graphs of his table (kinship relations) was filled in by Morgan, the other two (native terms and an English translation of these terms) were left blank to be completed by the scholar in the course of his work. In other words, the informants were asked such questions as: 'What do you call your father's father/the son of your father's brother?', etc.

In order not to miss any terms out, Morgan even included questions about relatives in the fifth collateral line. But the completeness of the programme is its fundamental fault. His point of departure in the process of establishing the meaning of terms is a previously formulated set of kinship relations (~). Moreover, it is an indisputable fact that these relations do not represent immutable and universal categories. The scholar working with Morgan's programme sometimes induces his informant to construct combinations of kinship relations which do not in fact exist for him.

I.N. Vinnikov makes a similar mistake when he asserts, in the introduction to his 'programme', that: 'there are two sorts of kinships a) by blood and b) by marriage', and that 'there are in turn two sorts of blood relationship a) in the direct line and b) in the collateral line', etc. (5) Having set himself the task of characterising the universal aspects of kinship systems, the author goes on to include features, characteristic not of all systems, but only of those of the civilised peoples of Europe. It is common knowledge, in particular, that the terminology of most of the Australian tribes contains no distinction between kinship by blood and by marriage, or between direct and collateral lines of blood relationship, etc. Descriptions of the kinship system of a given people, in which the ethnographer departs not from the categories derived from their own terminology, but from the specific features of another system which exists in his own language, are therefore based on false principles.

An attempt to overcome the drawbacks of Morgan's method, of using a list of kinship relations, was the so-called 'genealogical method' of gathering kinship terminology, worked out at the beginning of this century by W. Rivers. (6) Recognising the fallaciousness of an *a priori* formation of a set of kinship relations, which are then presented to the informant, Rivers proposed to get rid of not the relationship (∾) but the person A. This meant that the scholar as a preliminary step tracked down as many of the informant's relatives as he could, and gave each of them a place on a genealogical tree, a separate one of which was drawn up for each informant. After this, he asked questions about each of the relatives in turn, and the informant told him the kinship terminology he used for them. As the question was posed not as 'What do you call your father's brother's son?', etc., but as 'What kind of relationship is X for you?' the informant, it would seem, was not tied down to a previously constructed set of kinship relations and could call the person A by the name he would use for this person in an everyday situation.

This was the method recommended by I.N. Vinnikov for gathering terminology 'by means of questioning' (the second method in his 'programme'). The scholar studying kinship systems first selects a family at random and establishes the relations in which each member stands to the other members of the family, and then asks questions to determine the terms by which these people are designated. Then he establishes the relations in which each member of the given family stands to each member of the families related to that family, and the terms by which these people are designated, etc. (7) A.P. Dul'zon, who has used a basically similar method in gathering materials on the kinship system of the Kets, modified this procedure as follows:

1 Before interviewing, a list of all the Ket population, living in a given place, was drawn up from the statistics of the management of the collective farms.

2 A detailed genealogy of the members of each family was compiled, including their names, ages, nationalities, place of birth, year of death if they were no longer alive, place of residence if they lived somewhere else, etc.

3 The list of households was checked with these genealogies and used to construct lists of relatives for all the people selected for interviewing. The main work of establishing the kinship nomenclature was done through these previously prepared lists. This not only saved time, but also reduced the percentage of error. (8)

Rivers's genealogical method has become the most widely
used in ethnographical field work. However, it too has serious drawbacks. The chief of these is that when the informant gives the term he uses to indicate his kinship relation
with a given person, it by no means always follows that he
himself connects E and A through the same combination of elementary kinship relations that the ethnographer supposes from
the term. This drawback in the Rivers method was graphic-
ally demonstrated by M. Mead, who worked, in the 1930s,
among the Arapesh. For example, to the question of what the
Arapesh call the person A, who, from the ethnographer's point
of view, is the daughter of the daughter of the brother of the
father's father, the informant replies 'sister'. However, this
does not mean that the Arapesh arrived at this conclusion in
the same way as the researcher – by a convoluted mental
journey over the genealogical tree. He calls A by this term
only because this woman's brother lives in his village and is
therefore the informant's 'brother'. This 'brother' calls A
his 'sister' so the informant does too. (9)

To give another example: the kinship system of the Mbau
Fijians reflects a dual-marriage organisation of two exogamous
groups, connected by bilateral cross-cousin marriages (see
Figure 12.1). As a result, the kinship and affinal relations
coincide. In the figure, 4 represents the group of people of
the male sex in the father's mother's generation who do not
belong to the same moiety as Ego, 3 being the group of people
of the female sex of the same generation and from Ego's moiety.
Since the members of group 3 marry the members of group 4
and their sons (group 6) are the potential husbands of the
women of my generation and my moiety, group 6 includes, from
a genealogical point of view, four categories of relatives: the
sons of my father's sisters, the sons of my mother's brothers,
my sister's husband and my wife's brothers. (10) In fact,
when he refers to his relatives in group 6, the Mbau man does
not connect them with Ego in four different ways. For him,
all these relatives are connected with Ego by a single relationship – they are relatives of the same sex as himself, in his
generation, but from his mother's moiety.

'In short,' A. Hocart writes apropos of this,

what we seek most is the next of kin, and we run up and
down the family tree. The Fijians ... do not, because
there is no point in doing so. All they want is such information as will enable them to place each man on the correct
side in the right generation. An inquiry proceeds thus:
How are you related?
Of the same side and generation.
Why?
Because our fathers were of the same side and generation.

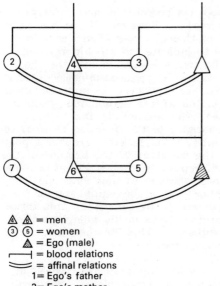

△ ▲ = men
③ ⑤ = women
▲ = Ego (male)
┌─┤ = blood relations
〓 = affinal relations
1= Ego's father
2= Ego's mother
3= Ego's father's sister
4= Ego's father's sister's husband
5= Ego's sister
6= Ego's sister's husband
7= Ego's wife who is also Ego's sister's
      husband's sister and his father's sister's
      husband's daughter

Figure 12.1 *The dual-marriage organisation of two exogamy groups in the kinship system of the Mbau Fijians*

Or else:
  We belong to successive generations on opposite sides,
  because he is of my mother's side and generation. (11)

This is sufficient proof of the fact that the ethnographer who uses the genealogical method of gathering kinship terminology measures the terminology with the yardstick of his own kinship system, rather than trying to see it from the point of view of the people who use the system studied.

N.A. Butinov remarked on this drawback of the genealogical method as early as 1951 and categorically stated that

  Soviet ethnographers must make a decisive break with this
  harmful tradition, and evolve a new method of recording kinship systems which will set down not only a system of
  abstract kinship terms but also the structure of the concrete
  social relations concealed in it. (12)

There is a theoretical possibility of working out such a method
of gathering materials on kinship systems. The point of
departure of the procedure of establishing the meaning of kinship terms can be not only the connection (~) between E and
A, formulated previously by the researcher (as in the Morgan
programme), or the person A whose relations to E the researcher establishes from the genealogical point of view (the
Rivers method), but also the term T taken on its own.

It was really this method I.N. Vinnikov had in mind when
he spoke of the first of the three systems recommended by
him:

> The first method presupposes close intercourse with the
> people, whose kinship system is studied, over a considerable
> period of time, and consists in the direct observation of the
> practical application of kinship terms. The person study-
> ing the kinship system, on hearing a kinship term in every-
> day speech immediately writes it down in the grammatical
> form in which the term occurred. He then establishes on
> the spot the kinship relation which exists (or used to exist
> if the person in question is dead) between the people who
> used the term and the person who was addressed or refer-
> red to by the term. (13)

However, this method of establishing the meaning of terms can
be fully adopted not just in participant observation, which is
unquestionably the most reliable method of ethnographical
field work, but also in interviews. The first method implies
the researcher's passive assimilation of the information he
seeks and, therefore, as a rule, demands a long stay among
the people studied. The ethnographer who pursues the
second method (interviewing) adopts a more active and fruitful
role. The informant is asked to name all the kinship terms
known to him in his own language. When a list of the terms
has been drawn up, the researcher asks the informant to explain the meaning of each term. This method of procedure
completely excludes the possibility of the scholar consciously
or unconsciously ascribing to the informant a category which
does not exist in the kinship system studied, since the latter
is free to explain the meaning of each term in the way he considers the most natural and usual.

This characterisation of the kinship system 'from within'
permits the scholar to discover features which totally escape
the ethnographer who uses the Rivers genealogical method.
For example, Swartz attracted attention to the fact that in the
kinship system of the Jivkese (Caroline Islands) the use of
some terms was determined not only by genealogical kinship,
but also by the 'situation' - in particular, the joint ownership
of land. (14)   It is quite possible that factors vital for some

systems have up till now been studied inadequately or not at all. However, if the factor really is important, the informant is free to point it out in the case when he explains the meaning of the kinship terms to the researcher. Thus, the Fijian defines many of the terms in his system not by the set of elementary kinship relations which exist for the European, but by a combination of two factors by which generation and which moiety of the dual-marriage organisation the person belongs to and so forth. In such a case, the task of the researcher is to determine accurately the set of factors which the informant uses to express the difference in the meaning of kinship terms.

However, there may be many cases where the informant determines the meaning of the term by a genealogical method, explaining, for example, that the term serves to indicate 'the son of the mother's brother', etc. This means that the terms in this system have already lost their original classificatory meaning and the relationship between A and E is interpreted by the informant himself as a relationship, between particular people, connected by individual kinship ties. But even here the study of the rules on which are based the set of elementary kinship relations which the informant himself operated can contribute to the understanding of the particularities of the system studied.

It goes without saying that the adoption of this method does not exclude the use of other means of gathering information on kinship systems in certain circumstances. After working out this method, W. Rivers used it to gather the basic material for such major works as 'The History of Melanesian Society'. However, in gathering data on Melanesian systems, Rivers also, on occasions, resorted to the traditional Morgan method - he explained the names the Melanesians used in terms of European kinship relations. However, Rivers commented that he only did this when he had no alternative (e.g. when there was no time to draw up genealogical schemas), and only in cases when he was already familiar with the essential features of the system. (15) In exactly the same way, if the scholar who adopts the above method becomes convinced that his informant is explaining his kinship relations from a genealogical point of view, and not in terms of any other characteristics, the scholar may use the Rivers or Morgan method for the purposes of clarifying and verifying his information. However, this is only admissible in cases when the main features of the system have already been explained to the researcher 'from within'. It must be explained that this method may only be successfully adopted when the scholar speaks the given language and uses it in all conversations with his informants.

This brings us to the question of the method of setting down
the meaning of the terms.   The kinship terms which exist in
the scholar's own language cannot be used to record the
meanings objectively.   W. Rivers quite correctly wrote, in
1914, that:

> English terms of relationship have no real equivalents in the
> languages of those who use the classificatory system while
> the terms of Polynesia and Melanesia are without real equiva-
> lents in our language.... It would seem as if the only really
> satisfactory plan would be to employ symbols for the differ-
> ent relationships and it is probable that the time will come
> when this will be done, and many parts of the description
> of the social systems of savage tribes will resemble a work
> on mathematics in which the results will be expressed by
> symbols, in some cases even in the form of equations. (16)

One of the first attempts at creating a conventional code for
setting down the meaning of kinship terms was the system
evolved by S.A. Tokarev in the 1920s. (17)

S.A. Tokarev correctly remarked that the scholar sometimes
unconsciously reduces the description of the system studied
to a translation of the terms from the given language to his
own.   However, the ethnographer who acts in this way is not
using a system of logically correlated scientific concepts, but
the kinship terms existing in his native tongue, which themselves need objective description.   The assertion that 'Among
the Iroquois a man calls his father's brother his father' is
totally incorrect. (18)   It is wrong because the corresponding
Iroquois term designates the father, his brothers (blood and
collateral), the husbands of his mother's sisters, and so forth
- i.e. it has a completely different content from the English
word 'father'. (19)

The system of coding the meaning of kinship terms which
S.A. Tokarev proposed to use to overcome the researcher's
subjectivity, was based on the supposition that 'all the end-
lessly varied kinship relations, of which only an insignificant
proportion have designations in known languages, can be reduced to the simplest relations.' (20)   The latter flow from
two forms of biological connections - marriage and birth include six types: father, mother, son, daughter, husband,
wife.   All one has to do is to invent convenient signs to
express these simple kinship relations, and, through them,
all the others.   In S.A. Tokarev's opinion, the most convenient signs are the Arab numerals: father = 1, mother = 2,
son = 3, daughter = 4, husband = 5, wife = 6.   All other
kinship relations can be reduced to those basic ones and explained by means of them.   For example, the father's father
is designated by 11, the mother's mother by 22, etc.

Although the relationships of brother and sister are not
simple, but derivative, S.A. Tokarev proposes to simplify the
system by including separate symbols for brother (group 7),
and sister (group 8).   In addition, if the kinship term
depends on the sex of Ego, the conventional letter 'm' is
placed in front of the corresponding index (if Ego is a man),
or 'f' (if Ego is a woman).

Other systems of coding terms with the help of numeral or
alphabetical indices were subsequently proposed by
A. Radcliffe-Brown (21) and George Murdock. (22)   A new,
more sophisticated and accurate version has been worked out
more recently by Yu. I. Levin. (23)

This code is based on three of the main elements in kinship
systems - child (C), parent (P), spouse (S).   Where it is
necessary to distinguish the sex of a given person, the symbols m or f are added to the corresponding index - e.g. Pm =
father, SfCm = son's wife, etc.   If it is necessary to indicate
the sex of Ego, the conventional sigms 'Em' (Ego-Man), and
'Ef' (Ego-Woman) are added to the index.   In contrast to
Tokarev's code, the set of symbols is read from Alter to Ego
(compare for example the designations for the father's sister:
18 according to Tokarev's and CfPPm according to Levin's
system).

An accurate method of recording both kinship and affinal
relations will help to clarify the structural principles of the
kinship system, which is itself very important in the comparison of different kinship systems.   Levin's code is more complete and more convenient than previously proposed methods
of setting down the meaning of terms.   It has already been
put into practice in the work of Soviet scholars. (24)

Finally we must mention another basic problem which virtually
every student of kinship systems encounters in his field work.

It was long ago remarked that every people has, as a rule,
not one, but a minimum of two kinship systems, different in
character, which function in different situational contexts.
Thus, in his study of the social system of the Melanesians,
W. Rivers drew attention to the fact that the terms with which
they addressed their relatives were different from the ones
they used for the same relatives in conversations with a third
party. (25)   On the basis of these observations, R. Lowie
introduced the practice of counterposing two categories of kinship terms ('terms of address' and 'terms of reference') in
ethnography. (26) H.L. Morgan, as is known, did not make
such a distinction.   His tables mainly analyse the 'terms of
reference' although he also mentions that, among the Iroquois,
relatives use not their names but kinship terms in addressing

each other. (27)   Morgan's opponent, George McLennan,
recognised only kinship terms which were used as a form of
address. (28)

It must be said that the distinction between the two categories of terms, introduced by Lowie, needs to be given a
different formulation.   It sometimes happens that the 'terms
of address' are used in referring to a relative in conversation
with other relatives, as well as in addressing him directly.
While the 'terms of reference' are used to designate relatives
in conversations with outsiders.   The set of contexts, in
which the different sub-systems, existing within one kinship
system, are employed, is thus quite complicated.   This was
recently underlined by D. Schneider, who gave a paper at the
International Congress of Anthropological and Ethnographical
Sciences, 'What should be included in a vocabulary of kinship
terms?'   At least as regards contemporary American terminology, the author claims, it is impossible to speak of the existence of a single sub-system of 'terms of designation'.   I can
call my relatives by different terms in different situations,
depending on whom I am talking to. (29)

About thirty years ago, H.T. Fei published his research on
the situational contexts in which kinship terms are used in the
Chinese system, which sheds light on this problem.   His main
conclusions can be reduced to the following:

1 The speaker can refer to a relative by the term he would
   use to address him directly (if the Ego, Alter and the
   interlocutor come from the same family and are of roughly
   the same age).

2 The speaker can refer to a relative by the term which
   the interlocutor would use to address this person directly
   (if all three people come from the same family but the
   speaker is older than the named and the interlocutor).

3 The speaker can call a relative by the 'term of reference'
   (if the speaker and the interlocutor are not related). (30)

This means that the scholar must list separately the terms
which he hears in the everyday speech of his informants and
those which they mention in the course of interviews.   Since
the scholar is usually not related to the informant, straight-
forward questioning will give him a list of the 'terms of reference'.   Terms which belong to different sub-systems must
never be listed together, as this will distort the general picture of how the kinship terms function among the people
studied.

The question of why the same relatives can be grouped

through different principles as indicated by the 'terms of address', on the one hand, and the 'terms of reference' on the other, has not yet been sufficiently investigated. B. Aginsky in his time suggested that one of the factors which stimulates the division into sub-systems might be the contradiction between the biological and social factors influencing kinship terminology.

In his investigation of the interpretation of kinship systems, he operated exclusively on the basis of the 'terms of address'.   In his view, the 'terms of address' correspond very closely to the actual social organisation and therefore define the norms of behaviour between relations more accurately than the 'terms of reference'. (31)

However, most contemporary scholars take the opposite view.   They make the point that historically the sub-system of 'terms of address' is always affected first by gradual changes in the system.   It is these terms which are liable to innovation.   The sub-system of the 'terms of reference' is more conservative and therefore preserves more vestiges of the previous stage of its evolution.   The 'terms of reference' are thus of more use to the scholar studying the course of development of the social system.

The data on kinship systems are summarised in the form of tables.   L. Morgan used tables made up of three columns: the first listing the kinship relations;   the second, the corresponding terms;   and the third giving an English translation of the terms.   The inclusion of the third column is not only unnecessary to the understanding of the structure of a given kinship system, but is also likely to mislead the people who use the tables.   A table with two graphs is therefore sufficient for summarising terminology gathered by a method which takes the term itself as the starting-point.   The first lists the terms of a given sub-system ('terms of address' or 'terms of reference') and the second explains the meaning of each term by means of a code.

A better method of collecting and setting down field material is an essential prerequisite for the achievement of one of the important tasks confronting Soviet ethnographers - the elaboration of a corpus of the kinship systems of peoples of the USSR.

NOTES

1   Amongst these, the most important to note are the works of D.A. Olderogge, S.A. Tokarev and Yu. M. Likhtenberg.
2   I.N. Vinnikov, 'A Programme for Collecting Materials on Kinship and Affinity Systems', Moscow-Leningrad, 1936.

3 Ibid., p. 16
4 Ibid., p. 19.
5 Ibid., p. 3.
6 W.H.R. Rivers, A Genealogical Method of Collecting Social and Vital Statistics, 'Journal of the Royal Anthropological Institute', vol. 30, 1900, pp. 71-2.
7 I.N. Vinnikov, op. cit., pp. 16-17.
8 A.P. Dul'zon, The Kinship and Affinity Terms of the Eniseisk Kets, 'Soviet Ethnography', 1959, no. 6, p. 87.
9 N.A. Butinov, Problems of Exogamy, in 'Tribal Society, Works of the Institute of Ethnography of the Academy of Sciences of the USSR', New Series, vol. 14, Moscow, 1951, p. 20.
10 W.H.R. Rivers, 'The History of Melanesian Society', Cambridge, 1914, p. 267.
11 A.M. Hocart, Kinship Systems, 'Readings in Anthropology', E.A. Hoebel (ed.), New York, 1955, p. 193.
12 N.A. Butinov, op. cit., p. 21.
13 I.N. Vinnikov, op. cit., p. 16.
14 M.J. Swartz, Situational Determinants of Kinship Terminology, 'Southwestern Journal of Anthropology', vol. 16, 1960, p. 394.
15 W.H.R. Rivers, 'The History of Melanesian Society', p. 265.
16 Ibid., p. 10.
17 On this, see S.A. Tokarev, A Contribution to the Methodology for the Study of Kinship Terminology, 'Moscow State University Herald', Historical-Philological Series, 1958, no. 4, p. 189.
18 H.L. Morgan, 'Ancient Society', Leningrad, 1934, p. 221 (Russian ed.).
19 Similar inaccuracies can be found in many contemporary works. See Ch. M. Taksami, 'Nivkhi', Leningrad, 1967, p. 205; N.A. Butinov, 'The Papausa of New Guinea', Moscow, 1968, p. 211; and others.
20 S.A. Tokarev, op. cit., p. 189.
21 A. Radcliffe-Brown, A System of Notation for Relationship, 'Man', no. 30, 1930, p. 93.
22 G.P. Murdock, 'Social Structure', New York, 1949.
23 Yu. I. Levin, The Description of a System of Kinship Terms, 'Soviet Ethnography', 1970, no. 4.
24 E.S. Semeka, A Componential Analysis of the Kinship System of a Society with Cross-Cousin Marriages, 'The Fifth All-Union Symposium on Cybernetics', Tbilisi, 1970, pp. 368-70.
25 W.H.R. Rivers, 'The History of Melanesian Society', p. 265.
26 R. Lowie, Relationship Terms, 'Encyclopedia Britannica', 14th ed., vol. 19, p. 84.
27 H.L. Morgan, op. cit., p. 132.
28 G. McLennan, 'Studies in Ancient History', London, 1886, p. 273.

29 D. Schneider, What Should be Included in a Vocabulary of
    Kinship Terms, 'Proceedings of the Eighth International
    Congress of Anthropological and Ethnographical Sciences',
    Tokyo-Kyoto, vol. 2, p. 89.
30 H.T. Fei, 'Peasant Life in China', 1946, p. 288.
31 B. Aginsky, Kinship Systems and the Forms of Marriage,
    'Memoirs of the American Anthropological Association',
    1935, no. 45, p. 95.

13 Systems of kinship terms and systems of social categories
*N.M. Girenko**

H.L. Morgan's discovery of a definite correlation between systems of kinship terms and the social system, so highly regarded by classical Marxism, gave ethnography a new source for studying the past, especially that of peoples with no written language. Since H.L. Morgan's time, a vast amount of factual material has been accumulated by ethnographers. This has led to new methods of studying the relationship between kinship and social systems. The study of kinship terms, and particularly their typological aspect, is in the process of becoming a relatively independent discipline within ethnography. Special adaptations of structural analysis are being developed and a special scientific method worked out. (1) This type of research, and, in particular, the formal-structural approach, is especially useful in typology. However, as M.V. Kryukov's work shows, (2) component analysis can also be successfully applied to the study of the history of kinship terms, at least when it is a case of the terminology of one ethos, preserved in written records. It is still not fully clear how suitable this method is for analysing the kinship terminology of peoples who do not have written records. Although systems of kinship terms have been studied for over a century, the question of what kinship terms represent, what laws determine the relationship between kinship nomenclature and systems of kinship relations has not yet been fully researched. The solution of this question would help to determine to what degree we can rely on this particular historical source, and how it should be used, and also to clarify to what degree formal-structural analysis can be applied to systems of kinship terms, how the results of such an analysis should be interpreted.

We will not discuss all existing approaches to the study of kinship systems, but limit ourselves to comparing the two traditional approaches, which, to a greater or lesser extent, touch on the relationship between systems of kinship terms and the social system.

The most traditional approach derives from the work of H.L. Morgan, where the kinship system is examined as a developing

* First published in 'Sovetskaya Etnografiya', 1974, no. 6, pp. 41-50.

system of family relations, whose dynamic is based on the social-economic development of the whole society.   However, H.L. Morgan himself remarked on the lack of correlation between the terminological schema and the actual system of family relations.   This contradiction was explained by the fact that the terminological schema reflects the system of family relations as it existed in the past.   This approach does not enable us to establish the correlation between the terminological schema and the actual social relations at any given moment or stage of the society's development;   nor does it make clear how one should interpret the presence of 'survival terms' in any given system of family relations.   Here, for example, is how W. Rivers defines the kinship system: 'Kinship relations are relations which are defined and can be described by means of genealogy.' (3)   Kinship relations are counterposed to final or marriage relations. (4)   In our view, the kinship system has been more precisely defined by the representative of another tendency (the functional) - A.R. Radcliffe-Brown in his preface to the collection articles entitled 'African Systems of Kinship and Marriage'.   A.R. Radcliffe-Brown writes:

> A kinship system is ... a network of social ties which represent the social structure of the society.   It is also true that the obligations of relations to one another, and equally the terms used in addressing or designating relatives, form part of this system. (5)

From this definition it clearly follows that kinship terminology reflects that part of the actual social structure which is covered by the 'network' of kinship nomenclature.   However, the author goes on to point out the difference between the relatively quickly changing nature of society and the comparatively stable, inert system of kinship terms. (6)   This necessary clarification contradicts the definition of the system given previously.   In A.R. Radcliffe-Brown's opinion, this contradiction is annulled by the fact that a kinship system is accepted as a system of norms and types of behaviour of different groups and individuals (relatives) towards each other.   It may be possible to use this approach to a certain exent for synchronising descriptions of kinship systems.   However, it excludes the possibility of examining systems of kinship terms as a historical source (since this definition virtually identifies the nomenclature and the kinship relations).   This leads A.R. Radcliffe-Brown to proclaim, 'We cannot uncover the history of African (social) institutions.' (7)   Nevertheless, studies based on the above definition provide systematised material which may be interpreted in completely different ways.

In spite of the discrepancy in theoretical premises, the two opposing approaches to the study of kinship systems have several basic points in common.

The relationship between kinship nomenclature and the system of kinship ties is treated in the following: (1) the kinship system in both cases is regarded as a system which is homogeneous in a phasic relation; (2) this system is based on blood and affinal kinship; (3) the system of kinship terms is also a homogeneous system in a phasic relation which reflects actual or past kinship relations. Here one should note that if we take A.R. Radcliffe-Brown's point of view that the kinship system is a system of types of behaviour, we have to discover the material causes of the origin and evolution of these types. If one uses the method of synchronomous observation, it does not make sense to speak of the laws of origin of any 'behavioural' kinship norms without this. On the other hand, with regard to the other tendency, it is known that a kinship system cannot be regarded merely as a system of family relations since 'the kinship term defines the status, the wealth, the right of inheritance, the position of responsibility occupied or, more precisely, rank etc.' (8) Here one should note that M.V. Kryukov is probably not quite accurate in his treatment of the views of D.A. Oldegrogge and is incorrect in identifying his point of view with that of Radcliffe-Brown. (9) The difference of principle actually consists in the fact that D.A. Oldegrogge suggests that a system of family relations is based on a definite aspect of social relations, whereas Radcliffe-Brown does not consider the question of the basis of the relations. (10)

However, a family system by no means always takes in the whole complex of social relations within a given social system. (11) In many cases one can only speak of a particular sub-system of the full complex of social relations - the social institution of kinship.

The relationship between these categories - the system of social relations and the social institution of kinship - varies according to the stage of social development reached. The nature of this change was precisely formulated by F. Engels in his work 'The Origin of the Family, Private Property and the State': 'The development of the family in the prehistoric times consisted in ... the continual narrowing of the circles - originally embracing the whole tribe - within which marital community between the two sexes prevailed.' (12) The circle of people who are regarded as relatives and whose mutual relations are defined by kinship terms tends to narrow, and means that in the process some groups of relatives, between whom marriage is forbidden, come to belong to different tribes. At the same time marriage becomes possible not only within one's own tribe (already as a primitive form of concentration of power), but also outside it. (13) Later, individual families of notables separate themselves from and counterpose themselves to the kin, and this leads to the final break-up of the kin-tribal organisation as a whole. (14)

The study of systems of kinship terms completely confirms the sketch of the social evolution of bodies of relatives suggested by F. Engels. The evolution of systems of kinship terms, in particular, shows that the social institution of kinship has a tendency to narrow. Thus, M.V. Kryukov concludes that the history of the development of kinship systems can be divided into two epochs, with an intermediate stage - the Arab (lineal) kinship system: 'the first of these is characterised by the classificatory systems of the Australian type, the second includes the whole of the later evolution of these systems.' (15) If the initial and final (relatively speaking) stages are represented as two poles of evolution, the terminology of systems nearer to the 'Australian' pole includes a wider social group within the general system of social ties than the terminology of systems nearer to the opposite pole. In the course of development, the social institution of kinship includes a decreasing number of actual (or potential) social ties in relation to the whole system of social relations. If, at the 'Australian' pole, the kinship terms express relations between groups of relatives, later the terms gradually acquire a more individual meaning; the genealogical succession of groups (and through this of individuals) comes to be treated as the genealogical or biological ties joining series of people - relatives. This can be seen most clearly from the systems of kinship ties of the so-called Arab (or lineal) type, e.g. the Chinese system. Here the system of social-kinship ties embraces quite a large body of relatives, but the ties are all purely individual and are differentiated by line and by generation. G. Dole has shown that there is a tendency for a lineal terminological schema to form from the fusion of the so-called bifurcatory and the later contemporary isolated type, and that this tendency is connected with the general process of the social-economic development of society. (16)

This leads to the question: is it correct to regard a terminological schema of kinship, nearer to the 'Australian' pole (under this heading we can include all the Turano-gavansk systems) as based on blood and affinal relations where it is known that all kinship ties become completely identified with genetical or biological ties only at a comparatively late stage of evolution of the social institution of kinship?

Some foreign scholars have treated the social institution of kinship from the point of view of blood relationship, creating a fundamental lack of correlation between the terminology and the social structure, since the structure is founded not on 'concepts' of individual biological ties but on the actual sex-age division of labour and on the primitive community of property. (17)

The economic aspect of the evolution of the social institution

of kinship is an independent subject of research. Studies
have been made of the historical development of various types
of organisation of economic activity. (18)

Does this mean that categories such as 'kinship' are completely inadmissible in the study of kinship systems nearer to
the 'Australian' pole? This seems not to be completely true.
The social ties existing in these societies should properly be
regarded as ties between kinship groups and the individuals
making up these groups. In our view, A.M. Hocart successfully, though not quite correctly, explained this in his refu-
tation of the concept 'of an extended treatment of kinship
ties' based on Fijian material: 'In the use of the term "tama"
to designate "father"; "vati" to designate "mother" we have
the term and not the survival of a genealogical (i.e. as we
understand it genetical) system.' (19) The Fijians use these
terms to designate a much wider group of people than, e.g.,
'the father', 'wife' of the contemporary Russian kinship
system. Even here, blood relationship exists (more precisely can be distinguished if necessary), but the Fijians do
not define it as a social tie independent of the group to which
the individuals belong. This view seems to have been held
by W. Rivers in spite of his definition of the kinship system
given above. (20)

The question of the criteria to be used in approaching the
analysis of a kinship system is in itself extremely difficult.
The difficulty is not removed by creating special methods of
recording kinship nomenclature. The most logical of such
methods known to us, and, at the same time, one of the most
difficult to read, is the one suggested by Yu. I. Levin. (21)
This method is convenient for defining the place of a given
term in an abstract genealogical schema and for coding the
terminology of a large number of systems of kinship terms
with the aim of further computer analysis. But does it
follow that the use of a code means that the record of the
kinship systems correspond more closely to reality? It would
seem not, neither in the case when 'living' systems are recorded and coded by the same nor (as in the majority of cases)
by different scholars. The code is itself a system and is
based on certain principles. Yu. I. Levin's code is based on
concepts of blood and affinal relationship (C = child, P =
parent). This is a very simple expression of genealogical
ties, although the author claims, 'We don't touch on ... the
contents of kinship systems.' (22)

We in no way consider the 'subjectivity' of the method of
recording kinship terminology proposed by Yu. I. Levin a
drawback. On the contrary, any system of codification is,
to a certain extent, a standard, and is used to 'measure'
phenomena to discover what amount of a deliberately chosen

quality they possess.   The point is what quality of systems of kinship terminology we choose and to what degree this quality corresponds to the standard.   In connection with this, doubts have been raised as to the possibility of describing any kinship system without comparing it with some known system or 'standard'.   This is true for example of M.V. Kryukov. (23)   Indeed, no 'unrelative' method of description has yet been found.

It is far more important in our view not to confuse the standard with the phenomenon itself.   Such confusion is caused for example by attempts to find blood relationships, as they are understood today, in stages of evolution of family-kinship bodies where these ties have not yet separated out from the general system of social relations.   It is the same with the treatment of the kinship system understood merely as a reflection of marriage norms or forms of marriage. As D.A. Oldegrogge remarked 'a kinship system is much more complicated and cannot be explained just in terms of them.' (24)

It seems to us (from the complex of phenomena hidden behind the kinship terminology) that it is possible to extract a set of basic factors, common to all social institutions of kinship.   First, the life support of the group covered by the kinship terms always has a particular internal organisation. This can be called the economic aspect.   The division of labour exists to a greater or lesser extent among the members of any social institution of kinship.   Second, every social institution of kinship has a traditional method of regulating the reproduction of the people who compose it;   this can be called the genealogical aspect.   Last, there are always regulations concerning changes in the social position of an individual or a group of people in relation to the other members of a social institution of kinship.   This can be called the age or biological factor (taking into account that people undergo changes from a biological point of view).

The social body, which as a rule consists of three actual generations, is reflected in the terminology as five terminological generations.   This is natural if it is considered that a terminological schema, as a means of verbally expressing various ties and social phenomena, is essentially egocentric. It reflects all the types of relationship in which 'Ego' can potentially participate.   The child is connected with the generation of his parents and grandparents.   The adult enters into relations with his children, and, when he's older, with his grandchildren.   In addition, he is in continuous relations with the older and younger members of his own generation. The fact that the terminological schema has five generations does not mean that greatgrandparents and greatgrandchildren

actually meet in the same social institution of kinship. In
reality, there is no 'zero generation' in the social group.
The whole system is just calculated from an egocentric point
of view with the help of the potentially possible types of relationship in which 'Ego' could participate.

All three aspects of the 'social organism' of kinship are inseparably connected. This social organism arises, develops
and functions as if on three planes simultaneously, although
at different stages of evolution one or the other aspect -
economic, biological, or genealogical - may be of more importance for the society. One or the other aspect of the group
or individual may be designated by a particular term depending on, and by virtue of, its 'social importance'.

That all types of kinship systems have a 'standard' of kinship and social ties for all types of kinship can be seen from
the existence of a basic kinship group which is the starting-
point for all ties in the social institution of kinship. This
interconnection of the 'standard' and the phenomena exists to
a significant degree in the isolation of the so-called nucleus of
the kinship group or 'nuclear' family. Thus, G. Murdock
considered the group of the father, mother and their children
the 'nucleus' of the system of kinship relations. (25) A similar definition of the basic group of social kinship is given by
Lévi-Strauss. (26) This view is typical of the ethnographers
of the English school. There is also the slightly different
approach of M. Fortes, who, looking at the social structure
only in the synchronomous plan, isolated the main sub-groups
within the system of kinship relations as a whole from the
point of view of people 'on the sidelines', and then analysed
the mutual interaction, function and co-ordination of such
groups. (27)

However, the views of A.R. Radcliffe-Brown are worth looking at again. He drew attention to the particular role played
by such categories of relations as siblings within the social
institution of kinship. In his preface, Radcliffe-Brown stated
that 'the principle on which classificatory kinship terminology
is based, can be called the principle of the unity of the group
of siblings.' (28) This group goes beyond the limits of the
conventional European family. Radcliffe-Brown explains this
as follows 'Thus, in a given system the son can be taught to
regard the group of this father's siblings as a unified group,
in relation to which he sees himself as "son".' (29) O. Dempwolff came to a similar conclusion about the basis of the kinship principle and the role of the generation groups in the
functioning of the African kinship system (i.e., in the given
case, Turano-gavan) as early as 1909, when he was studying the connections between totemism and kinship systems. (30) He explained this phenomenon by the religious

concepts of the Africans 'who consider everyone who is their
kinsman by clan or totem as their brother.' (31)   O. Dempwolff identified these concepts.   However, in the social life
of the Africans, e.g. in East Africa where the so-called
'extended' (relative to the European kinship system) group of
siblings is widely represented, one can find explanations of
such groups of siblings which seem to us better-founded.
For example, one can draw attention to the activity of groups
of particular sexes and ages in carrying out joint tasks -
agriculture, hunting, herding cattle, and, in the past, armed
raids.   There are reasonable grounds for supposing that, in
the recent past, the activity of these groups was much wider
and that they had much greater social importance. (32)   As
well as such 'formalised' groupings, the traditional sex-age
demarcation exists both within the contemporary household
and groups of relatives.   Among some ethnoses, members of
one age group within an initiated generation (age set. T.D.)
until very recently formed separate settlements and represented a largely independent social-economic unit.   The Nyakusa
are a classic example of this. (33)   Until recently, so-called
houses of young men and women, male and female 'clubs', existed in many communities.   There, people of the same generation and age formed much closer ties among themselves than
with their parents.   All this suggests that the unity of the
group of siblings is based upon the framework of social life
and has its roots in the general principle on which the social
organisation, and, in particular, the social institution of kinship is based.   Movement along the social ladder was impossible outside these groups.   Marriage, which was seen as an
act of entering on adulthood, could only take place within the
limits of a particular initiated generation (age set. T.D.),
but with restrictions imposed by local ideas of exogamy.

If we accept the thesis that the evolution of the kinship
system leads to the narrowing of the social organism of kinship - and we have full grounds for accepting it - it is
obvious that the relationship 'group of parents-group of children' cannot represent a widening of the activity of the behavioural norms from the 'nuclear' family to a larger group of
people.   A more realistic suggestion is that the so-called
'nuclear family' in this case is of less social importance for the
individual than his membership of a wider group, i.e. of the
group of siblings, descendants of similar groups.   The evidence of ethnographical research since the discarding of the
patriarchal theory favours this solution.

V.M. Misyugin drew attention to the role played by the
sibling group in the social systems of the peoples of East
Africa, in his analysis of the nature of the development of the
social relations of the Swahili. (34)   Unlike most of the African ethos, the history of the Swahili can be traced not only

from ethnographical comparisons but also from local written
records.   As far as one can judge from these sources, the
'ndugu' group (as V.M. Misyugin calls it, using the Swahili
term for siblings), based on ties similar to those of a sibling
group, was at different stages of the evolution of the social
relations of the Swahili, both an exogamous and an endogamous
group. (35)   Thus, the basic meaning of this term (as a category indicating membership of this group) was 'equal to me',
'the same as I'.   In the Swahili language today, the term
'ndugu' is sometimes used to designate relatives whom one is
forbidden to marry, and, figuratively, it is used to describe
people outside this criterion, e.g. a fellow-tribesman.   The
latter is more noticeable in inter-ethnic relations.   The old
meaning, 'member of my age group', is preserved in the wedding songs of the Swahili, in which the bride and groom are
called 'ndugu'. (36)

   The laws of inheritance of the title of chief, the laws of
land use, the nature of the customs of levirate (a woman marries her dead husband's brother. T.D.) and sororate (a man
marries his wife's sister. T.D.) among many of the peoples of
this region, convince us that the most socially important group
in many kinship systems was, in the not so distant past, the
group of siblings and not the 'nuclear family'. (37)   In these
kinship systems it can be shown to be the basic group of 'Ego'
or the kinship nucleus, joining people who have identified
social ties reflected in the kinship terminology.   In this case,
the kinship system corresponds completely to the social organism, consisting of basic nuclei with social ties explained in
kinship terms.   It seems to us that the idea of the correlation
of the kinship system and the basic kinship nucleus enables us
to avoid bringing the principle of individual biological ties into
this social sub-system as socially important.   This, however,
does not prevent the correlation of kinship systems of different stages of social development with the relatively, or, more
precisely, potentially, final stage of their development - the
contemporary isolated type or the conventional kinship system,
e.g. as mentioned in a code.   The genealogical or biological
connection between ancestors and descendants exists really
(or can exist as a variant) in both cases, but has different
degrees of social importance which perhaps allows us to compare systems of different stages of development.   The discovery of the causes of the formation of various sorts of ties
within the social institution of kinship is the ethnographer's
goal in each case.   N.A. Butinov spoke of the necessity 'of
working out a new method of recording kinship systems which
would set down not only a system of abstract kinship ties, but
also the structure of social relations hidden behind it.' (38)
It seems to us that now it is not so much a matter of working
out a method of recording terms, as of exploring the essence
of different sorts of social ties, in the degree to which they
can be reflected in systems of kinship terms.

Kinship systems are not dead, petrified structures.   They change with the whole social-economic structure of society, although relatively more slowly than the actual productive relations.   This can partly be explained by the greater schematisation, the formal and traditional nature of the system. However, changes are recorded in ethnographical surveys and serve as a basis for clarifying our ideas on the nature of the development of the social institution of kinship. (39)   The inertia of the kinship system is also due to the fact that each new characteristic of the system arises within the previous traditional form and thus bears the stamp of the previous stage.   The relationships between individuals and groups within a kinship system are not only greatly formalised but are also fixed in the linguistic terminology of the people concerned.   Kinship terminology, as a linguistic phenomenon, is even more conservative than the actual system of kinship relations a social phenomenon.   At any given moment, the system of kinship terms reflects actual relations and ties within the social institution of kinship, but expresses them through social categories which arose in the previous stage of social development.   New elements of terminology clearly originate from the impossibility of using the old categories, or from their inadequacy.   This means that both groups of terms relating to different stages of formation of the kinship system as a whole, and terms and categories which do not have analogies in the system of the previous period, can be found within one system of kinship terms.   The fact that systems of kinship terms are systems of social categories also means that they can be regarded as a reliable source for the history of the social institution.   On the other hand, this feature of the system of kinship terms means that it can be regarded not as a homogeneous but as a heterogeneous system, in the sense that its separate elements relate to different stages of its formation and bear the stamp of these stages.

The basic kinship nucleus - the sibling group - can be seen as one highly conservative type of relationship within the kinship system.   This group changes as the kinship system evolves.   Thus, in accordance with the 'movement' of the system towards a lineal structure, it shrinks, or, under certain conditions, when bifurcatory generation systems are formed, appears to widen.   However, its basic principle is preserved: it is a body of people with identical social ties within the social institution of kinship.   It also preserves its fundamental dual structure.   The dual structure of the basic group of 'Ego' is here called fundamental since the unity of two mutually connected social categories is one of its characteristics.   This dual membership (a social phenomenon) is obviously based on the duality of sexes (a biological phenomenon).   In many systems of kinship terms, the words for siblings express not only membership of a certain sex - as e.g. 'sister', 'brother' - but also membership of the opposite sex. Many of the ethnos of Melanesia use such a terminology for the basic group of 'Ego'; it is also widely found on the African continent. (40)   Thus, among the Nyamwezi (East Africa) the term 'ilyumbu' means 'sibling of the opposite sex', (41) and, according to the sex, 'Ego' and 'Alter' can be translated into Russian as both 'brother' and 'sister'.   The term for sibling has a similar meaning among some peoples, whose languages contain grammatical indices for sex.   For example, among the Konso (Ethiopia), the term 'alaua' means 'brother' and the term 'alauda' can be used to mean 'sister'. (42)   Or, among the Tuaregs (Sahara), the term 'amekkar' approximately corresponds to the Russian 'brother', and the term 'tamekkart' to the Russian 'sister'. (43)   (Both systems of terms belong to the Turano-gavan system.)   In both these examples the affixes express a particular grammatical kin relationship.   The coincidence of the fundamentals of these terms does not appear to be an accidental or isolated phenomenon.

The temporally heterogeneous character of systems of kinship terms, as systems of social categories during different stages of the evolution of the system, may perhaps enable us to come to the conclusions about the nature of the social structure of the period when the given term appears.   Such fragmentary reconstructions would, of course, need to be used in conjunction with other systems of a similarly heterogeneous nature.   Among these one could include some aspects of folklore, rituals connected with marriage, burial, the election of elders, production rituals and many other ethnographical sources for the study of people's traditional culture.

NOTES

1   For a brief examination of methods of formal-structural analysis, see M.A. Chlenov, Formal Methods of Studying Systems of Kinship in Contemporary American Ethnography, 'Ethnological Research Abroad', Moscow, 1972, pp. 146-69.
2   M.V. Kryukov, 'The Kinship System of the Chinese', Moscow, 1963.
3   W.H.R. Rivers, 'Social Organisation', London, 1923, p. 53.
4   Ibid., p. 52.
5   A.R. Radcliffe-Brown, D. Ford (eds), 'African Systems of Kinship and Marriage', London, 1950, p. 13.
6   Ibid.
7   Ibid., p. 2.
8   D.A. Oldegrogge, Basic Features of the Development of Kinship Systems, 'Soviet Ethnography', 1958, no. 1, p. 25.
9   M.V. Kryukov, op. cit., p. 48.

10   See, for example, D.A. Oldegrogge, From the History of
     Family and Marriage (the System of Lobola and Different
     Forms of Cousin Marriage in Southern Africa), 'Soviet
     Ethnography', 1947, no. 1, pp. 13-29.
11   See Yu. I. Semenov, The Category of the 'Social Organ-
     ism' and its Importance for Historical Science, 'Problems
     of History', 1966, no. 8, p. 94.
12   K. Marx and F. Engels, 'Collected Works', vol. 20, p. 51.
13   H.L. Morgan, 'Ancient Society', New York, 1877, p. 513.
     The appendix to this work (L. Morgan's debate with
     McLennan) shows that Morgan did not make a terminologi-
     cal distinction between the concept 'tribe' as a social
     structure, combining separate social-kinship organisms in
     a single social organism, and 'tribe' as an ethnic commu-
     nity in the state of development typified by the kin-tribal
     organisation.
14   K. Marx and F. Engels, 'Collected Works', vol. 20, p. 108.
15   M.V. Kryukov, op. cit., p. 270.
16   See, for example, G.E. Dole, The Lineage Pattern of Kin-
     ship Nomenclature: Its Significance and Development,
     'Southwestern Journal of Anthropology', vol. 21, no. 1,
     1965, p. 55.
17   See K.P. Kalinovskaya, The Correlation of the Function
     and Structure of Age Groups among the Galls, 'Soviet
     Ethnography', 1972, no. 4, pp. 137-8.
18   See N.A. Butinov, The Division of Labour in Primitive
     Society, 'Problems of the History of Primitive Society',
     Moscow-Leningrad, 1960, pp. 80-108.
19   A.M. Hocart, The Kinship System, 'Anthropos', 1937,
     no. 2, p. 551.
20   The dynamic process of the emergence of consanguinal
     biological ties, as socially important in the process of the
     evolution of kinship collectives, can be seen clearly from
     W.H.R. Rivers's course of lectures, ed. B. Perry,
     W.H.R. Rivers, op. cit., pp. 188-91.
21   Yu. I. Levin, The Description of a System of Kinship
     Terms, 'Soviet Ethnography', 1970, no. 4, pp. 18-30.
22   Ibid., p. 18.
23   M.V. Kryukov, op. cit., p. 23.
24   D.A. Oldegrogge, The System of Ikit, 'Works of the Insti-
     tute of Ethnography of the Academy of Sciences of the
     USSR', vol. 54, Moscow, 1960, p. 163.
25   G.P. Murdock, 'Social Structure', New York, 1949, p. 92.
26   See, for example, C. Lévi-Strauss, 'Structural Anthropol-
     ogy', New York, 1967, pp. 44-6.
27   M. Fortes, The Structure of Unilineal Descent Groups,
     'American Anthropologist', vol. 55, no. 1, 1953, pp. 25-9.
28   A.R. Radcliffe-Brown, op. cit., p. 23.
29   Ibid., p. 24.
30   O. Dempwolff, Totemismus in Deutsch Ostafrica, 'Deutsches
     Kolonialblatt', 1 January 1909, pp. 22-6 (D.A. Oldegrogge

kindly provided me with a detailed synopsis of Dempwolff's article).

31 Ibid.
32 See K.P. Kalinovskaya, 'The Age-Groups of the Peoples of East Africa, Their Structure and Function', Leningrad, 1972, Synopsis of a Candidat Thesis.
33 M. Wilson, 'Good Company. A Study of Nyakyusa Age-Villages', London, 1851.
34 V.M. Misyugin, A Syakhil Chronicle of the Medieval State of Pate, 'Works of the Institute of Ethnography', vol. 60, Moscow-Leningrad, 1966, pp. 52-84.
35 Ibid.
36 S.A. Farsi, 'Ada za Harusi Katika Unguja', Nairobi, 1967, pp. 28, 31.
37 See, for example, N.D. Yongolo, 'Maisha na Desturi za Wanyamwezi', London, 1953, pp. 57-8.
38 N.A. Butinov, Problems of Exogamy, 'Works of the Institute of Ethnography', vol. 14, Moscow, 1951, p. 21.
39 See, for example, W.H.R. Rivers, 'Kinship and Social Organisation', London, 1914, p. 68.
40 For examples of this terminology among the peoples of the Bantu language group (23 examples), see D.A. Oldegrogge, The Kinship System of the Bakongo in the Seventeenth Century, 'Collected Papers on African Ethnography', vol. 3, Moscow, 1959, p. 33.
41 W. Blohm, 'Die Nyamwezi', vol. 2, Hamburg, 1933, p. 33.
42 C.R. Hallpike, 'The Konso of Ethiopia', London, 1972, p. 106.
43 J. Nikolaisen, The Structural Study of Kinship Behaviour with Particular Reference to Tuareg Concept, 'Folk', vol. 3, Copenhagen, 1971, p. 107.

Main bibliographical sources

Articles in the following are published centrally and distributed throughout the USSR:

'Sovetskaya Etnografiya' (new series) ('Soviet Ethnography'),
1946-present.   Published by USSR Academy of Sciences'
Publishers, Moscow-Leningrad, contributions accepted from all
republics of the USSR.
'Narody Mira' ('Peoples of the World').   Began 1954.   Contributors from all republics.   Wide coverage, e.g. Africa,
the Caucasus.
'Rasy i Narody' ('Races and Peoples').   Published by USSR
Academy of Sciences, diverse contributors.
'Trudy Instituta Etnografii Imeni Miklukho-Maklaya' ('Works of
the Institute of Ethnography named after Miklukho-Maclay').
Began 1934.   New series: 1947-present.   Publishes contributions from members of the Leningrad and Moscow branches
of the Institute of Ethnography of the USSR Academy of Sciences.
'Sbornik Muzeya po Antropologii i Etnografii' ('Collected Works
of the Museum of Anthropology and Ethnography').   Began
1900.   St Petersburg, Imperial Academy of Sciences.   Vol.
IX 1930, then vol. X 1949 and from then continuous publication.
'Kratkiye Soobshcheniye' ('Brief Communications').   USSR
Academy of Sciences Institute of Ethnography, Moscow and
Leningrad branches.   Began 1946.
'Polevye Issledovanie' ('Field Research').   USSR Academy of
Sciences Institute of Ethnography, Moscow branch.   Vol. I,
1974.   In progress.

Articles in the following are published locally and are held
only in the principle libraries of the USSR and in their own
location:

'Trudy' ('Works').   Journal of every State University containing articles in ethnography in the history section.   For
example:
  'Trudy LGU' - Leningradskogo Gosudarstvenogo Universiteta
  (Leningrad State University).
  'Trudy MGU' - Moskovskogo Gosudarstvenogo Universiteta
  (Moscow State University).
  'Trudy Tashkentskogo Gosudarstvenogo Universiteta' (Tashkent State University).

Each union republic has a State University which publishes its 'Trudy' in the local language and in Russian in its capital city.

'Izvestiya' ('News').   Bulletin of each Academy of Sciences. The history sections include works in Ethnography.   For example:

'Izvestiya Akademii Nauk Tadjikskoy SSR', Bulletin of the Academy of Sciences of the Tadjik SSR.

'Izvestiya Akademii Nauk Gruzinskoy SSR, Bulletin of the Academy of Sciences of the Georgian SSR.

Each union republic has an Academy of Sciences in its capital city and publishes summaries and some whole articles in Russian.

Random selections in English translation of Soviet authors can be obtained through: S. and E. Dunn (eds), 'Soviet Anthropology and Archaeology'.   Started 1962.   Publ. M.E. Sharpe Inc., White Plains, NY 10603, USA.

DISCAR